Elusive Paradise

The Millennium Prize

Diana Nemiroff

with an essay by Johanne Sloan

NATIONAL GALLERY OF CANADA
OTTAWA, 2001

Message from the Sponsor

On behalf of all those who have generously contributed under its Circle program, the National Gallery of Canada Foundation is pleased to be sponsoring the special exhibition *Elusive Paradise: The Millennium Prize*.

The National Gallery of Canada Foundation was created in 1997 for the purpose of raising endowment and annual funds for the Gallery. It is fitting that the Foundation be involved in this celebration of excellence in contemporary art from Canada and around the world, and in the presentation of the first international prize for the visual arts in Canada.

Elusive Paradise offers us a rare opportunity to reflect on who we are and where we are today. We congratulate everyone at the Gallery who has sustained the grand vision of mounting this exhibition and competition, particularly its organizer, Diana Nemiroff, Curator of Modern Art. We are also honoured to welcome to the National Gallery the ten invited artists: Geneviève Cadieux, Janet Cardiff, Tacita Dean, Liz Magor, Shahzia Sikander, Jana Sterbak, Valeska Soares, Yoshihiro Suda, Diana Thater, and Jeff Wall.

The diverse visions presented by these artists mirror, in a sense, the wide range of backgrounds of the Foundation's supporters, who proudly share in common a great passion for the arts. To all of them, we express our heartfelt thanks.

John E. Cleghorn, Chair of the Board of Directors, National Gallery of Canada Foundation

Foreword

The decision to create an international prize to mark the turn of the millennium has its origin, first and foremost, in the desire to identify and celebrate outstanding artistic achievement. In choosing to recognize an artist in such a tangible way, the National Gallery joins a number of other museums and arts organizations around the world. Many long-standing international exhibitions, such as the Venice Biennale and the Carnegie International, award prizes to one or more of the participating artists in recognition of the excellence of their work in the exhibition. In the case of the Venice Biennale, in which artists are selected by their own country and show in separate pavilions, the award carries some of the competitive national connotations also associated with the Olympic Games, whereas the Carnegie's award earmarks a particular work for purchase by the museum and is a means of building the collection. Other more recently created prizes include The Turner Prize, which is administered by the Tate Gallery and is awarded to an artist resident in Britain for an outstanding exhibition in the previous year, and The Hugo Boss Prize, which is administered by the Guggenheim Foundation, is open to artists internationally, and is awarded for creative achievement over an entire career rather than for a single work or exhibition.

The National Gallery shares with these institutions the intent to create a showcase for contemporary art. We anticipate that the publicity around the prize will bring the latest developments in contemporary art to the attention of a broader public than the admittedly small audience of committed gallery-goers who keep up with the trends in the art magazines and travel to international art exhibitions such as the Venice Biennale and Documenta in Kassel, Germany. The exhibition is an occasion to identify timely issues in contemporary art, and to emphasize the relevance of art to the world in which we all live. One way in which it differs from the others mentioned above is its focus on a specific theme, the "elusive paradise" of Arcadia. The subject underlines the utopian connotations of the millennium, and reminds us of the central place that nature continues to play in the creative imagination. Through it, we are all invited to imagine the perfect world.

An important objective from the beginning was to communicate the solid accomplishments of Canadian artists by creating an international forum in which they would have a strong presence. This goal seems especially important now, as art in our time takes on an increasingly international character. Artists take their place on a global stage, and must communicate in a world that is culturally and linguistically diverse. The situation offers, at its best, opportunities for creative cross-fertilization of unprecedented scope and intensity to which, we hope, the present exhibition will contribute.

In order to achieve these objectives we invited an international panel of experts in the visual arts to meet with us on several occasions to share their thoughts about possible exhibition models. Lynn Gumpert, Director of the Grey Art Gallery at New York University, Ivo Mesquita, newly-named Director of the Museu de Arte Moderna in São Paulo, Didier Ottinger, Curator of Modern Art at the Centre Georges Pompidou, and Chantal Pontbriand, editor of the contemporary art magazine *Parachute*, have contributed many valuable insights during this process, and graciously accepted the difficult task of deciding on the eventual winner of the Millennium Prize. One observation that emerged from our meetings was the need for a theme that would balance the interest and excitement of a prize with an exhibition that would be anchored in a place and a history, yet discerning in regard to contemporary art trends. This was the challenge that Diana Nemiroff, the National Gallery's Curator of Modern Art, accepted when she assumed the direction of the project. I would like to extend my thanks to all the members of the panel for their help in shaping the project, and especially to Diana Nemiroff for imparting her vision to the final exhibition.

A Prize for the Millennium would have remained a dream were it not for the participation of the National Gallery of Canada Foundation. The generosity of all who have contributed to the Foundation has made this dream a reality, and we are very grateful to them. Yet even while we recognize the distinctive achievement of the prizewinner, it is important to acknowledge the significant contributions of all the artists to the exhibition and to contemporary art in general. Collectively and individually we are all nourished by the creative vision of each of the artists in the exhibition, whose accomplished works offer both immediate delight and an occasion to reflect on the world that lies before us as the third millennium begins.

Last but not least I would like to thank all the staff of the National Gallery whose professionalism and dedication have contributed, directly or indirectly, to the success of the exhibition and this catalogue.

Pierre Théberge, C.Q., Director

Preface

It is common to observe that contemporary art reflects contemporary realities, and while this is true to an extent, it is equally true that art pushes beyond or behind immediate realities. As often as not, contemporary art challenges us because it presents a vision of the world that is unexpected and unsettling; even its beauties are an implicit criticism of the tendency to rush through the world without taking sufficient account of the details that make it meaningful. Bearing in mind the inquiring, critical tendency of the art of the last century, which has frequently sought to open new dimensions of reality to perception, I have chosen a subject whose suggestions of earthly perfection are deliberately utopian, in a desire to provoke, at the beginning of the twenty-first century, a reflection on the ideals of refuge and harmony that nature still has the power to embody. These are the ideals that make the idea of Arcadia a powerful one, even today. They lie, largely unacknowledged, behind contemporary debates on the development of natural resources and the future of the environment, and figure in the background of discussions on the meaning of place in an era of globalization.

In proposing the subject of Arcadia to the ten artists in the exhibition, I knew that they would surely address both the idealizing and the elusive character of the theme, and that dystopic echoes would be heard alongside any sweet hymns to nature. Indeed, the vision of nature that emerges from the exhibition is a complex one. Charged with an awareness of history and of the transformative role of technology, the works of art in the exhibition also make room for the pleasures of the senses, creating quiet private places of reflection. The metaphorical gardens of this twenty-first century Arcadia could not have been envisioned in quite the same way at any other time in history: they reflect us even while leading us to imagine other worlds.

Throughout the process of realizing the exhibition I have benefited from the interest and assistance of many people inside the National Gallery and without. Firstly I am grateful to the director, Pierre Théberge, for his conviction that contemporary art should occupy a place of first importance among the activities of the National Gallery, and for his confidence in my vision of the exhibition and selection of artists. An international committee of advisors joined us on several occasions for substantive discussions about the present directions of contemporary art and the project of a prize for the millennium. I wish to thank Lynn Gumpert, Director of the Grey Art Gallery of New York University, Ivo Mesquita, newly-named Director of the Museu de Arte Moderna in São Paulo, Didier Ottinger, Curator of Modern Art at the Centre Georges Pompidou in Paris, and Chantal Pontbriand, editor of *Parachute* magazine, published in Montreal but read around the world, who have all given of their time and expertise during the development of the exhibition. Their judgement will be put to the test, as they have accepted the difficult task of selecting the winner of the Millennium Prize.

I have had the privilege of working with a dedicated team within the National Gallery whose knowledge and enthusiasm have greatly contributed to the success of the exhibition. Getting the exhibition into the galleries and making it look both beautiful and effortless has been the responsibility of numerous people. Yves Théoret, exhibition manager, has met the challenge of keeping this complex project on track during all its stages through his intelligent coordination of the details and the overall picture. David Bosschaart designed the exhibition spaces and was responsible for the lively graphic design; he has succeeded in assuring the unity of an exhibition with several locations throughout the building. Ceridwen Maycock and Christine LaSalle provided efficient coordination of the shipping arrangements for the exhibition. Jacques Naud and his team in Technical Services installed the exhibition, meeting the demands of the artists, the curator, and the schedule with their usual professionalism. The expertise of Mark Paradis and the staff of Multimedia Services has been essential to meeting the technical requirements of the individual works. My thanks go out to them all.

The events surrounding the exhibition are an occasion to honour and celebrate the work of the artists and to develop a deeper understanding of the exhibition's themes. I would like to extend my appreciation to Barbara Dytnerska, who has developed a stimulating education program that addresses the subject of the exhibition as well as diverse needs of our public with imagination and flare. Emily Tolot and Sylvie Tremblay in Special Events made the opening festivities and the prize ceremony memorable and enjoyable events, and I am grateful to them.

The exhibition will live in memory and have a place in the history of the National Gallery because of this book, whose appearance and content are the result of the collaboration of many talented individuals. I would like to thank my secretary, Shirley Proulx, and my assistant, Iris Amizlev, for their help with many different aspects of the project, and especially for assembling the photographs and lists of exhibitions, which, I hope, will make this catalogue a useful reference tool for the future. I am grateful to Johanne Sloan of McGill University for her insightful essay, which explores the complex meanings of landscape in modern and contemporary art with an incisive intelligence that demonstrates her deep knowledge of the subject. Translation was provided by Danielle Chaput and Bérengère de Guernon, who have faithfully rendered the voices of the authors while creating a French version that reads with ease. The English and French texts were edited with a sure and sensitive hand by Usher Caplan and Claire Rochon, and the quality of the illustrations was ensured by Colleen Evans. Emmeline Debay of Timmings & Debay has shown an admirable understanding of the exhibition in her beautiful design, which gives equal proof of her understanding of the art of the book. Finally, I am grateful to

Serge Thériault, Chief of Publications, for his commitment to the overall quality and excellence of this publication.

Many people beyond the National Gallery have been closely connected with the realization of the exhibition. I wish to thank the staff of the following galleries for their assistance on many levels with the individual artists: Galerie René Blouin, Montreal (Geneviève Cadieux and Yoshihiro Suda); Galeria Camargo Vilaça, São Paulo (Valeska Soares); Deitch Projects, New York (Shahzia Sikander); Equinox Gallery, Vancouver (Liz Magor); Frith Gallery, London (Tacita Dean); Marian Goodman Gallery, New York (Tacita Dean and Jeff Wall); Susan Hobbs Gallery, Toronto (Liz Magor); Gallery Koyanagi, Tokyo (Yoshihiro Suda); LiebmanMagnan, New York (Valeska Soares); Luhring Augustine, New York (Janet Cardiff); and David Zwirner, New York (Diana Thater).

Every exhibition depends for its success on the generosity of lenders, and this one is no exception. I would like to express my deep appreciation to the collectors and museums who have parted with precious works from their own collections to make this presentation possible, including the Art Gallery of Ontario, Toronto; Bruce Bailey, Toronto; Galerie Jöhnen & Schöttle, Cologne; Gary and Tracy Mezzatesta, Los Angeles; the Mugrabi collection, New York; and the Vancouver Art Gallery, Vancouver.

On behalf of the artists, I would like to recognize here the precious contribution of the individuals and organizations who have collaborated in the production of their work. In particular, I would like to acknowledge The Fabric Workshop and Museum in Philadelphia, which collaborated with Jana Sterbak on the realization of *Oasis*, in the context of its Artist-in-Residence Program. I would also like to thank the artist's assistant, Denis Labelle, for his research and technical assistance, and the Canada Council for the Arts for their contribution to the project. Grateful mention should be made of Theresa Bergne of Field and the musicians and singers of the Salisbury Cathedral Choir who have worked with Janet Cardiff on her reworking of Thomas Tallis's *Spem in Alium Nunquam Habui*, as well as George Bures Miller, who provided technical assistance. The support of James Lingwood and Jane Hamlin has also been invaluable. Apart from organizations whose mandate is to assist artists in the creation of their works, there are occasionally businesses in the private sector whose interest in the technical challenges of a particular artist's work motivates them to provide timely assistance in kind. Both the National Gallery and Janet Cardiff are grateful for the ongoing support of B&W Loudspeakers, and in particular for their generous donation of forty-two speakers for Cardiff's audio installation in this exhibition.

Finally, my thanks go to the artists who accepted my invitation to participate in this exhibition. It has been a privilege and a pleasure to work with them and to present their works here at the National Gallery of Canada.

Diana Nemiroff, Curator of Modern Art

Statement of the Jury

The jury was by turns impressed and seduced by *Elusive Paradise: The Millennium Prize*. We would like to extend our congratulations to its organizer, Diana Nemiroff, Curator of Modern Art at the National Gallery of Canada, for a brilliantly conceived and superbly installed exhibition.

In the context of the major issues animating contemporary art at the dawn of the twenty-first century—notably the exploration of how the human, the artificial, and the natural are interrelated—the ten artists represented in the exhibition offer us a reconsideration of nature and imaginatively open a window onto the place we occupy in it.

In the course of our deliberations, we were invariably attracted by the resonant lyricism of the exhibited works, all of which inspire a renewed vision of the arcadian ideal. Here are ten distinct voices each responding to the challenge of the theme of an "elusive paradise" and making an important contribution to the development of contemporary artistic expression.

Given the excellence of the exhibition, selecting one artist was not easy. Our discussions included consideration of the significance, impact, and ramifications of such an award. As a result of our deliberations the jury decided, by a majority vote, to award the National Gallery of Canada's Millennium Prize to Janet Cardiff.

Forty-Part Motet skilfully combines the languages of music and sculpture with contemporary communications technology, profoundly altering our perception of the space. The jury was deeply moved by this work. Using the most immaterial and most intimate of materials, the human voice, the artist has produced an experience of pure transcendence. The expressive possibilities of this work hold great promise, and we hope that the awarding of the Millennium Prize will enable Janet Cardiff to advance further along the paths on which she has boldly embarked.

We would also like to congratulate the National Gallery of Canada for establishing the Millennium Prize and to thank the National Gallery of Canada Foundation for its generous financial support.

Members of the Jury
Lynn Gumpert, Director, Grey Art Gallery, New York University
Ivo Mesquita, Director, Museu de Arte Moderna, São Paulo
Didier Ottinger, Curator of Modern Art, Centre Georges Pompidou, Paris
Chantal Pontbriand, Editor of the contemporary art magazine *Parachute*, Montreal

Jury Chair
Pierre Théberge

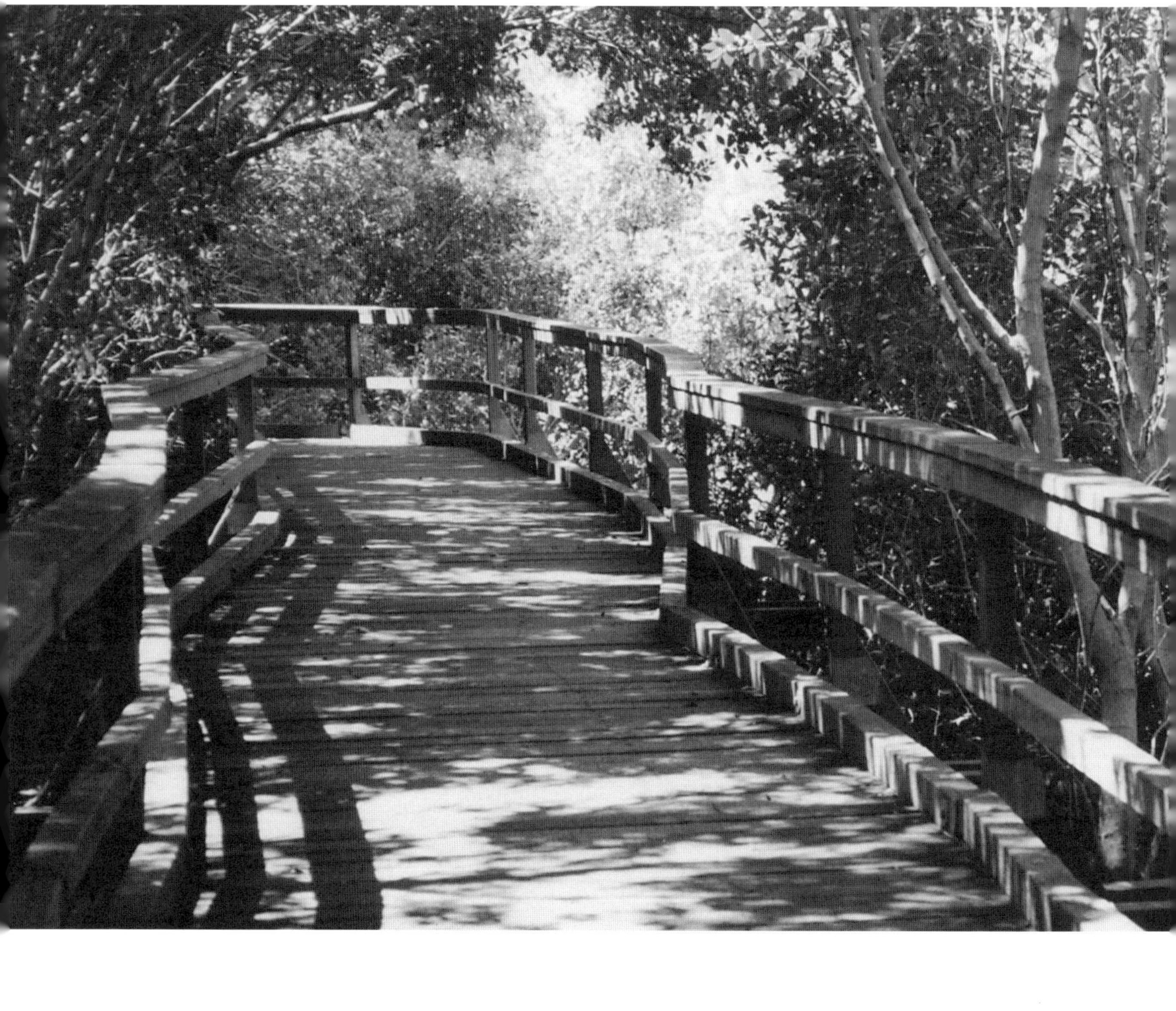

Mangrove swamp and boardwalk, Brisbane, Australia (photo Diana Nemiroff)

After Arcadia

Ours is not a century of paradises.[1]

What can Arcadia—narrowly associated with classical pastoral poetry and with certain paintings of the seventeenth-century French painter Nicolas Poussin—have to say to contemporary art at the start of a new millennium? It is all too clear that the twentieth century, just past, was an age not of utopias but of dystopias. Picasso's *Guernica*, a denunciation of the Fascist-instigated bombing of Republican Spain painted for the Spanish pavilion at the 1937 Exposition Internationale in Paris, throws into relief the primary themes: man against machine, the subjugation of human values to totalitarian ideologies, the cruelty and suffering of war. Yet Matisse (Picasso's arch-rival in many eyes) was the author of two supremely arcadian paintings in the early years of the century, *Luxe, calme et volupté* (fig. 1) and *Le bonheur de vivre*, and along with his compatriot Pierre Bonnard showed that the arcadian tradition inherited from the Renaissance had not yet been exhausted. However, as John Elderfield has convincingly argued, there is more than idyllic relaxation in these paintings.[2] Their central drama is the recovery of a childlike intensity of vision that could connect the emotions inspired by the external world to their original, atavistic inner sources. Thus, Baudelaire's "Invitation au voyage," from which Matisse drew the title of *Luxe, calme et volupté*, is not only an invitation to a distant, ideal place, but also a recovery of an inner, primal harmony that is projected upon external reality.

I believe that both aspects of the arcadian myth, the primitive and the pastoral, along with a darker vision of disunity and conflict, have informed art in the twentieth century, especially art that that takes nature as its primary subject. Arcadia summons up utopian ideas of perfection associated with nature but at the same time evokes the transience of experience and loss. If today technology promises new utopias, the desire for

[1] Henri Michaux, *Light through Darkness*, trans. Haakon Chevalier (New York: The Orion Press, 1963), p. 3.
[2] John Elderfield, *Henri Matisse: A Retrospective* (New York: The Museum of Modern Art, 1992), particularly pp. 33–37 and 53–56.

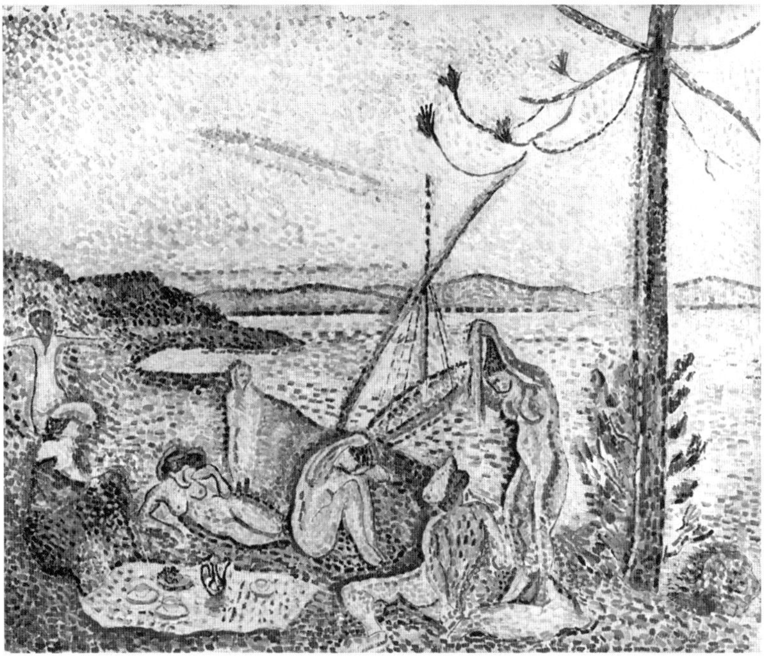

refuge from modern life is not just an eccentric impulse but widespread. In more abstract terms, Arcadia implies order, an ideal balance of human and non-human, yet its opposite, disorder, is never completely absent. In this sense, every period of history has had its Arcadia. But before looking at the works in this exhibition through the framework of a contemporary vision of Arcadia that has both a utopian and a dystopian side, I would like to explore the history of the idea, in order to show how it has affected not only art and literature, but also our everyday understanding of the natural world.

The Historical Arcadia

The original Arcadia was of interest to poets for its remoteness. A hilly region in central Greece, it was known in antiquity as a rough, uncultivated place peopled by hunters and goatherds whose only art was that of music, played on pipes to while away the lonely hours. Its inhabitants were healthy in their diet and egalitarian in their customs, though Ovid described them as bestial and uncouth. Their god, Pan, was half-man, half-beast, known for his musical skill and also for his unbridled sexuality. He was associated with the fecundity of nature but also its cruelty, and in Plato's *Phaedrus* he represents totality and many-sidedness. Thomas Rosenmeyer, in his book *The Green Cabinet*, states that, "he had come to stand for a world whose wholeness is a function of its contradictions."[3]

fig. 1 Henri Matisse, *Luxe, calme et volupté*, 1904–1905, oil on canvas, 98.5 x 118 cm, Musée d'Orsay, Paris © Estate of Henri Matisse/SODART (Montreal) 2001

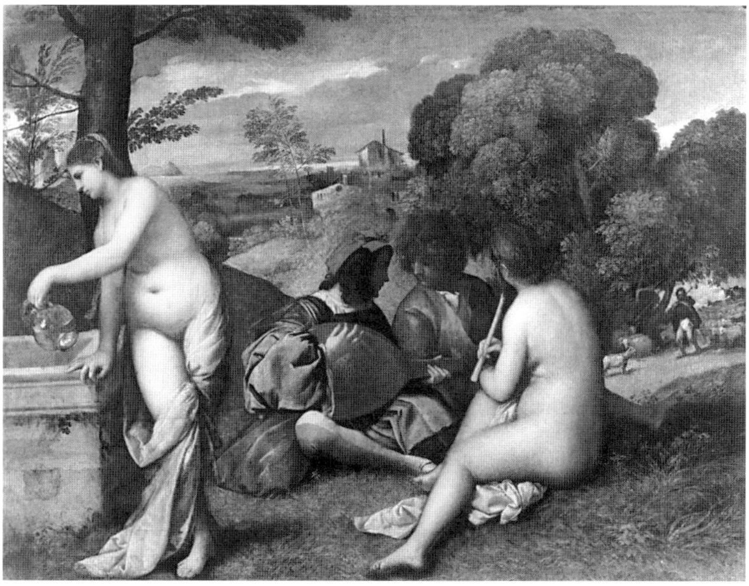

The harsh primitivism of this wild Arcadia was transformed by the Roman poet Virgil, whose *Eclogues* depict an idealized utopia, a composite landscape whose features are a suitable backdrop for poetic reverie. His Arcadia is not a place on the map but a spiritual landscape where myth and reality are joined—"the land of the gilt-edged weekday," as Bruno Snell comments sardonically.[4] Here the herdsman is not preoccupied with practical activities, but fills his leisurely hours with tender songs of love. The Arcadia that Virgil depicts is a locus of withdrawal from reality, including the political realities of the day. In the background lie civil war and dispossession following the death of Caesar, and the first *Eclogue* begins with an invitation to the exiled Meliboeus to pause for a while before resuming a journey leading to the uncertainty of unknown lands. However, Virgil does not deal with political problems head on. His Arcadia lies outside of history, poised mid-way between Rome's origins in the legendary past and a future Golden Age in which peace and harmony rule. Its mediating character is made clear, as Leo Marx observes, by its spatial symbolism.[5] It is described as a green hollow, surrounded by echoing woods, situated between the city of Rome and the inhospitable bare rocks and marshlands that lie beyond.

[3] Thomas Rosenmeyer, *The Green Cabinet: Theocritus and the European Pastoral Lyric* (Berkeley and Los Angeles: University of California Press, 1969), p. 243. [4] Bruno Snell, *The Discovery of the Mind: The Greek Origins of European Thought*, trans. T.G. Rosenmeyer (Cambridge: Harvard University Press, 1953), p. 291. [5] Leo Marx, *The Machine in the Garden* (New York: Oxford University Press, 1964), p. 22.

fig. 2 Titian, *Le concert champêtre*, c. 1509–1510, oil on canvas, 110 x 138 cm, Musée du Louvre, Paris

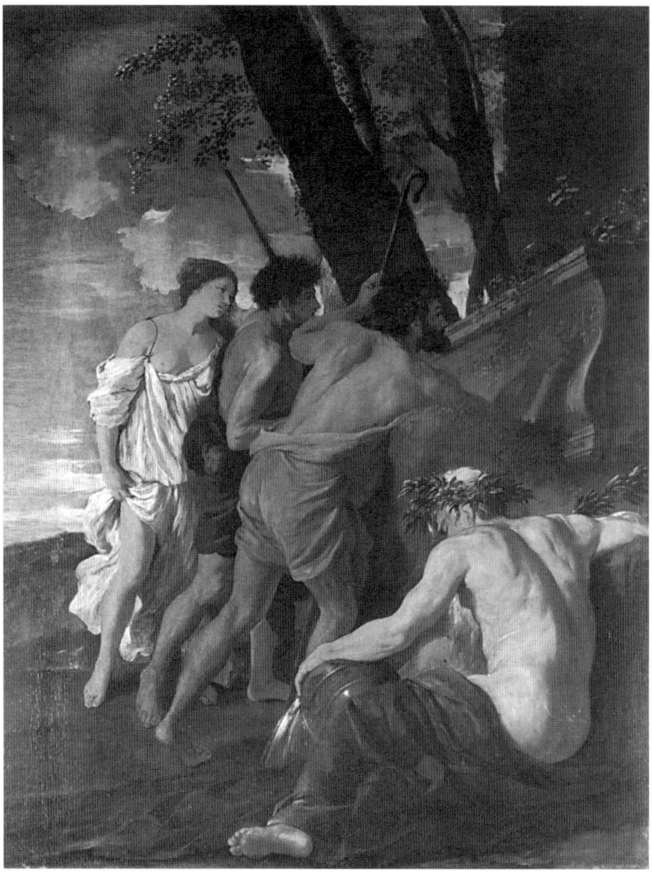

Virgil's Arcadia embodies the pastoral ideal that was handed down to the Humanist poets and painters of the Renaissance. It is an idyllic place of love and leisure, a land of dreams where nature satisfies all man's material needs in a perpetual spring or summertime of harmony and ease. Only the pain of unrequited love dims its pleasures, and the poet sings with sweet sadness of love's unfulfilled longings. But by the Renaissance, Arcadia's blissful utopia was removed not only in space but in time. It had become an object of nostalgia, like the whole Classical world. The elegiac feeling peripherally present in Virgil became a central quality of Renaissance poetry, and Arcadia was painted in melancholy terms as a realm lost forever.[6]

The Renaissance produced many variations on the pastoral theme in the visual arts, notably the lovely *Concert champêtre* (fig. 2) usually attributed to Giorgione, which

6 Erwin Panofsky, "*Et in Arcadia Ego*: Poussin and the Elegiac Tradition," in *Meaning in the Visual Arts* (Garden City, N.Y.: Doubleday Anchor Books, 1957), pp. 303–304.

fig. 3 Nicolas Poussin, *The Shepherds of Arcadia*, c. 1628–1629, oil on canvas, 101 x 82 cm, Devonshire Collection, Chatsworth. Reproduced by permission of the Duke of Devonshire and the Chatsworth Settlement Trustees (photo Photographic Survey, Courtauld Institute of Art) translated its qualities of detachment and suspension of purpose into delicately felt renditions of landscape peopled with shepherds and courtly lovers. In the following century, Claude Lorrain found a means of transmuting the twilight haze of Virgil's *Eclogues* into a golden light that suffused his landscapes with an air of unreality evocative of a Golden Age. But the most significant seventeenth-century interpretation of the arcadian theme came with Poussin, who initially linked it to the Christian Vanitas motif through the device of a skull placed on a tombstone inscribed with the words *Et in Arcadia Ego*, "Even in Arcadia, there am I" (fig. 3). Poussin borrowed the skull as well as the inscription from Guercino, who a few years earlier had painted two shepherds startled by their discovery in the woods of a skull on a block of crumbling stone (fig. 4). In Guercino's painting the inscription is on the side of the stone visible to the spectator but not the shepherds, and it functions like a caption spelling out the meaning of the scene, which is to be understood as a *memento mori*, or reminder of death. Though Poussin adds various Classical allusions, including a shepherdess, to his picture, its warning remains the same. However, as Panofsky shows in his masterful study of Poussin's treatment of the theme, his second version of *The Shepherds of Arcadia* (fig. 5) breaks with the moralizing medieval tradition.[7] The skull is gone, and so is the element of surprise. Here, "the Arcadians are not so much warned of an implacable future as they are immersed in mellow meditations on a beautiful past," and the transition is made from moralism to openly expressed elegiac sentiment.[8] In the absence of the death's head, the meaning of the phrase *Et in Arcadia Ego* is obscured. Instead of "I [Death] am even in Arcadia," it can understandably (though incorrectly, from a grammatical point of view) be interpreted to mean "I too dwelled in Arcadia"—not a warning, but a bittersweet reminder of past pleasures.

Gradually the idea of death disappeared altogether, and all that remained of Arcadia was love and the dream of a bucolic life of simple pleasures. Then, in the nineteenth century, the taste for factual observation brushed away poetry, although Constable at the beginning of the century painted his local landscape with a naturalness of feeling and observation that was essentially pastoral, as did the Barbizon painters in the forest of Fontainebleau somewhat later. The essentials of the arcadian theme were, however, adaptable to different contexts, and it is instructive to compare Seurat's measured celebration of suburban weekend pleasures in *La Grande Jatte* (fig. 6) with Puvis de Chavanne's classicizing *Pleasant Land* (fig. 7). Lawrence Gowing views the pastoral form as "an imaginative vessel for the meaning of a human environment," and each painter in his own way

[7] Panofsky, *op. cit.*, p. 312 ff. [8] Ibid., p. 313.

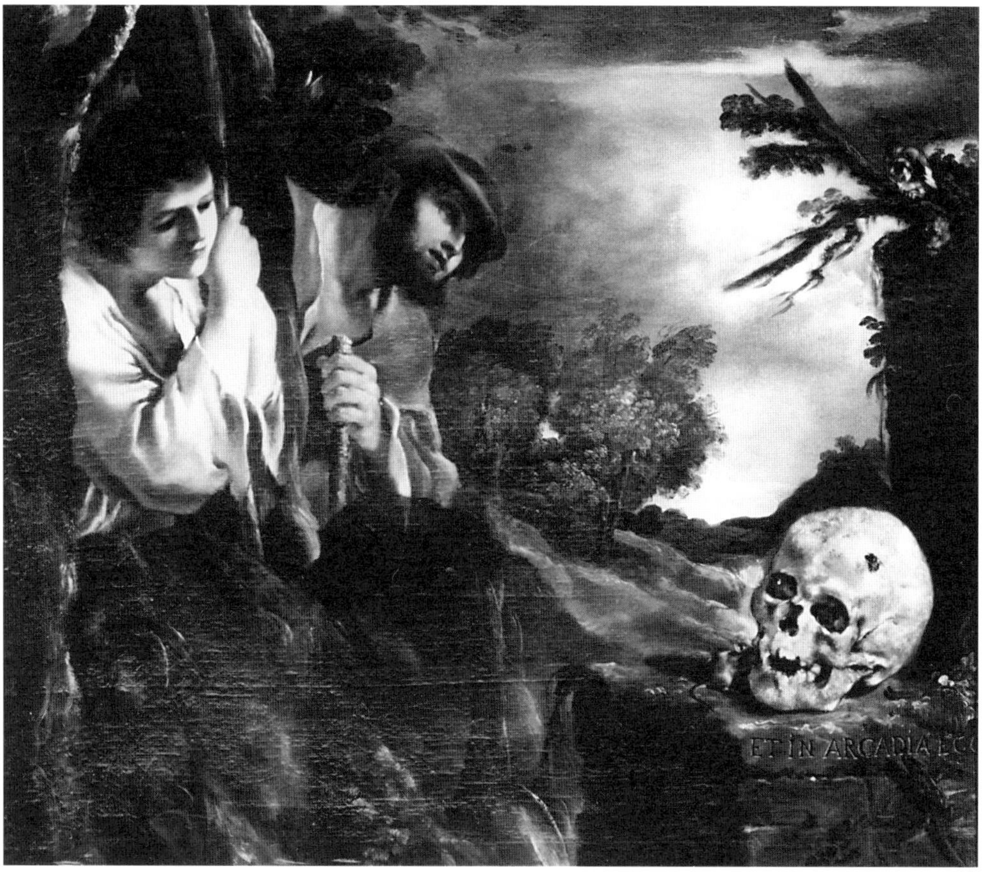

discovers the quality of detachment and the "art of relationship" that is its essence.[9] As for the primitive Arcadia, by the end of the nineteenth century it had once again become an actual place, and to discover it one can do no better than to look at any of Gauguin's Breton or Tahitian paintings.

A Natural Paradise

Parallel to its depiction in art and literature, the arcadian vision and its variants were also being realized in the landscape. There is probably no better introduction to this subject than Simon Schama's *Landscape and Memory*, a masterful argument for the persistence of myth and memory in the experience of nature throughout human history.[10]

[9] Lawrence Gowing, "The Modern Vision," in Robert C. Cafritz, Lawrence Gowing, and David Rosand, *Places of Delight: The Pastoral Landscape*, exh. cat. (New York: Clarkson N. Potter, 1988), p. 189. [10] Simon Schama, *Landscape and Memory* (Toronto: Vintage, 1996).

fig. 4 **Guercino,** *The Arcadian Shepherds* (*Et in Arcadia Ego*), 1618, oil on canvas, 82 x 91 cm, Galleria Nazionale di Palazzo Corsini, Rome

In his final chapter, entitled "Arcadia Redesigned," Schama's discussion ranges from the creation of park-like private estates and picturesque gardens that combined nature and art in an extravagant pursuit of sublime effect in eighteenth-century England to the taming of the forest of Fontainebleau in the nineteenth century with marked trails for hikers and Frederick Law Olmsted's creation of a vast metropolitan Arcadia in New York's Central Park. According to Schama, "There have always been two kinds of arcadia: shaggy and smooth; dark and light; a place of bucolic leisure and a place of primitive panic." "It's tempting," he adds, "to see the two arcadias perennially defined against each other; from the idea of the park (wilderness or pastoral) to the philosophy of the front lawn (industrially kempt or drifted with buttercups and clover); civility and harmony or integrity and unruliness?"[11]

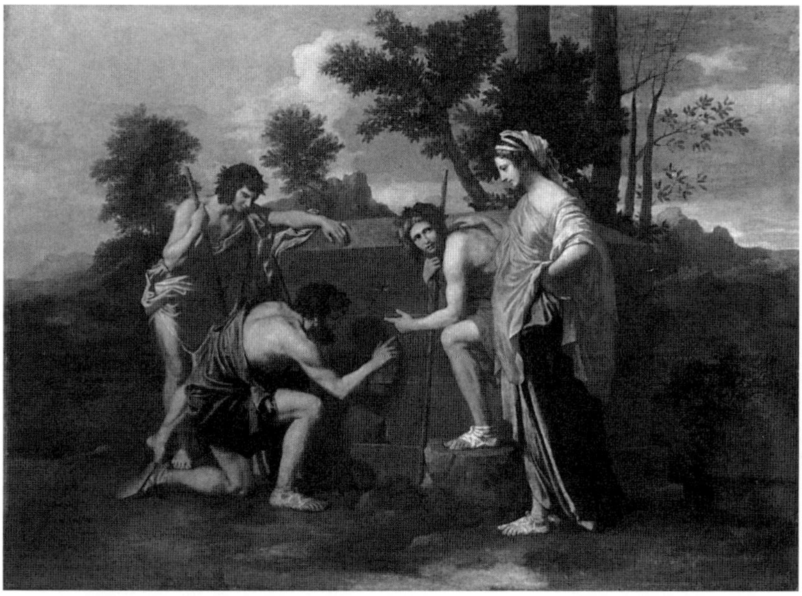

Schama's definition of these man-made natural retreats as Arcadias is, of course, metaphorical. But it is a revealing metaphor, because it seizes upon their underlying commonality as landscapes designed to fit the changing vision of the natural world as a place with intrinsic human meaning. Arcadia is designed (and redesigned, as Schama points out in his title) to wrest a meaningful order out of chaos and to satisfy the human

[11] Schama, pp. 517 and 525.

fig. 5 Nicolas Poussin, *The Shepherds of Arcadia*, c. 1638–1640, oil on canvas, 85 x 121 cm, Musée du Louvre, Paris desire for a sense of wholeness. Such a desire may be universal. It certainly is not limited to the Greco-Roman construction of Arcadia. The early Christians, for example, imagined the place of humankind's redemption as a heavenly Garden of Eden, and took their name for it from the Persian *pairidaeza*, or paradise, a rectangular or square walled garden or park intersected by two channels of water. The Persian garden was a distillation of springtime, a green oasis in a dry country. Its walls (there were sometimes two sets, outer walls that kept game in and poachers out, and inner walls to keep the game away from the plants) defined a park for hunting and an intimate garden for love and intellectual pursuits. At the same time they kept out the rest of the world.

But the enclosed garden laid out in four quarters was itself a world and was understood to represent wholeness in the Middle Ages. Although the early Christians believed that all nature was poisoned at the Fall, in the Renaissance it was argued by many that nature had merely been scattered, and Creation was regarded as a puzzle that could be put back together by the study of God's works. This aim was greatly aided, as John Prest has demonstrated in his fascinating study of the origins of the botanical garden,

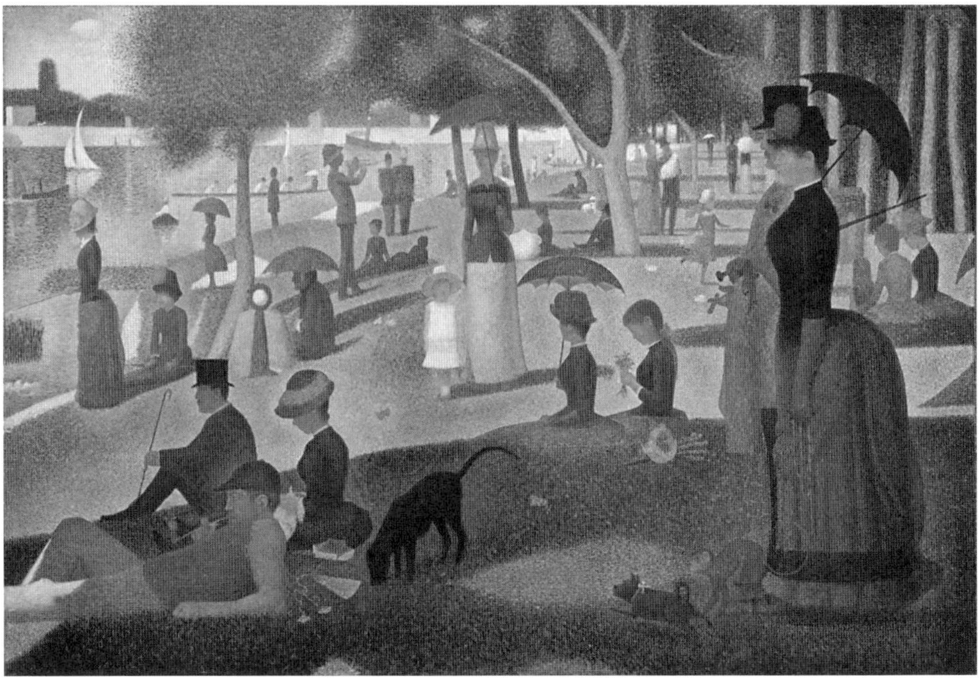

fig. 6 Georges Seurat, *A Sunday on La Grande Jatte*, 1884–1886, oil on canvas, 207.6 x 308 cm, The Art Institute of Chicago, Helen Birch Bartlett Memorial Collection

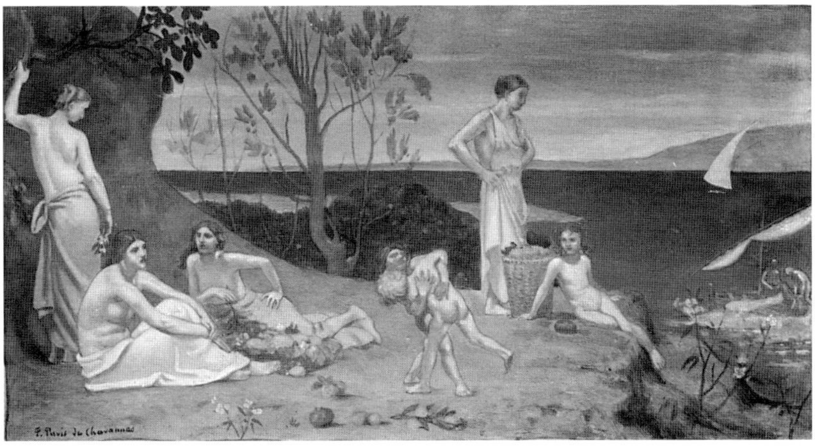

by the discovery of the Americas.[12] The many new plants and animals found there were thought to be the missing pieces of the puzzle, and gardeners sought to collect as many as possible for the new botanical gardens, which were conceived as re-creations of the Garden of Eden.[13] The idea of these gardens, some of them very ambitious, was nothing less than the recovery of knowledge and power over nature. On the model of the reflection of the great in the small, the knowledge of nature was thought to be the route to self-knowledge.

The chief formal characteristic of such gardens, which were part allegorical, part scientific, was their regularity and order. Nature before the Fall was imagined in contrast with the disorderly world that people saw around them, which was noticeably lacking in coherent form. Gradually, this view changed. The link between disorder and the corruption of nature at the Fall was challenged by those who argued that God himself had made nature so varied, and gardeners stressed the idea that nature likes variety. At first, variety was sought through carefully planned contrasts with artificially created wildernesses—groves of trees laced with winding paths were placed within the walls of the garden. But by the eighteenth century the idea of naturalness, modelled on the pastoral ideal, came to dominate, especially in England, and the landscape garden was born. The

[12] John Prest, *The Garden of Eden: The Botanic Garden and the Re-Creation of Paradise* (New Haven and London: Yale University Press, 1981). [13] Ibid., p. 6. Although animals had to be excluded from the botanical garden for practical reasons, the continuing belief in the "Great Chain of Being," linking the mineral world, plants, animals, and man in a continuous progression to God, led to collections of rocks and animals being established alongside the gardens, many of which had extensive menageries. See Prest, pp. 52–54.

fig. 7 Pierre Puvis de Chavannes, *Pleasant Land* (*Doux pays*), 1882, oil on canvas, 25.7 x 47.6 cm, Yale University Art Gallery, New Haven, The Mary Gertrude Abbey Fund landscape garden expressed the ideal that there should be no division between garden and landscape. Instead, each should flow naturally into the other. In one sense, the walls of the formal garden came down, but in another, they were merely concealed, for the creation of parks for the landed gentry and the nouveaux riches involved the expropriation of vast amounts of common land and the careful exclusion of real agriculture from the picture. Behind the creation of Arcadia for a few lay the dispossession of the common farmer. The ideal unity it represented concealed a larger social disunity.

With dispossession and disunity, we find ourselves back at the starting point of Virgil's *Eclogues*. Indeed, the situation gave rise to a new kind of poetry, the so-called anti-pastoral. But for most the practical response was migration, to the city or to America, which held out the promise of a new, arcadian utopia to be wrested from the wilderness.

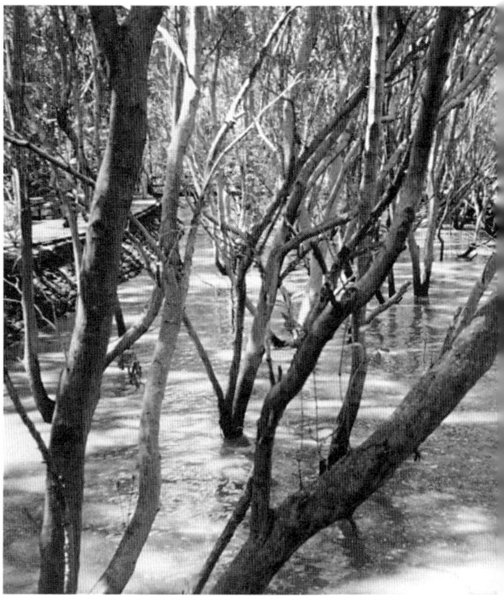

The Modern Arcadia

In the view of one American writer on gardens, the main contribution of his country to the world landscape are the wilderness preserve and the front lawn.[14] Both, as Simon Schama notes, can be vehicles of Arcadia. Which is not to say, simplistically, that the one represents the pastoral and the other the wild or primitive Arcadia, despite Freud's comment linking wilderness parks and the unconscious:

The creation of the mental domain of phantasy has a complete counterpart in the establishment of "reservations" and "nature-parks" in places where the inroads of agriculture, traffic, or industry threaten to change... the earth rapidly into something unrecognizable. The "reservation" is to maintain the old condition of things which has been regretfully sacrificed to necessity everywhere else; there everything may grow and spread as it pleases, including what is useless and even what is harmful. The mental realm of phantasy is also such a reservation reclaimed from the encroaches of the reality principle.[15]

[14] Michael Pollan, *Second Nature*, cited in Evan Eisenberg, *The Ecology of Eden* (Toronto: Random House, 1998), p. 249. [15] Sigmund Freud, *General Introduction to Psychoanalysis*, cited in Marx, p. 8.

fig. 8 Mangrove swamp and boardwalk, Brisbane, Australia (photo Diana Nemiroff)

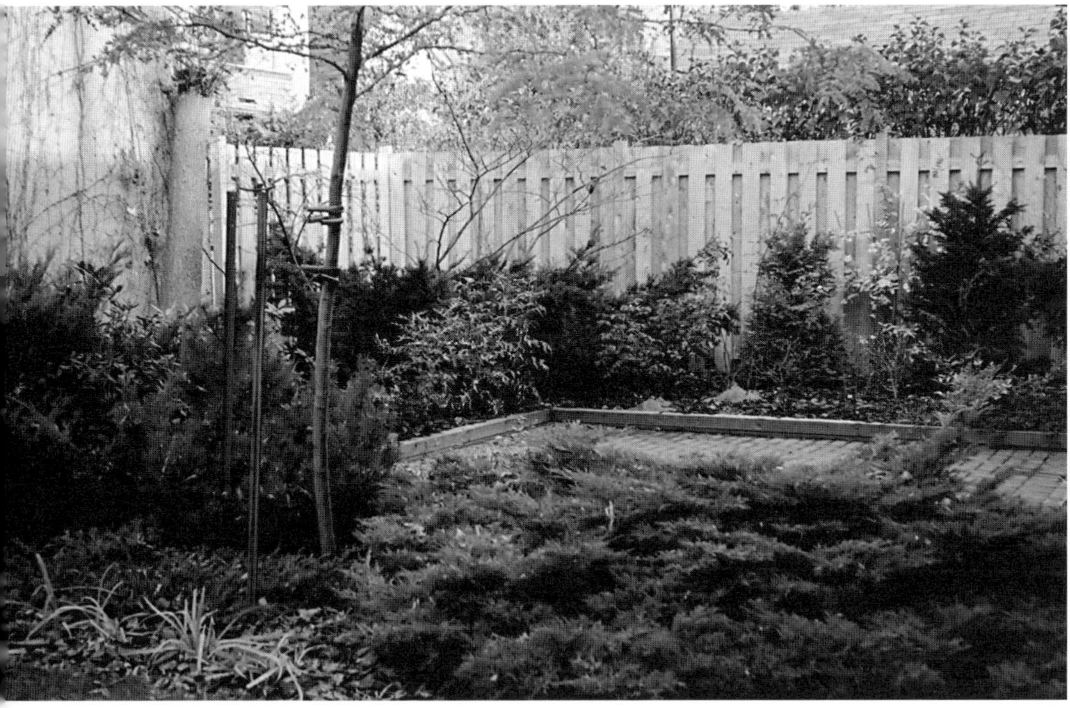

Rather, both—if one takes the lawn metonymically to stand for the suburb—are midpoints between non-human nature and civilization, and both are complex and changing places.

In his influential book on the pastoral in American life and literature, Leo Marx distinguishes between two kinds of pastoral, the one popular and sentimental, the other imaginative and complex. "Each," he says, "does represent something of the yearning for a simpler, more harmonious style of life, an existence 'closer to nature,' that is the psychic root of all pastoralism—genuine and spurious."[16] It is easy to find examples of popular pastoralism. On a recent visit to the Internet, for instance, I found that typing the word "arcadia" took me either to the sites of innumerable small American towns called Arcadia, or to real estate agents who have incorporated Arcadia and its bucolic associations into their prospectus for peace and happiness in the country, the dream house. Around us, the desire to return to nature has caused the market for country cottages to boom, while for the more adventurous, wilderness outfitters offer a cornucopia of equipment suited to every fantasy, from hiking and camping to mountain-climbing and white-water rafting.

16 Marx, p. 6.

fig. 9 Urban garden, Ottawa (photo Diana Nemiroff)

However, the flight from the city has pushed the suburb further and further into the working countryside, with sometimes disastrous results. The citizens of Walkerton, a rural hamlet in southwestern Ontario, had harsh proof of this last year when seven people died as a result of drinking water that was contaminated by runoff from local livestock operations. Agriculture is now run on an industrial scale. Those green fields that looked so inviting on Sunday afternoon outings in the family car stink of manure, and the waste from herds of a thousand or more hogs or cattle is difficult to keep out of the pastoral paradise. Similarly, the wilderness preserve is threatened by its very popularity. We now realize, for example, that the wildlife in Banff National Park, in Alberta, is menaced by the tourist development of the town at its heart. The park's roads are virtual walls cutting through the habitats of some wild animals, while others have become our camp followers, attracted by the prospect of an easy meal. Alarmingly frequent stories about hikes in the woods interrupted by sometimes fatal bear attacks make the idea of an arcadian wilderness (where at the very least the creatures live in harmony with man and each other) difficult to hold on to. Yet none of this lessens the desire behind the dream.

As the dream of refuge in nature becomes more elusive, the arcadian middle landscape is changing. Although there is resistance in some quarters, suburbs are more densely built and city-like than they once were. Even the supremacy of the car is challenged by new urban planning. Nor is the green lawn the perfect democratic symbol it used to be, as the dangers of pesticides and monoculture are more widely known; more and more people are sowing meadows in their front yards, or creating small, partly paved outdoor areas surrounded by blooming plants in pots or borders, in a modest return to the paradise garden (fig. 9). The real wilderness cannot be replaced, as its biological diversity is the source of the world's survival in the future, but environmental groups are beginning to convince city governments of the value of preserving wetlands on the fringes of the urban conglomeration (fig. 8) and are drawing attention to the importance of cleaning up the waterways that connect outlying suburbs and towns to the metropolitan centre. In closing his lengthy examination of the Western landscape imagination, Schama quotes Thoreau, most of whose walking and ruminating in nature took place within a few steps of his backyard in Concord: "It is in vain to dream of a wildness distant from ourselves. There is none such. It is the bog in our brain and bowels, the primitive vigor of Nature in us, that inspires that dream."[17] Thoreau's words underline the close bond between the inner, psychic landscape and the outer, natural world.

[17] Schama, p. 578, quoting from Robert L. Rothwell, ed., *Henry David Thoreau: An American Landscape*.

Fleeing from the oppressive constraints of the urban environment to the countryside, however short the distance, is not necessarily to be dismissed as an escapist flight from the complexities of modern life (which, as we have seen from Virgil's *Eclogues*, is a very old impulse). It may also be, especially in the hands of artists, an attempt to draw complex meanings out of apparently simple situations—what William Empson called "the pastoral process of putting the complex into the simple,"[18] in his book *Some Versions of Pastoral*, which was itself an attempt to enlarge the meaning of pastoral for modern literature. For example, I was struck by an extended, lyrical description of the happiness inspired by his visits to the countryside in the memoir of the Hungarian poet George Faludy.[19] The passage occurs immediately before a harrowing account of his arrest and imprisonment by the Communist authorities on invented charges of spying. The contrast is not only one of happiness and suffering. Faludy's description of the ancientness of the Hungarian countryside and his simple enjoyment of its pleasures, when contrasted with the paranoia and irrational cruelty of the post-war regime, has the effect of evoking, symbolically, political values of integrity and legitimacy that contest the right of the authorities to remake Hungarian society in the Stalinist image. Nor is this the only such contrast in Faludy's book. His exile during the war in North Africa also takes on the character of an idyllic interlude, in which the political determination to save Hungary from Fascism, which preoccupied him prior to the outbreak of war, is juxtaposed with endless days passed in leisure (*otium*), love, and storytelling that were, finally, more in harmony with his poet's temperament. Indeed it was this temperament, and the store of civilization that it absorbed in such interludes, that equipped him to resist the ordeal of the labour camp with which the memoir concludes.

Pastoral and Anti-Pastoral

The juxtaposition of contending values and perspectives is at the heart of the pastoral mode. While the popular pastoral can be escapist and sentimental, the pastoral mode in art or literature often involves "implicitly or explicitly, a critical exploration and counterbalancing of attitudes, perspectives, and experiences."[20] In looking back at the representations of Arcadia I have described, it is striking to note the tensions at their core

[18] William Empson, *Some Versions of Pastoral* (Norfolk, Conn.: New Directions, 1938), p. 23. [19] George Faludy, *My Happy Days in Hell* (Don Mills, Ont.: Totem Press, 1985). [20] Patrick Cullen, *Spenser, Marvell, and Renaissance Pastoral* (Cambridge: Harvard University Press, 1970), p. 1.

(beginning with the sudden appearance of the exiled Meliboeus in the green hollow of Virgil's *Eclogues*), whether the source be unrequited love, the inevitability of death, or the more contemporary intrusions of industry and pollution. Even the terms used to describe it seem to come in paired opposites: primitive and pastoral, wild and idyllic, park and garden, natural and artificial. Ambivalence seems natural to it. If Arcadia represents the search for wholeness, it appears that wholeness, like Pan, the god who is half-beast, half-man, is fraught with contradictions. Arcadia—the perfect mid-point between wilderness and civilization—is culture's view of the natural world, which in the end is perhaps the only one available to us. Dissonance is probably inevitable.

What versions, then, of Arcadia may be found in recent art? The poetry of shepherds playing pipes and chasing after shepherdesses has been obsolete since the eighteenth century, though the natural setting remains. Yet, according to W.J.T. Mitchell, landscape

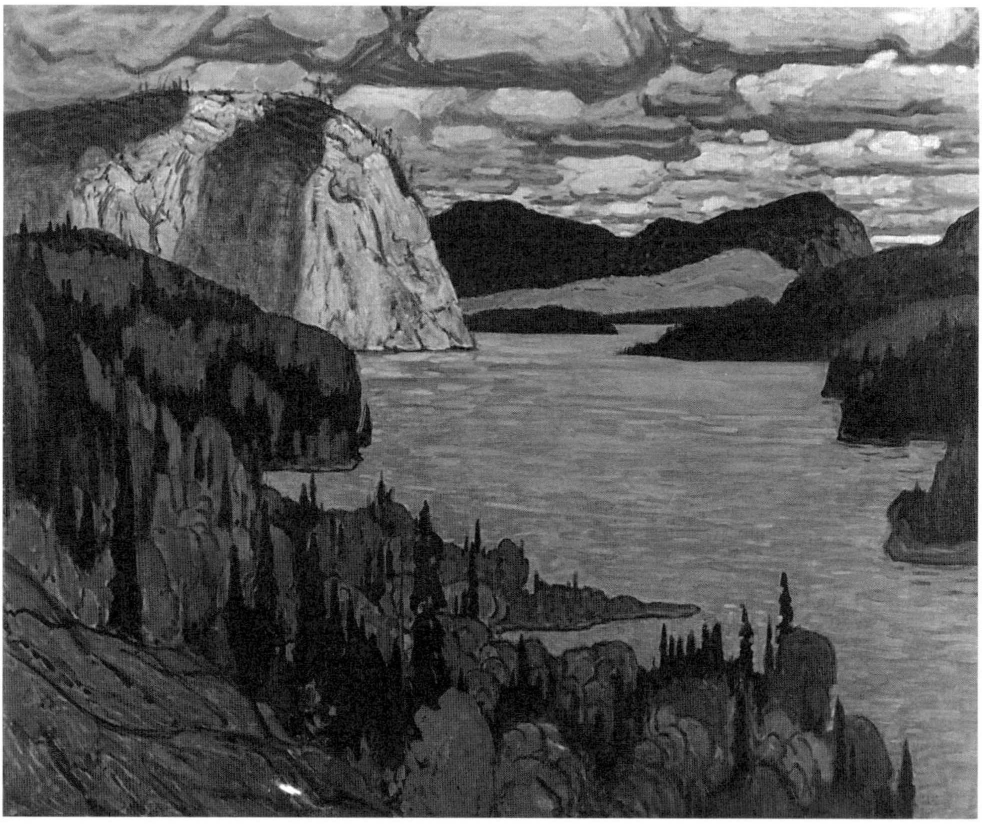

fig. 10 J.E.H. Macdonald, *The Solemn Land,* 1921, oil on canvas, 121.9 x 152.4, National Gallery of Canada, Ottawa

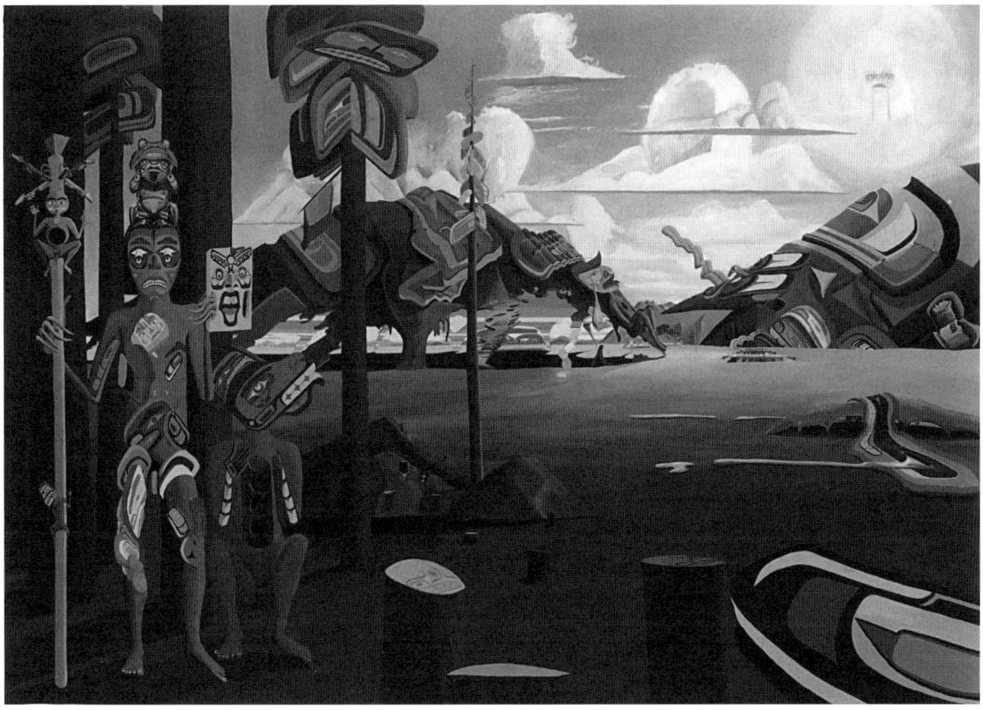

is an exhausted medium.[21] Mitchell is referring to landscape as an instrument of cultural power that "naturalizes a cultural and social construction, representing an artificial world as if it were simply given and inevitable,"[22] and not its representations in painting, photography, and (I would add) cinema. While I doubt that landscape was ever—except for the self-consciously naturalizing parks of eighteenth- and nineteenth-century Europe—conceived other than to be read symbolically, though perhaps not in the way he has in mind, his suggestion that landscape in the European tradition may be exhausted for the purposes of serious art is of greater interest. Mitchell's hypothesis is that landscape representation is bound up with imperialism, and the importance of the genre in ancient Roman, Chinese, and modern European civilizations lends support to his argument. Yet like capitalism, whose processes offer him analogies for his Marxist analysis, landscape's fate has been more complex than he allows. As a genre, it is true, landscape painting no

21 See his essay "Imperial Landscape," in W.J.T. Mitchell, ed., *Landscape and Power* (Chicago and London: University of Chicago Press, 1994), pp. 5–34. Of particular interest here are his nine "theses on landscape," in which he states: "Landscape is not a genre of art but a medium … of exchange between the human and the natural … a natural scene mediated by culture … Landscape is an exhausted medium, no longer viable as a mode of artistic expression." 22 Ibid., p. 2.

fig. 11 Lawrence Paul Yuxweluptun, *Scorched Earth, Clear-cut Logging on Native Sovereign Land. Shaman Coming to Fix*, 1991, acrylic on canvas, 195.6 x 275 cm, National Gallery of Canada, Ottawa

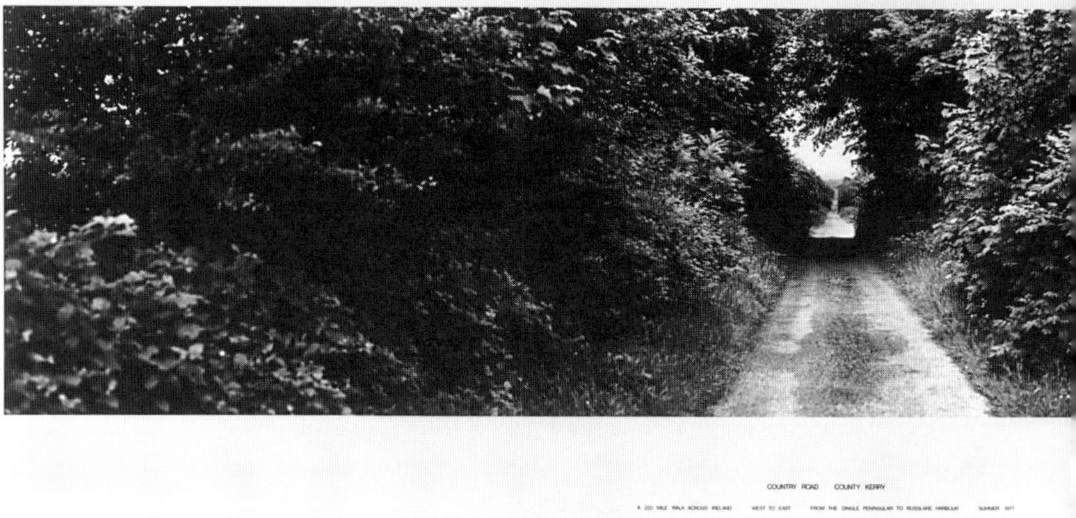

longer occupies a place in the forefront of contemporary art as it did in the nineteenth century. Even into the twentieth, the Canadian example of the Group of Seven (active in the second and third decades of the century) suggests it could still play an important role because of its capacity to symbolize the identity of a young nation (fig. 10). As a cultural medium, however, it is still potent now, not least for Aboriginal peoples and environmental activists who have used the communicative power of the landscape image, straight or transformed by art, to appeal directly to the feelings, both spiritual and political, that most of us harbour about nature and our relationship to it (fig. 11).

But what about the *art* of landscape today? Is Mitchell right to say that landscape in the European tradition is exhausted for serious art? There are two parts to the answer to this question. The first is a qualification about *genre*: the explosion of media and the traditional categories of art in the twentieth century make it impossible to limit the subject of the relationship of the human and the non-human to a discussion about painting. Since the advent of Conceptual art and related movements such as Land Art in the late 1960s, landscape as subject and as medium (or material) has been omnipresent in serious art. Hamish Fulton's and Richard Long's landscape walks, which Fulton, for his part, insists are "the art" no less than the photographs and texts exhibited in galleries, are an example (figs. 12 and 13). They seem to emerge from an English pastoral tradition of ease and intimacy with nature, although the Romantic identification with Nature's moods

fig. 12 **Hamish Fulton**, *Country Road, County Kerry*, 1977, gelatin silver print, 97 × 247.3 × 4.4 cm (framed), National Gallery of Canada, Ottawa © Hamish Fulton

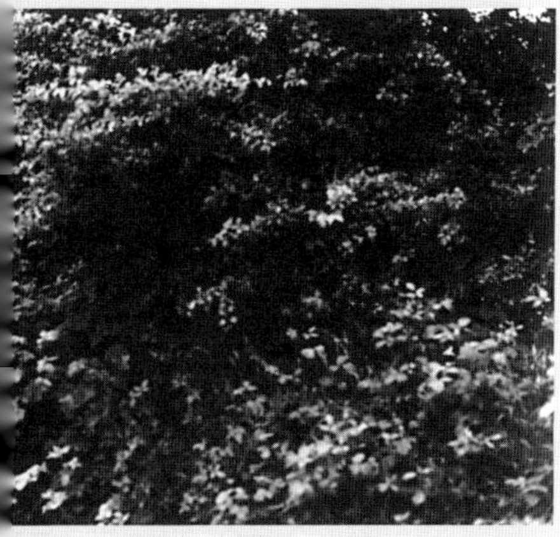

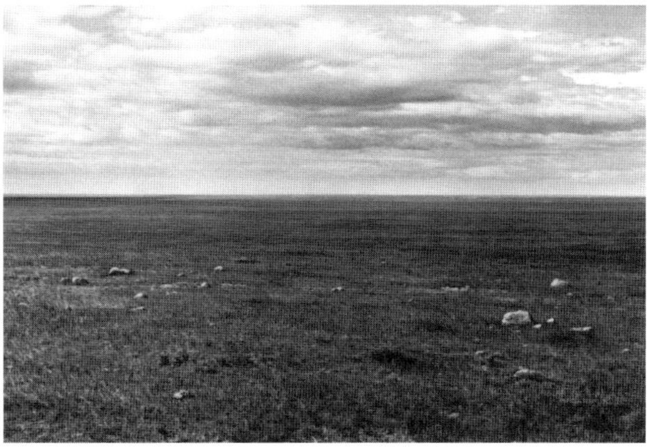

and hidden places has been replaced by the calmer relationship of diaristic—and often poetic—observation. Still, both artists move through the landscape in apparent tranquillity, and this harmony with their environment, which extends from familiar backways to remote outposts, is fully pastoral in character. At the other extreme lies Robert Smithson's earthwork *Spiral Jetty* (p. 36), hauled from the earth, briefly visible, and finally submerged in an inland sea. Smithson's vision of nature's sublimity, his grasp of its non-human, entropic logic, are emphatically anti-pastoral. In his accompanying essay, he wrote, sardonically, "*Et in Utah ego*," substituting for Arcadia a specific geographical place and geological landscape, while evoking a dizzying dissolution of self in the next line.[23] Both of these opposing modes belong to the contemporary vocabulary of landscape.

The second part of the answer to the question must address the issue of painting. A certain type of idealized landscape painting, representing an immediate and uncomplicated relationship with the natural environment, has been displaced into photography of the sentimental amateur or corporate commercial variety. (Or has it given way to direct experience as the availability of travel brings the exotic locale nearer?) In this sense Mitchell is right. However, another kind of landscape painting has emerged which is both a continuation and a critique of the European tradition. Here, Gerhard Richter and Anselm Kiefer may serve as examples, although they are very different artists, and perhaps neither

[23] Nancy Holt, ed., *The Writings of Robert Smithson* (New York: New York University Press, 1979), p. 113.

fig. 13 Richard Long, *A Straight Hundred Mile Walk on the Canadian Prairie*, 1974, photograph with added text in graphite on cardboard, 50.6 x 75.9 cm, National Gallery of Canada, Ottawa © Richard Long would think of himself as a landscape painter. Richter's work is always realized through the mediation of photography, and his greatest landscape work is not a painting but rather an encyclopaedic compendium of photographs of his environment entitled *Atlas*. These fragmented observations of people and places constitute a personal and at the same time socially and historically specific reportage of everyday life in Germany today, and they serve as the basis of his representational paintings. In his landscape paintings, he sometimes evokes the Romantic tradition of Caspar David Friedrich, and at other times the bucolic country themes that abound in nineteenth-century painting (fig. 14). However, Richter's landscape paintings have a characteristic detachment that is due partly to the absence of actors peopling these scenes and partly to the interposition of photography. While these images have inherited from the nineteenth century the bias toward observation of the real, the slight blurring that so often occurs in them distances reality and creates a sense of removal. If Richter simultaneously evokes and dissociates himself from the naturalistic landscape traditions of the previous century, Kiefer summons up and confronts more dangerous ghosts. Coming in the wake of the most terrible period of German imperialism, he creates landscapes of devastation that may be read like books. Marked by stains recalling blood and burnt remnants, and littered with names of gods and heroes, they are at once history paintings and complex allegories of guilt and redemption. Formally, their characteristically high horizon line denies any kind of transcendent relationship with the land. Instead, there is the suffocatingly close atmosphere of memories long buried and finally unearthed (fig. 15).

It is not, in my view, wrong to describe Richter's images as pastoral: they are somehow timeless in feeling, calling up a vision of integration and harmony , yet permeated with the sadness of the unattainable. Kiefer, on the other hand, belongs—like Smithson, with whom he shares his grasp of the inhuman, although it comes from a different place, in history rather than geology—to the anti-pastoral, in fact anti-humanist, strain in twentieth-century landscape art. Perhaps we can go further and identify two threads that weave themselves in and out of twentieth-century representations of nature. One might be called the objective thread. It is certainly prosaic, in the sense of being straightforwardly descriptive, although this does not preclude a certain terse poetry. This strand is evident, I think, in Conceptual art, although it could be traced back to the empiricism that motivated much of nineteenth-century art and seems to come out of a belief in the possibility of a direct relationship to nature. The other thread comes out of Symbolism. Poetic or allegorical, its material representations are symbols of a reality that is felt to lie beyond appearance. Its landscapes are the landscapes of the psyche or of the recesses of human as well as natural history. Whether these two strands can be woven together to make a contemporary version of Arcadia, in which the utopian and dystopian poles are balanced, is the question I wish to ask with this exhibition.

A Green Thought in a Green Shade[24]

This question is raised against a background of discussions about the natural world that can be summed up in simple terms. The older, utopian discourse (which for some time now has had its dystopian side as well) concerns technology's place in the world and its effects on it. Everyone acknowledges that the power of technology is transformative; arguments arise as to whether the transformation is for better or for worse. One observation that is often raised in the context of art is that technology has allowed the substitution of a mediated knowledge of the world, especially nature, for direct experience. Not only is our understanding of nature shaped by culture; nature is itself a cultural construct and thus an indication of the division and separation at the root of our being. This is true, but should be understood as nothing new. Every technical advance, whether of a practical kind, such as the plough or the motor car, or of an intellectual nature, such as the printed book, has permitted us to do and know more about the world at the cost of some degree of removal from it. However, today the older impulse to satisfy the desire for direct contact by seeking refuge in nature or by going back to the land (and its implicit rejection of the oppressive constraints of civilization) is joined by the admonitions of the environmental movement, which in their extreme form warn of the imminent destruction of nature through technology. In such a context the landscape of Arcadia—understood philosophically as a half-way point—offers a useful perspective from which to balance the opposing imperatives of the city and the wilderness. Many present-day artists, including several in this exhibition, address these polarities. Thus, for example, the works of Liz Magor and Jana Sterbak ironically undermine the idea of nature as refuge, while Diana Thater has consistently used technological means (here a video wall image of the sun composed from a NASA photograph shot from a space telescope) to make statements about our position as observers, interpreters, and makers of fictions about nature.

24 This phrase comes from Andrew Marvell's poem "The Garden." It is worth quoting several more lines from the poem, as they suggest very well the points I am making in this section: "The mind, that Ocean where each kind/Does straight its own resemblance find;/Yet it creates, transcending these,/Far other worlds, and other seas;/Annihilating all that's made/To a green thought in a green shade."

The other, newer conversation is occurring around the meaning of place in a culture and economy that are increasingly global in reach. Not only has the cultural aftermath of colonialism forced a reconsideration of Eurocentrism, overturning the authoritative model of centre and periphery, but the pressures of globalization have focussed attention on the specific and shared characteristics of the local environment and culture. Identity is often considered to be shaped by place in ways that are unduly reductive, yet the focus

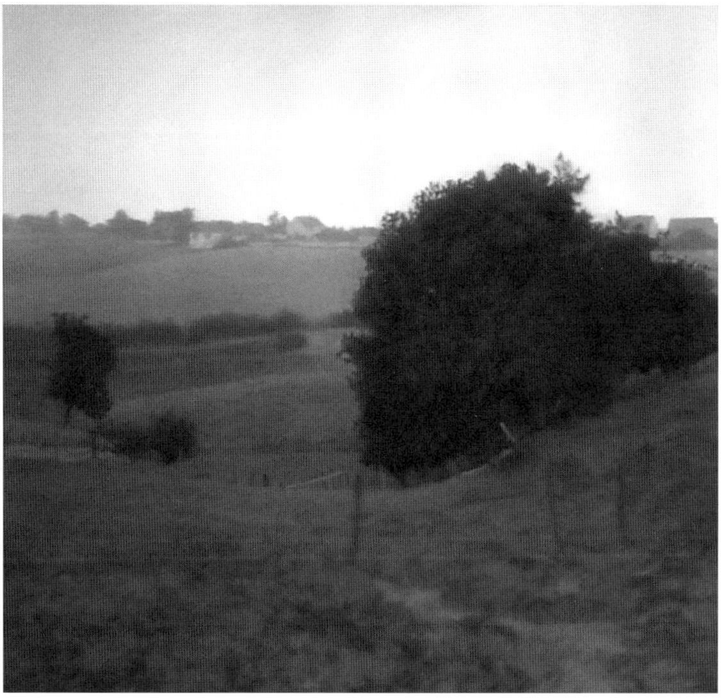

on place also leads to an enlarged understanding of the variety of our cultural roots. In addition, it is well to admit, in an era of shifting borders, the depth of the human attachment to place and the almost mythic dimension of the land in the human imagination. Arcadia can contribute to this conversation by balancing the cultural end of the equation with the natural. It is an imaginative construct that acknowledges the need to invent other worlds, even while reflecting critically on this one. The landscapes that Jeff Wall has contributed to this exhibition operate on both levels, offering visions of innocence and escape as well as unsettling images of the effect of the resource industry on the environment. For her part, Shahzia Sikander, who studied traditional miniature painting in her

fig. 14 Gerhard Richter *Wiesenthal*, 1985, oil on canvas, 90.5 x 94.9 cm, The Museum of Modern Art, New York, Blanchette Rockefeller, Betsy Babcock, and Mrs. Elizabeth Bliss Parkinson Funds

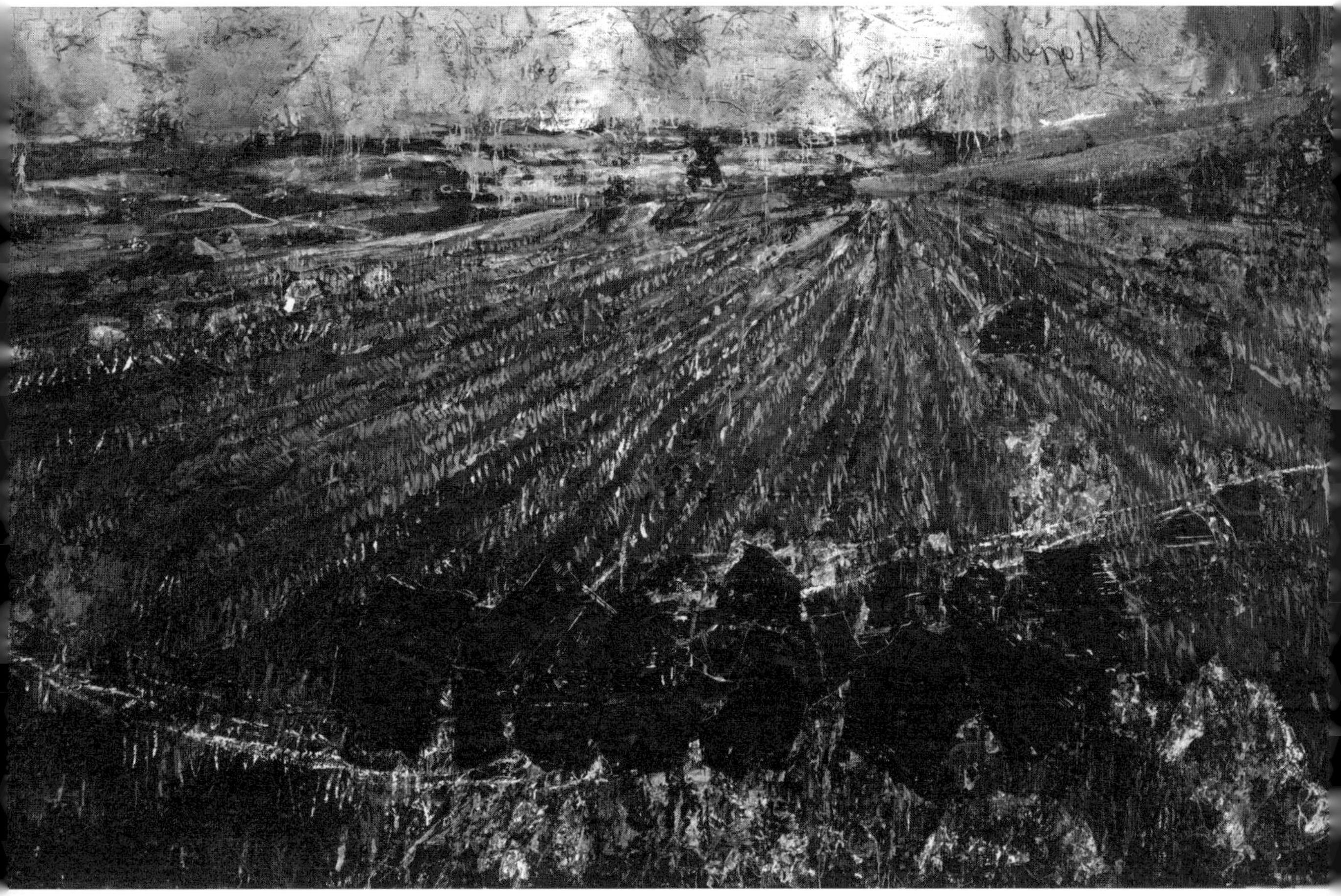

fig. 15 **Anselm Kiefer**, *Nigredo*, 1984, oil, acrylic, emulsion, shellac, and straw on photograph on canvas, with woodcut, 330 × 555 cm, Philadelphia Museum of Art, Gift of the Friends of the Philadelphia Museum of Art in celebration of their 20th anniversary

native Pakistan, uses the classical Persian motif of the garden to rethink feminine identity in a world of change.

One of the interesting aspects of the present exhibition—though it was not a conscious consideration in the selection of the artists—is the strong feminine presence it displays. I wonder if this is not also a significant aspect of rethinking Arcadia now. The melancholy of the classical Arcadia turns on the complaint of unrequited love on the part of the male poet. The pastoral space is basically a masculine one predicated on the absence or inaccessibility of the beloved lady, in which nature is both stage and echo for the lover's laments. At the same time, nature is presented as the Great Mother stripped of her dark and threatening side. Yet woman as subject scarcely exists in Arcadia. It would be retrogressive to suppose that the answer lies in an *other*, feminine arcadian space. Rather, Geneviève Cadieux, for example, deliberately constructs spaces that deny the unbroken wholeness of the natural landscape. Her photographs are oblique glances at ordinary things that speak without idealization or melancholy. Valeska Soares, on the other hand, fully indulges in the sensual surfaces associated with femininity, while balancing these with a cool gaze at the conventional structures of romantic fantasy.

Another issue that arises in looking at the exhibition—and it is an issue important to any discussion of Arcadia—is that of beauty and the related subject of visual pleasure. The strands of twentieth-century art that I have traced here do not, in their emphasis on prosaic observation or on poetic or allegorical symbolism, exclude beauty, but it is not a quality that is often pursued for itself. Perhaps one reason is the separation of the beautiful from the sublime that Modernism inherited from Kant. The aesthetic of power represented by the sublime held more force for the past century; whereas the sublime is great, the beautiful may be small, even diminutive, and hence lacking in power. It is linked, as one can see from the contemporary criticism of Matisse, with hedonism and luxury, and thus offends the modern sensibility, which associates toughness, struggle, and irony with truth.[25] However, as the philosopher Elaine Scarry argues, beauty may well be allied with truth in its own right, because it "ignites the desire for truth" by giving us the experience of conviction. Moreover, in her view, "through its beauty, the world continually recommits us to a rigorous standard of perceptual care,"[26] out of which can come an attention on our part to assuring its continuance. For example, Yoshihiro Suda's minutely detailed carvings

25 See Elderfield, pp. 15–22, for an extended discussion of the competing views of reality represented by such opposing pairs in criticism of Matisse and in modernism in general. 26 Elaine Scarry, *On Beauty and Being Just* (Princeton: Princeton University Press, 1999), pp. 52 and 81.

of flowers or even humble weeds in the exhibition offer an intimation of perfection that is usually unattainable. In the unlikely context of a bare-walled museum gallery, we come upon them unexpectedly like greetings from another world, and our sense of aliveness is heightened by the discovery.

Still, beauty and any such perfection is elusive. As Henri Michaux observes in the quote that prefaces this essay, "ours is not a century of paradises," and this is true as well for Arcadia. We cannot imagine perfection without some scepticism, some degree of withdrawal. But isn't this detachment one of the attributes of Arcadia? It certainly doesn't prevent the mind from imagining other worlds or from chasing after the elusive phenomena of this one, as Tacita Dean's patient attempt to capture the sun's eclipse from the Cornish coast in her film *Banewl* in this exhibition poignantly shows. In her reprise of Thomas Tallis's *Spem in Alium*, Janet Cardiff moves beyond the visual world, using sound alone to recreate a vision of Paradise that four hundred years ago many still believed attainable, through virtue and faith in the afterlife. In the contemporary world such certainties elude most of us. The arcadian dream of harmony here on earth may serve as a timely reminder that hope rests now in the balance of earth and mind alone, "a green thought in a green shade."

Diana Nemiroff

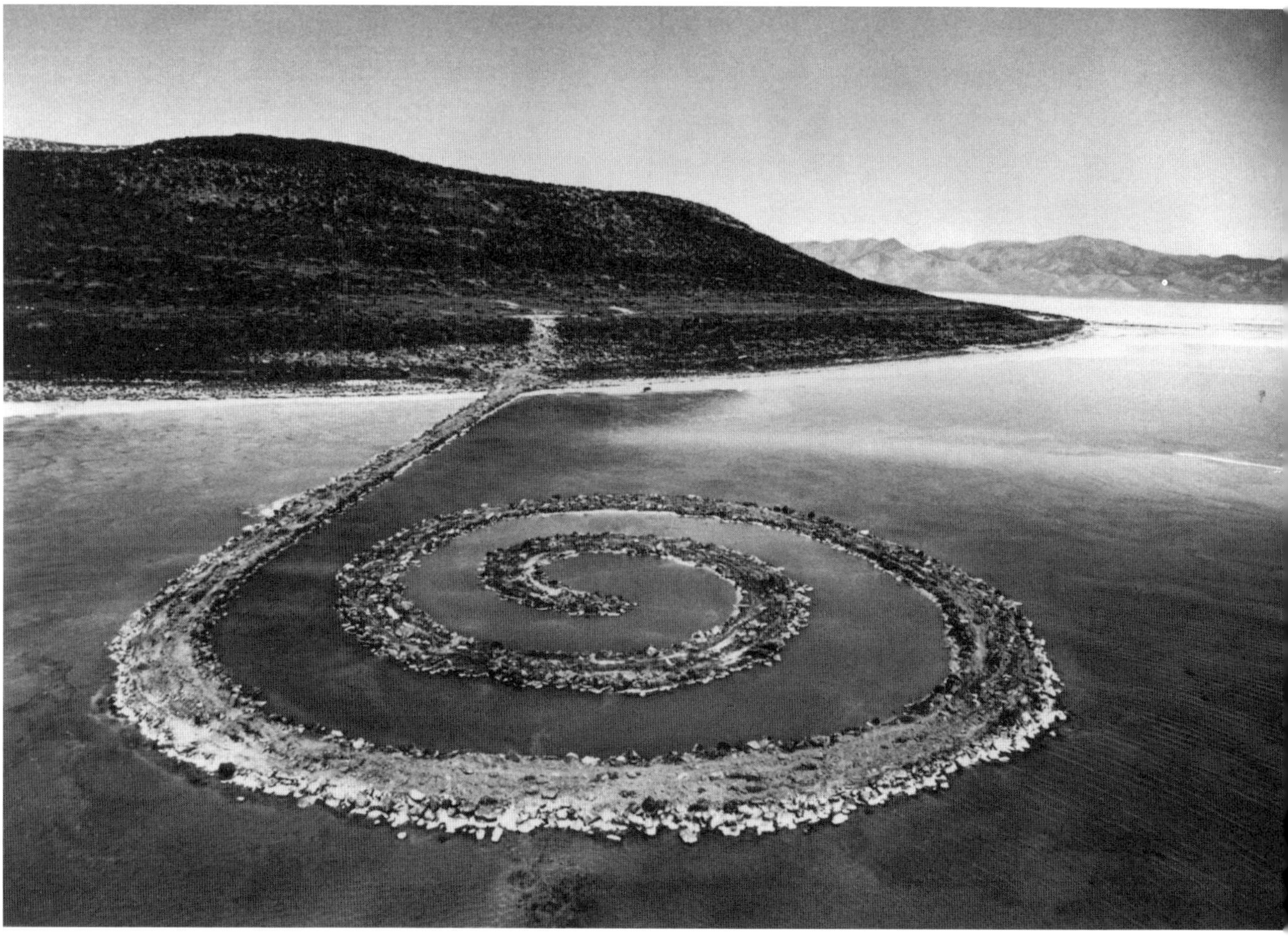

Robert Smithson, *Spiral Jetty*, Great Salt Lake, Utah, April 1970, black rock, salt crystals, earth, red water (algae), 1 × 4.5 × 450 m, Estate of Robert Smithson, courtesy of the James Cohan Gallery, New York, collection of the Dia Center for the Arts, New York (photo Gianfranco Gorgoni)

Outside Matters

In the early days of Impressionism, the artist Claude Monet set himself adrift in a customized painting-boat (fig. 1), leaving behind solid ground and the studio's filtered light and belaboured techniques, and leaving behind as well Parisian intrigue and politics. It was from this position of outside-ness that the artist would grapple with nature's most elemental and insubstantial phenomena. Water, light, and atmosphere would be transformed into modern colours and shapes. In this way, nature would eventually make its way back to the metropolis. About a hundred years later, in 1970, Robert Smithson conceived his *Floating Island*, an unrealized project that was meant to wend its way around the borough of Manhattan, pulled by a little tug-boat. Complete with trees, bushes, rocks, earth, and a meandering path, Smithson's "island" was an apparently real piece of nature, presented without undue aesthetic embellishments (fig. 2). At the same time, this floating landscape generated its own poetics of skies and earth in motion, and so Monet's and Smithson's landscape projects would seem to have some commonality. In the twentieth century, however, the stakes are quite different when artists decide to situate themselves, their practice, or their artworks outdoors. What might be the value, at the present time, of seeking outside spaces, or natural spaces? This question has been addressed by the philosophers Deleuze and Guattari in *A Thousand Plateaux*, where they argue that "one cannot write sufficiently in the name of an outside. The outside has no image, no signification, no subjectivity." Even if it isn't really possible to escape from language, society, and the symbolic order of things, it is still necessary to imaginatively posit oneself in an "other" place. The concept of outside-ness would therefore continue to have great metaphoric value.[1]

Throughout the nineteenth century artists rushed to set up their easels outdoors. There was immense rhetorical power attached to the notion of *pleinairisme* (open-air painting). This had become a gesture enacted against academies and other institutions of art, which decreed that in order for nature to be transformed into art there was need of

[1] Gilles Deleuze and Félix Guattari, *A Thousand Plateaux* (London: The Athlone Press, 1988), p. 23.

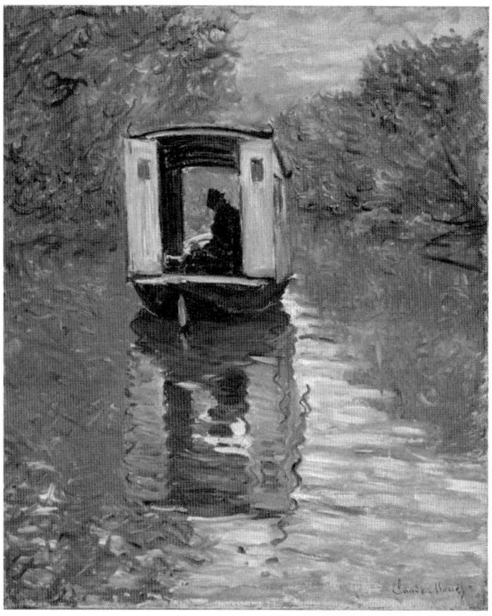

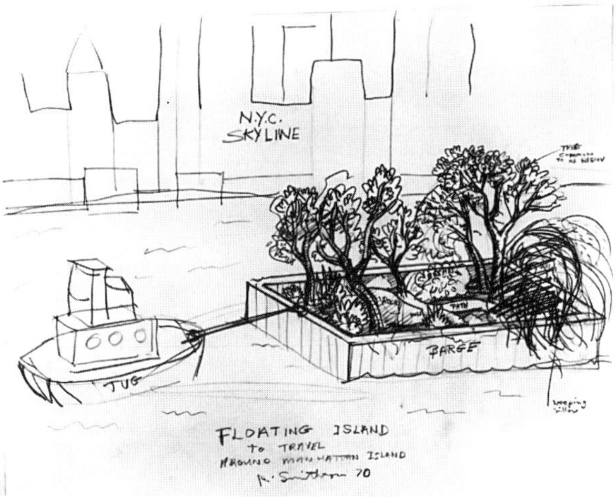

a narrative structure, derived from a stock of religious, mythological, and literary stories. Nature was therefore narrativized. Most modern artists were determined to divest their landscapes of saints, goddesses, and heroes, but it was not always so easy to shrug off this cast of characters, who seemed to show up whenever an artist so much as glanced at a bit of scenery. Referring to a pastoral scene by Camille Corot, Émile Zola once remarked that much as he admired the painter's technique he only wished Corot would kill off once and for all the nymphs who continued to wander through his otherwise naturalistic country environments (fig. 3).[2] This attitude is characteristically modern, and indeed it can be said that modern landscape art was founded on the wish to de-narrativize nature. Perhaps nature didn't have to appear in the guise of an idealized past, and perhaps it was not necessary for people to carry around in their heads previously-formed pictures of Arcadia, Eden, Cythera, or Atlantis. Instead, during the nineteenth century, it became desirable to head out-of-doors on one's own, and to confront nature on its own. The apparently direct encounter between an individual and the realm of nature could be radical and modern, aesthetically productive, and even utopian.

Nature as a concept is notoriously difficult to grasp. Is it a place, an essence, a system? The book of nature can provide us with structure, order, encoded information. A more romantic approach would say that nature is what exists just beyond culture, history,

[2] See Michael Clarke, *Corot* (London: South Bank Centre, 1991), p. 8.

fig. 1 Claude Monet, *The Boat Studio* (*Le bateau-atelier*), 1876, oil on canvas, 72 x 59.8 cm, The Barnes Foundation, Merion, Pennsylvania **fig. 2 Robert Smithson**, *Study for Floating Island to Travel around Manhattan Island*, 1970, pencil on paper, 48.3 x 61 cm, Estate of Robert Smithson, courtesy of the James Cohan Gallery, New York, collection of Joseph E. Seagram & Sons

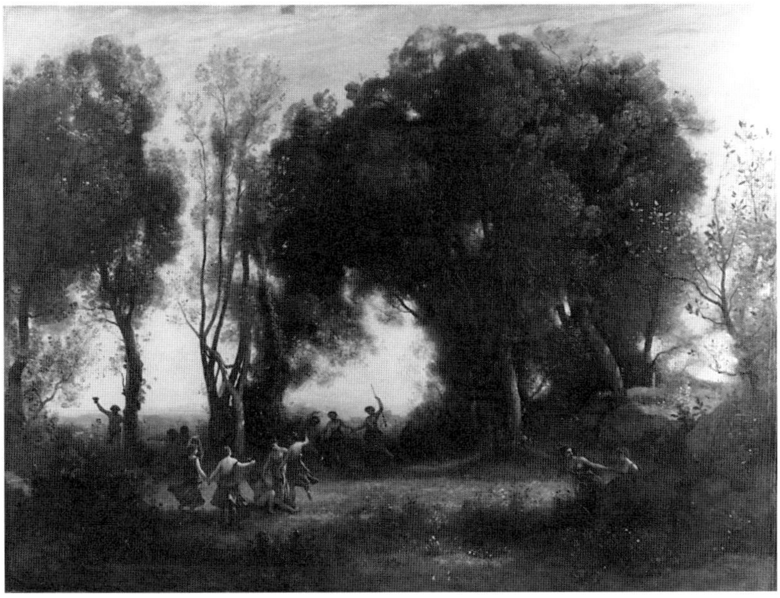

civilization, convention, and habit; making contact with this realm can therefore be challenging and liberating. The very questioning of what nature might mean is indeed worked into the practice of modern landscape art. Landscape art can be approached as a form of visual knowledge. To return to Monet's radiant maelstroms of paint (the works he would have produced while in his boat-studio and as a result of other *plein-air* experiences), this natural universe is not a static and unchanging background, nor does it serve as a restful antidote to modern urban life. Instead, in these paintings the whole atmosphere is animated; nature seems to be in constant motion. In the late nineteenth century, the outside could be made strangely electric, perhaps as much so as the newly electrified and industrialized city.

Leaving the city to find inspiration or rejuvenation in nature is nothing new in the history of occidental culture, but we should ask how this aesthetic gesture has acquired different meanings over time. Robert Smithson participated in the aesthetic rediscovery of natural spaces and phenomena by North American and European artists working under the banners of Earthworks, Land Art, and what can be described more generally as "conceptual landscape art," during the 1960s and '70s. For some twentieth-century artists there was a primitivist appeal to working in the desert or forest, as if imitating non-European native markings on the land allowed them to tap into a mythic substratum of nature. Thus, like some of their nineteenth-century counterparts, such artists seemed to

fig. 3 Camille Corot, *Une matinée (La danse des nymphes)*, c. 1850, oil on canvas, 98 x 131 cm, Musée du Louvre, Paris turn to nature even as they turned away from the complexities of modern life. The gesture towards nature or an outside space can have a more ambiguous kind of aesthetic allure, however, in that conceptual landscapes don't always provide a window onto a lush and inviting green space. Many Earthwork artists, Minimalist sculptors, and Conceptualists, for instance, headed for the outdoors because they wanted to unmoor artworks from their museological fixity. An art object removed from its wall-bracket or pedestal and taken outside the normative gallery setting would enter into a whole new set of relations with its surrounding environment. As Rosalind Krauss has remarked, "the ambition of minimalism was... to relocate the origins of sculpture's meaning to *the outside*, no longer modelling its structure on the privacy of psychological space but on the public, conventional nature of what might be called cultural space."[3] There are many ways, then, to interpret how artists situate themselves and their artwork either outdoors or outside. In the contemporary era, artists' outward moves are not always seeking primary contact with nature, in an unspoiled outdoor environment, and yet the value of reaching for a heterogeneous "outside" remains.

Smithson's artwork is particularly fascinating because he problematized questions of exteriority, site, and site-specificity while continuing to engage with landscape fictions. Smithson's *Floating Island* (which exists only as a drawing) is unusual because it is a landscape-in-motion. If Monet did his utmost to provide the illusion of movement and change in nature, Smithson literalized this aesthetic gesture. At the same time, this rectangular landscape can be thought of as a miniaturized replica of New York City's Central Park, which Smithson greatly admired—largely because the park arose out of the same kind of used-up, entropic environment that he himself was drawn to. The park was worth mimicking because it was a stupendous piece of artifice, not a lost natural paradise.[4] And so a replicated bit of scenery would circumnavigate the city, while at the same time corresponding to forces, spaces, and desires emanating from within the city. If the *Floating Island* does function as a type of ideal natural space, this might be by virtue of its inaccessibility. Around and around the diminutive island goes, without anyone setting foot on it—and so it remains a site of imaginative refuge.

[3] Emphasis mine. Rosalind Krauss, *Passages in Modern Sculpture* (Cambridge: MIT Press, 1977), p. 270. [4] Smithson's body of writing is an essential part of his practice; he was often critical of so-called ecologists who wanted to "return" to a prelapsarian, pure state of nature, because this was an undialectical understanding of how landscapes appear and are used over time. See "Frederic Law Olmsted and the Dialectical Landscape," in *Robert Smithson: The Collected Writings*, ed. Jack Flam (Berkeley: University of California Press, 1996), pp. 157–171.

Landscape and Utopia

Pastoral is a dream of time — of leisure sewn into exertion, snatched from it easily, threaded through the rhythms of labour and insinuating other tempos and imperatives into the working day.[5]

Sometimes it is obvious that landscape art is supposed to transport us into the past. We know by a work's title, by certain architectural signifiers, or by those telling mythological presences, that a particular grove and patch of sky is a distinctive kind of Greco-Roman place, cut off from us by thousands of years. Artists re-presented such sites again and again, and it can be said that landscapes have often been possessed of a retrospective gaze; it is as if an ideal state of nature could be located only in the distant past. Once upon an arcadian time, the story goes, nature was reconciled with human needs and desires. In such a place, there is no such thing as gruelling or exploitative labour. Here people are always lolling about on verdant hillsides, and there is evidently an abundance of leisure time, especially for dreaming, poetry, music, philosophizing, and lovemaking.

But then, the landscape genre in the occidental tradition has provided viewers with all manner of dream-like environments and artificial paradises. Wandering through a museum, it is not always possible to pinpoint the exact temporal and spatial coordinates of the pleasant green spaces on display. If landscape art's fictive geographies can suggest a long-lost golden age, at other times they seem to announce a future state of things. And sometimes it is all rather ambiguous: the pastoral dream seems to exist in the interstices of time, somewhere outside of the world as we know it.

Although powerful strains of nostalgia have undoubtedly informed it, landscape is a remarkably malleable genre, both spatially and temporally. Prior to the nineteenth-century rise of nation-states and the assertion of national schools of landscape painting, the iconography and pictorial effects of landscape art moved back and forth across borders. Artists all over Europe constructed what were in effect montage-landscapes: they would copy bits of iconic paintings by Claude Lorrain or other masters of idealization — a particularly graceful tree, a historically-resonant temple, a distinctive kind of late-afternoon light — and conjoin them to images of nature that were more specific, local, and empirically observed. Indeed, what all neo-classicists set out to accomplish in some sense was a

[5] T.J. Clark, *Farewell to an Idea: Episodes from a History of Modernism* (New Haven and London: Yale University Press, 1999), p. 70.

synthesis, so that their time and place would be linked to another, more illustrious, time and place. It is not the case, therefore, that we can draw a line within the history of art between realistic pictures of nature on the one hand and fantastically synthetic ones on the other. Even in the most realistic-looking landscape representation, the "here and now" is inevitably interwoven with images and memories of other places and other times. Landscape art is full of these kinds of allusions and associations, of scenes that are witnessed, imitated, and/or half-remembered.

The politics of landscape appreciation have been much discussed in recent years. The practices of borrowing and pastiche mentioned above have not always been so innocent. This is certainly the case with regard to landscape architecture, whereby ersatz or authentic bits of classical ruins were distributed throughout English, French, or German estates, where they might well be accompanied by more exotic teepees or pagodas. The ideal landscape form would thus expand beyond its Mediterranean origins, developing a kind of omnivorous global consciousness. John Barrell has written, moreover, that landscape art often relegated peasants to the "dark side of the landscape," while the owners of the land positioned themselves as true inheritors and re-interpreters of the arcadian dream. W.J.T. Mitchell has questioned the very art-historical definition of landscape as the selective isolation of natural scenery, given that this art form has so easily hidden social conflicts and historical traumas beneath a mantle of sumptuous greenery.[6] At certain historical moments, the landscape sensibility coincided only too neatly with the historical projects of colonialism and imperialism.

These aspects of landscape's history cannot be glossed over, but it is equally important to recognize countercurrents and alternative perspectives within the Euro-American tradition. For instance, in the remarkable landscape art of Rubens there is no spurious reconciliation of nature with human desire and social imperatives. What is made visible to viewers are people struggling with recalcitrant tools, vehicles, animals, and the earth itself, while all around the plant-life grows in a chaotically entwined profusion (fig. 4). Everything moves, grows, changes before our eyes. Rubens's landscapes evoke the myriad points of conflict or tension *between* natural and cultural things. The paintings indeed seem close to a contemporary understanding of ecosystems, in all their changeable, interlocked vitality. It is only in the far-off background that all this muddy materiality is provisionally left behind, and we can discern a horizon-space that is crystalline and unearthly.

6 See John Barrell, *The Dark Side of the Landscape* (Cambridge and New York: Cambridge University Press, 1980), and W.J.T. Mitchell, "Gombrich and the Rise of Landscape," in *The Consumption of Culture 1600–1800*, ed. Ann Bermingham and John Brewer (London and New York: Routledge, 1995).

It was during the nineteenth century, however, that the social and aesthetic meanings of landscape art expanded dramatically, so much so that the genre became a central focus of modernist painting. At times, it is possible to make direct links between politics and the aestheticization of nature. The simple but glowing works of the Barbizon school, for instance, were taken up by certain utopian socialists as visionary glimpses of a post-revolutionary world.[7] The quotation at the top of this section, from T.J. Clark, suggesting that "pastoral is a dream of time," is part of a lengthy commentary on a late-nineteenth-century painting by Camille Pissarro. Clark discusses Pissarro's anarchist affiliations, and he also examines the qualities of shadow, light, and colour that make this a mesmerizing modern image. In this way he is anxious to prove how a seemingly nostalgic, slow-moving evocation of nature might critically intervene in the politics of modernity.

When there are few geographic coordinates, or where there is temporal uncertainty, can this ambiguity actually enhance the allure of landscape art? If we catch a glimpse of flowery meadowland through a half-open door, or a glimmer of a horizon in the far background of a picture, there is nonetheless the promise of something ... perhaps of beauty,

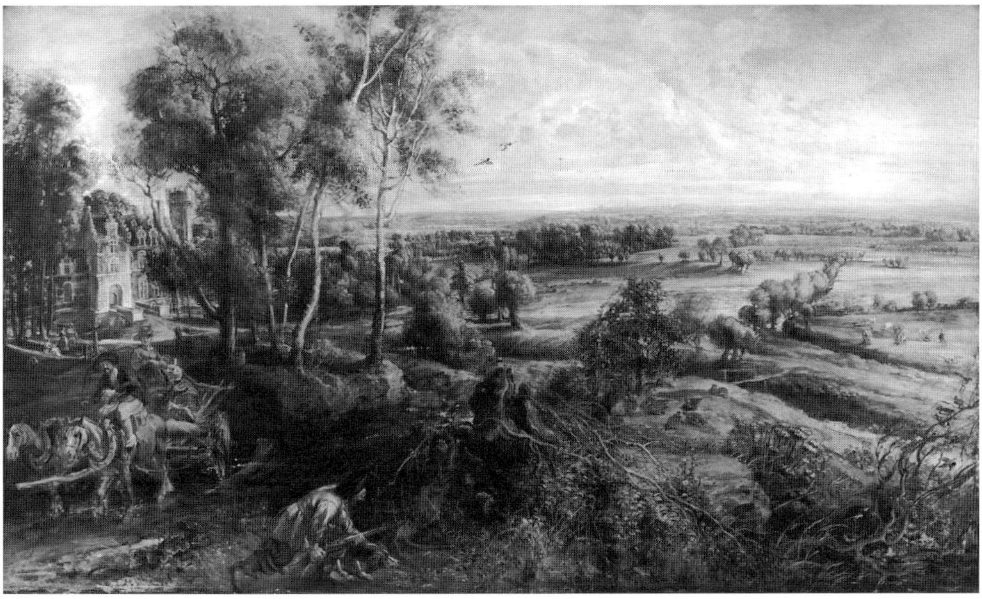

fig. 4 **Peter Paul Rubens,** *An Autumn Landscape with a View of Het Steen in the Early Morning*, c. 1636, oil on oak panel, 131.2 x 229.2 cm, National Gallery, London

[7] The followers of Charles Fourier, in particular, admired Barbizon forest scenes, not as escapist fantasies, but as harbingers of future peace and social justice. See Neil McWilliams, *Dreams of Happiness: Social Art and the French Left 1830–1850* (Princeton: Princeton University Press, 1993).

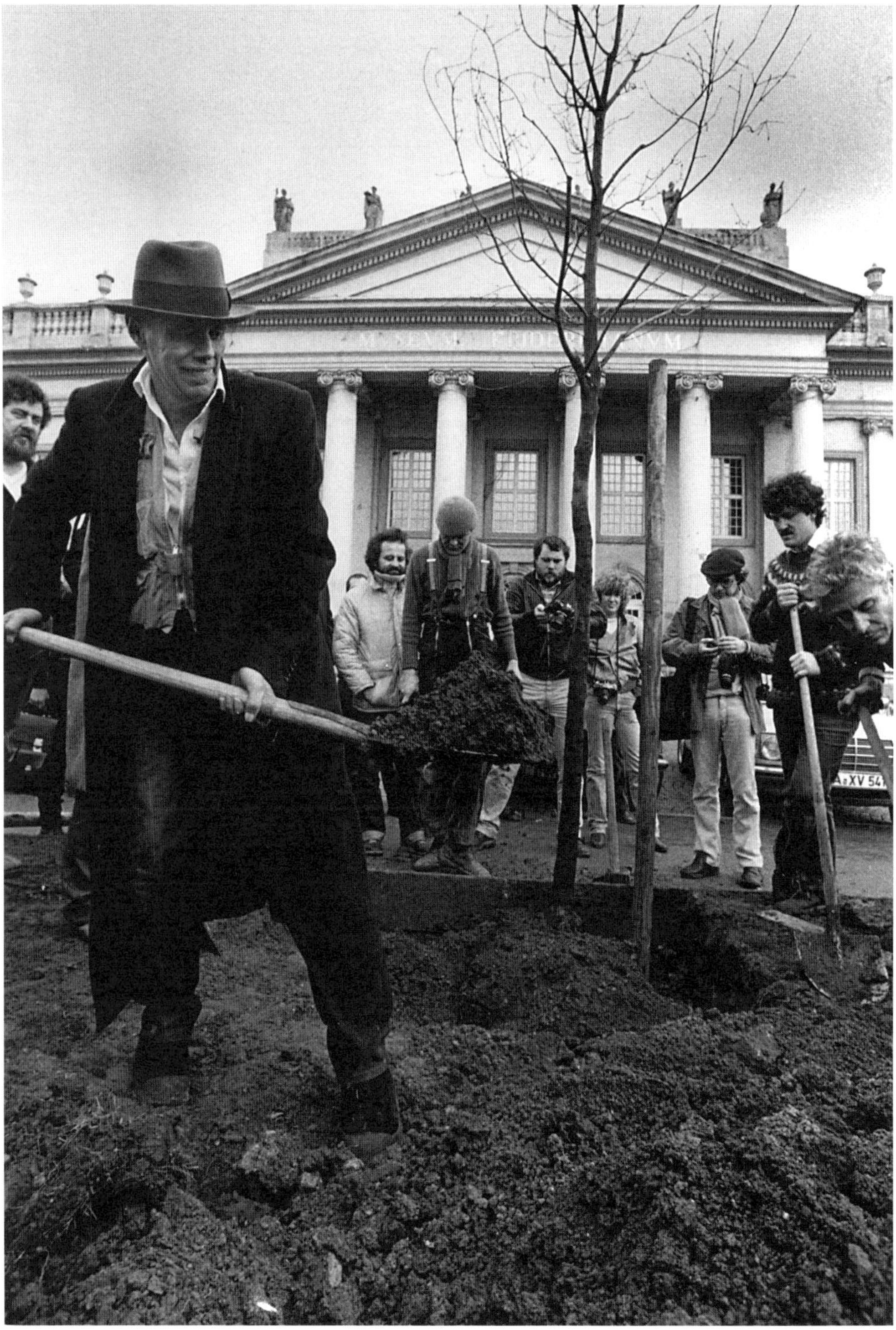

fig. 5 **Joseph Beuys** planting an oak tree as part of the *7000 Oaks* project at Documenta 7, Kassel, Germany, 18 March 1982 (photo Dieter Schwerdtle)

escape, or harmony with nature. Louis Marin has in fact pointed to the horizon in landscape art as an exemplary model for the utopian impulse. This is an understanding of utopia that does not necessarily correspond to a specific place, image, or object. For the utopian is more likely to appear, Marin suggests, as the interval or "gap between two frontiers or two continents, old and new worlds."[8] It is such instances of horizon-like openness *within* texts or images that fuels the desire for "other" unseen places, other places that are realms of freedom and pleasure.

Landscape as Concept

In the early part of the twentieth century, the landscape genre was regarded by many avant-garde artists as a retrograde, kitsch form of artistic expression. It was only in the late 1960s and '70s that a serious focus on nature and landscape aesthetics was rekindled in Europe and in North America. It can be argued that geo-aesthetic concepts such as "space," "place," "environment," "site," and especially "site-specificity," now utterly commonplace in contemporary art, can be historically linked to the landscape genre. Joseph Beuys is a unique figure from this era, in that he attempted to forge a link between political activism, environmentalism, and contemporary aesthetic concerns—with the ritualized planting of trees entitled *7000 Oaks*, for instance (fig. 5). Beuys even went beyond such specific gestures to envision an "ecological *Gesamtkunstwerk*," consisting of a kind of convergence of social and individual desires, together with the neglected energies of animal life and the non-human material world.

Many British and American artists were part of this turn to nature, while on this side of the Atlantic the importance of Canadian artists to the development of a new conceptual landscape aesthetics has perhaps not been fully recognized. The work of Joyce Wieland and Michael Snow in particular remains highly relevant to contemporary investigations, including much of what is presented in the current exhibition. While Smithson was dreaming up his *Floating Island*, and working on the more celebrated *Spiral Jetty*, Wieland and Snow were using photography, film, installation, performance, and a range of other media to explore the aesthetics of place, ecology, spectatorship, and nationalism.

In order to re-invent landscape, Wieland, Snow, Smithson, and their contemporaries had also to grapple with the legacy of the genre—that is to say, they had to come

[8] Louis Marin, "Frontiers of Utopia: Past and Present," *Critical Inquiry* 19 (Winter 1993), p. 417.

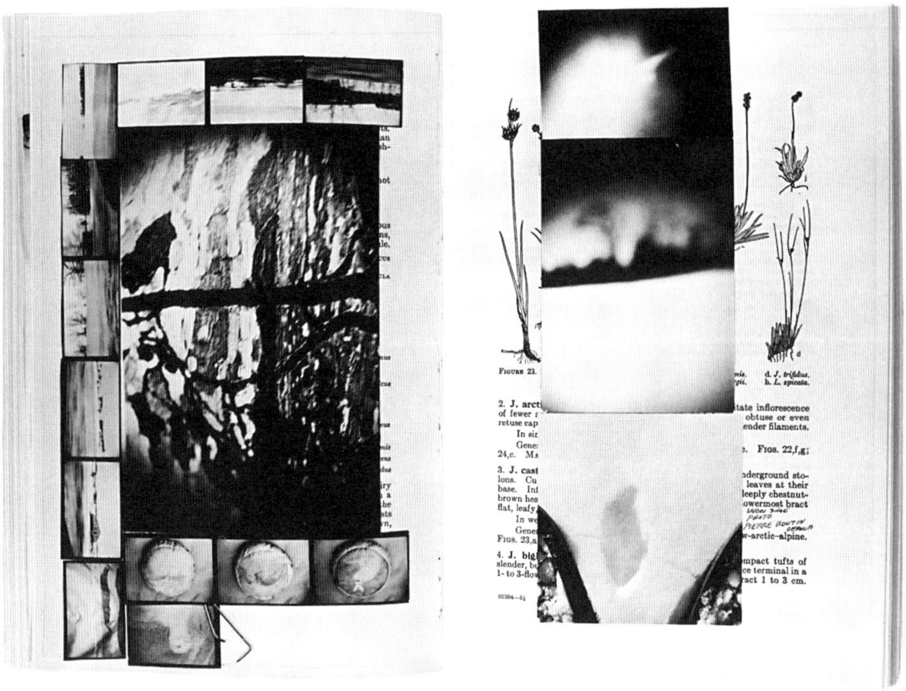

to terms with the overly familiar motifs, textures, spatial illusionism, and ideological assumptions of landscape painting. Their conceptually-oriented art considers images, whether historic or contemporary, within a field of signification. Thus each of their artistic framings of nature exists in relation to other paintings, photographs, utterances, spaces, buildings, and so forth. Sometimes the artworks present us with what seem to be extremely fractured views, although, as noted above, the glimpse or evocation of a place beyond has been crucial to landscape aesthetics. On the other hand, we often find a proliferation of views, readings, and interpretations. Smithson for example, produced a photographic work entitled *400 Seattle Horizons*, and Wieland made a quilted piece entitled *109 Views*. In Wieland's book-work for the 1971 exhibition *True Patriot Love*, meanwhile, there was simultaneously a surfeit of images, and a sense that each image was in itself mysteriously incomplete in its capacity to represent the visible world. Black-and-white photographs were overlaid onto the pages of a government publication about Arctic flowers: there are snowy vistas, the pattern of snow-shoe tracks, and stretches of blurry scenery, as if the camera were perpetually trying to capture something just outside the frame (fig. 6). Also, there are repeated sequences of a Tom Thomson painting, texts in English, French, Inuktitut, and Gaelic, and snapshots of the artist assuming the persona

fig. 6 Joyce Wieland, *True Patriot Love* (Ottawa: National Gallery of Canada, 1971), pp. 60–61 © Joyce Wieland of the Canadian heroine Laura Secord. There is a layering of stories, histories, and art-histories, of voices and points of view. The landscape comes in and out of focus as the pages turn, and there is a sense of movement through time and space. At times the landscape seems to be viewed from a moving vehicle, and it acquires a very modern kind of anonymity. Other images close in on details, suggesting the slower, embodied tempo of a walk into the landscape. The speed varies, but these entry-points are, in a way, consistent with how traditional forms of landscape art invite the spectator to enter and "travel" around the virtual space of the artwork.

With this book-work, Wieland's approach to landscape corresponds closely to what Smithson so aptly described as the "dialectic between site and non-site." This important theorization relates to conceptual landscape art as a whole: "sites" are the specific geographic locations, and "non-sites" are the maps, codes, texts, images, and various other modes of representation that might describe a given site. It is important to recognize, according to Smithson, that the two categories never quite match up, because "between the actual site... and the non-site exists a space of metaphoric significance."[9] And so the viewer is drawn into a landscape space that is associative and accumulative, where he or she can continue the process of making meaning.

A spectator who confronts painted, photographed, or projected scenes of isolated geographic sites is seemingly given the opportunity to perceive nature on its own—as an entity severed from civilization, from human nature, from the perceptual matrix of human vision. In the contemporary period, this aesthetic isolation was taken to an extreme in Michael Snow's project, *La région centrale* (1970–71). Snow installed a customized movie camera in a remote part of northern Québec, so that it might endlessly record the inhospitable terrain. Images of the bundled-up artist alongside his robotic machine have entered into the lore of twentieth-century art, reminiscent, perhaps, of how nineteenth-century *pleinairistes*, brushes poised mid-air, were captured by cameras for posterity (fig. 7). This landscape-machine and its visual product seem de-humanized, not only because human culture was absent from the surveyed scenery, but because the camera moved up, down, and around every which way, not respecting the horizontal and vertical axes on which any kind of picturesque vision must be founded.[10] This natural site was not

[9] Smithson, *Collected Writings*, p. 364. [10] Although Snow's gyrating apparatus had its own life as an art-object, about three hours' worth of the collected film footage was indeed publicly exhibited. The movement of *La région centrale* has been described as "figure-8s, arcs, scallops, sweeps, zigzags, horizontal shifts, Mobius strips, tipping and rocking of the image within the frame, along with a shaking effect and angling or tilting of the image within the frame" (Regina Cornwell, *Snow Seen: The Films and Photographs of Michael Snow* [Toronto: Peter Martin, 1980], p. 111).

filtered and softened through an artist's subjectivity, it was not anchored by orthogonal pictorial structures, it was not interpenetrated in any explicit way by myths, stories, or histories. It is as if Snow had attempted to divest his project of all those qualities that render the non-human world meaningful, and perhaps even beautiful. And yet, Snow himself insisted on situating his work within a painting tradition, for he announced about this project, "I want to make a gigantic landscape film equal in terms of film to the great landscape paintings of Cézanne, Poussin, Corot, Monet, Matisse, and, in Canada, the Group of Seven."[11] Perhaps *La région centrale* reminds us that, whatever the location of the scenery, whatever the medium, landscape representations always involve more than a sense of "being there." On the contrary, even the simplest act of framing a scene implies a process of metaphoric *dislocation*. It is worth remembering that throughout the 1970s both Snow and Wieland continued to develop projects where the landscape was set in motion in different ways. Wieland would go on to make her own version of the great Canadian landscape film, *The Far Shore* (1976), which unlike Snow's project, would embrace narrative and sentiment. For his part, Snow's *Plus tard* transformed a roomful of iconic Group of Seven paintings into a kind of moving panorama, or, to use Alexander Wilson's phrase, into "events in automotive time."[12]

Ecology — The Inside View

Landscape art doesn't need to arise out of a materially-evident plot of land, nor will it always provide an illusionistic arrangement of trees, earth, sky, and so forth. Even so, the ecological consciousness of recent years has changed things. Even as we acknowledge landscape art's dislocations and hallucinatory qualities, the fragility of natural ecosystems leads us to consider anew the very ground we walk on, the water we drink, the air we breathe. With the prospect of ecological ruination, the materiality of nature asserts itself.

It has often been intriguing to artists that the non-human natural world can mimic the malleability of human history. At the beginning of the twenty-first century, however, there is a more and more disquieting awareness of how catastrophically mutable natural spaces and phenomena can be. There is not only the matter of pollution and the depletion of natural resources, but also the re-shuffling of genetic material in laboratories. Such dystopian developments have had an enormous influence on how nature is perceived and represented.

[11] Quoted in Cornwell, p. 114. [12] Alexander Wilson, *The Culture of Nature* (Toronto: Between the Lines), p. 34.

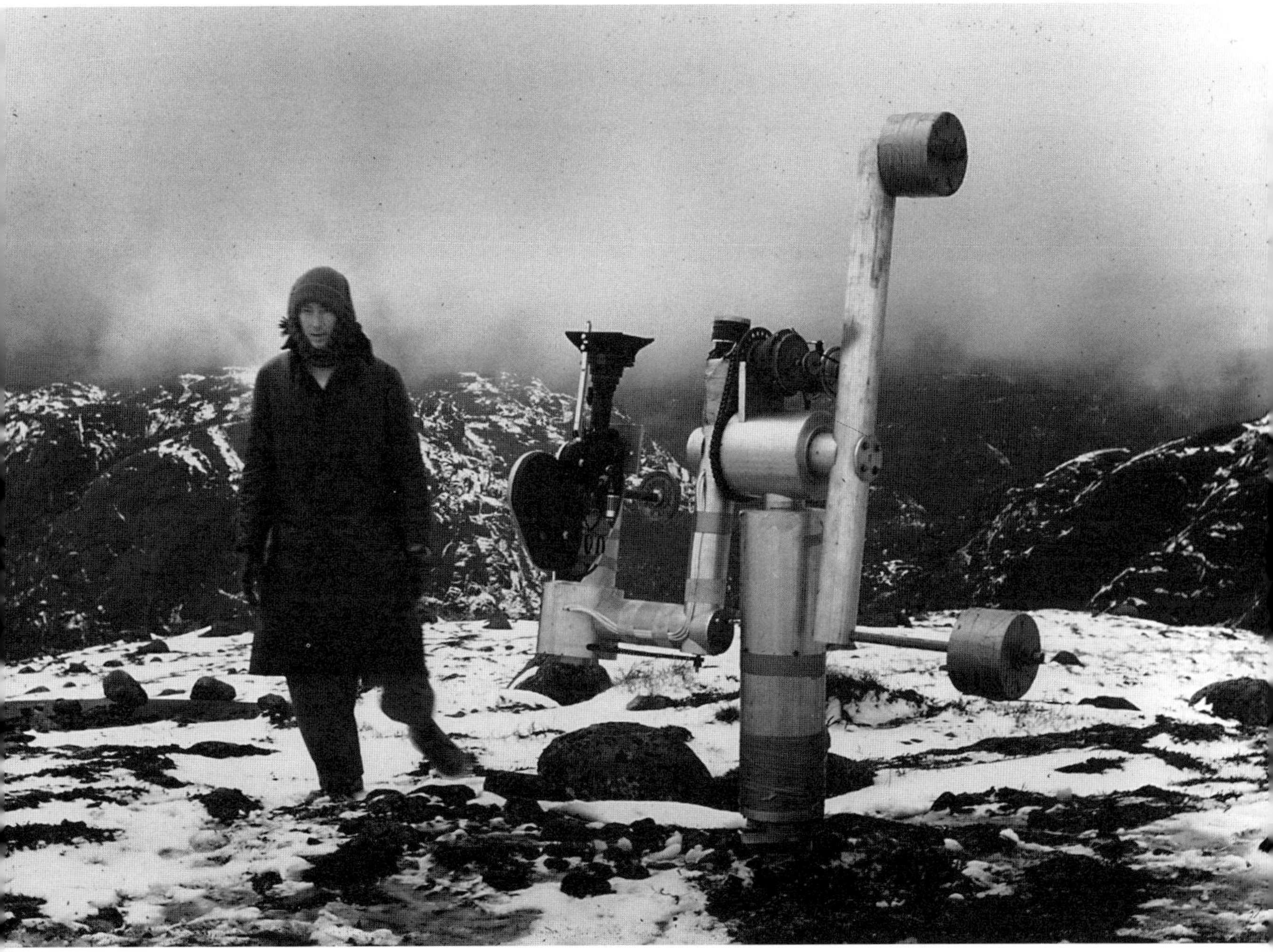

The idea of rising above or stepping back to get an adequate perspective on the world has been a central conceit of landscape representation. But what is the optimal distance for viewing natural sites and phenomena? There is a strange and wonderful painting by the seventeenth-century artist Salvator Rosa that suggests just how close it is possible to get: we are shown the philosopher Empedocles throwing himself into the crater of Mount Etna for the sake of knowledge. As spectators of landscape, we usually seem to float above and outside a fictive natural space, but here we are pulled down, plunging directly into the earth. In this remarkable image the relationship between figure and ground is as unstable as it can be. Part of the fascination with volcanoes in centuries past

fig.7 Production still during filming of Michael Snow's *La région centrale*, 1970 (photo Joyce Wieland)

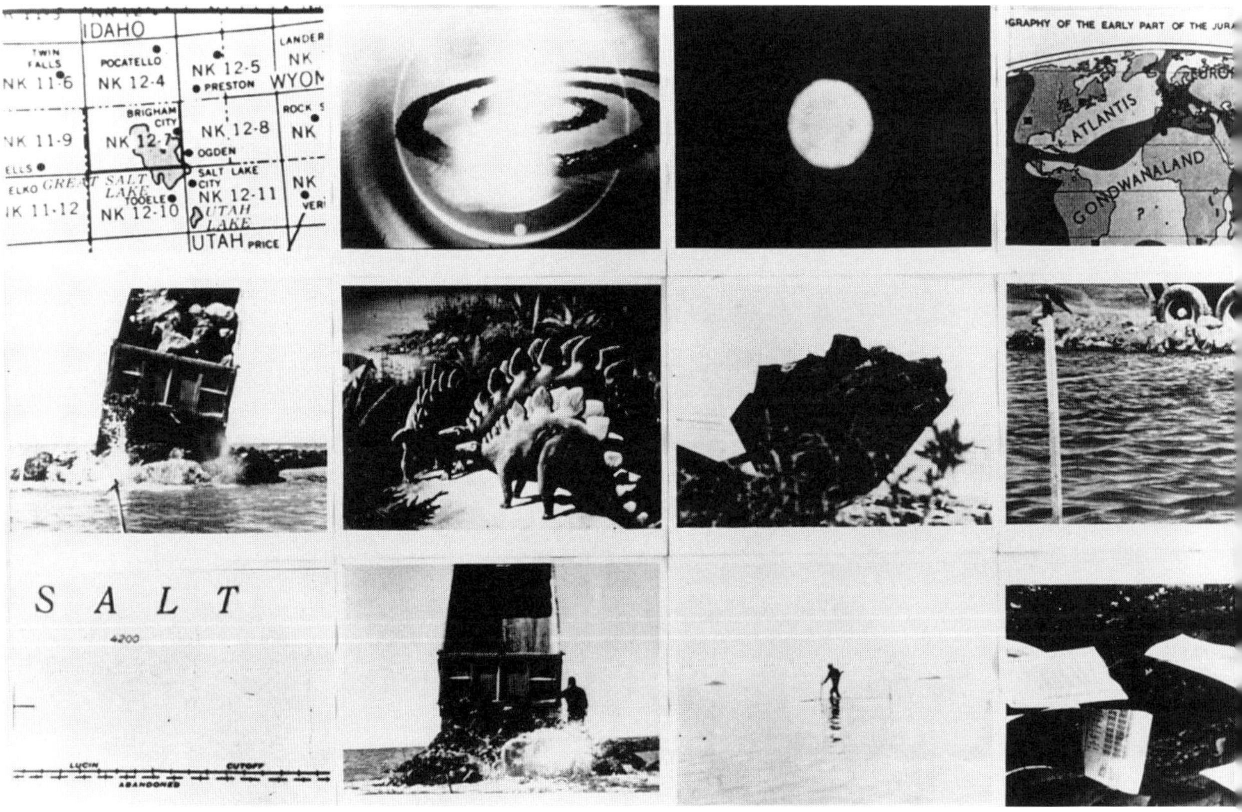

fig. 8 **Robert Smithson,** *Spiral Jetty* film stills, 1970, black-and-white silver gelatin prints, 3 panels, 64.1 × 110.5 cm each, Estate of Robert Smithson, courtesy of the James Cohan Gallery, New York, collection of Museet for Samtidkunst, Oslo

was that it seemed possible, momentarily, to glimpse nature from up close and inside, to witness something of the planet's inner power and structure. And so there is the possibility that landscapes can, in a manner of speaking, get turned inside out, unearthing a network of natural, social, and psychic systems. What was previously underground, or hidden beneath a strip of beautifying turf, can become visible.

These days, it is the movies that most often capitalize on the inner workings of nature, transforming these elemental energies into a form of spectacular visual entertainment. The blockbuster films of recent years have featured monster hurricanes, tornadoes, volcanoes, and the like. The narratives tend to be rudimentary: a few ordinary, well-meaning people are exposed and on the run, and then a repertoire of marvellous special effects is deployed. An underground fire bursts through city streets, or a ferocious wind hurls objects through space; water, air, and earth heave sublimely. We watch these set-pieces avidly, admiring in equal parts the artificiality, the technical wizardry, but also the apparent naturalism. Our appreciation has little to do with knowledge of specific sites, eco-systems, or communities, because here nature appears as a timeless, uncontrollable force.

In this context, contemporary kinds of ground-level landscape art provide other layers of meaning, so that nature appears to have a range of historical, utilitarian, commemorative, oneiric, or utopian meanings. Works of art can provide outside points of view, giving a sense of perspective about how nature intersects with human history; and then there are inside positions, an immersion in the earth itself. Outside or inside—from which position do we gain more knowledge, or derive more imaginative pleasure? Smithson's *Spiral Jetty* consisted of a film, photographs, drawings, a torrent of words, and a pile of rocks—and it remains an exemplary work of landscape art to the present day, even if the rocks themselves can no longer be seen on Great Salt Lake (fig. 8). The artist wasn't attempting some kind of primary contact with wilderness, because this site had been used and subsequently abandoned by oil prospectors. It was therefore a historical site, already registered in human history, which Smithson only continued to frame and re-frame. Gradually, however, the images and words of *Spiral Jetty* succeed in luring the viewer inwards and downwards, into a kind of geotropic swoon that seems likely to result in a bodily absorption into the earth. Smithson did not avoid showing aerial overviews of his rocky promontory, but it was clearly not through such loftiness that knowledge or aesthetic pleasure would be achieved.[13] The language in the *Spiral Jetty* essay certainly

[13] It is of interest that *Spiral Jetty* appeared at about the time that American astronauts' first bluish photographs of the earth were widely publicized. Smithson once referred to the moonshot as a demoralizing, "very expensive non-site" (Smithson, *Collected Writings*, p. 268).

emphasized this tension. While at times the shape, colour, and material composition of the project is described in quasi-scientific or archaeological terms, Smithson would also resort to extremely lurid prose: "Chemically speaking, our blood is analogous in composition to the primordial seas. Following the spiral steps we return to our origins, back to some pulpy protoplasm, a floating eye adrift in an antediluvian ocean."[14] This downward spiral can be understood as a strategy for relinquishing visual mastery; no longer is there a virtual eye in the sky, seeing and knowing everything. Instead, *Spiral Jetty* sinks us into an "antediluvian" earth, and into a much deeper past than the scant few-thousand-year regression of arcadian landscape painting.[15]

Perhaps it is a genuinely utopian project, at the present time, to re-imagine our inherited archive of arcadias and other natural dream-worlds. The landscape-related artworks of Smithson and many contemporary artists seem to momentarily bring nature, history, and utopia together, through different kinds of social space and across timelines. The on-going relevance of this approach was eloquently described by Ernst Bloch, as he traced the utopian impulse from its early days, when the planet was not yet fully mapped and it seemed possible that remote idyllic places still awaited discovery. Bloch spoke of recuperating some remnants of discarded maps, stories, images, and objects, for it was amongst this rubbish-heap of historical longings that one could still find glimmers of a world beyond. It is not a question of transcending the material, the historical, the earthly, and the bodily. For even if no far-off corners of the world remain to be discovered, Bloch argued that utopia still exists *in* the earth, in the materiality and thing-ness of the everyday world around us. "Almost nothing has survived of the geographical dream in its old form. Nevertheless, the earth has not been fully learnt, nor, in spatio-temporal terms, fully expressed."[16]

Johanne Sloan

[14] Smithson, *Collected Writings*, p. 148. [15] The 1999 acquisition by the Dia Center for the Arts of the *Spiral Jetty* site in Utah could mean, unfortunately, that an effort might be made to reverse the artwork's sublime, entropic disappearance. [16] Ernst Bloch, *The Principle of Hope* (Oxford: Basil Blackwell 1986), p. 760.

Catalogue

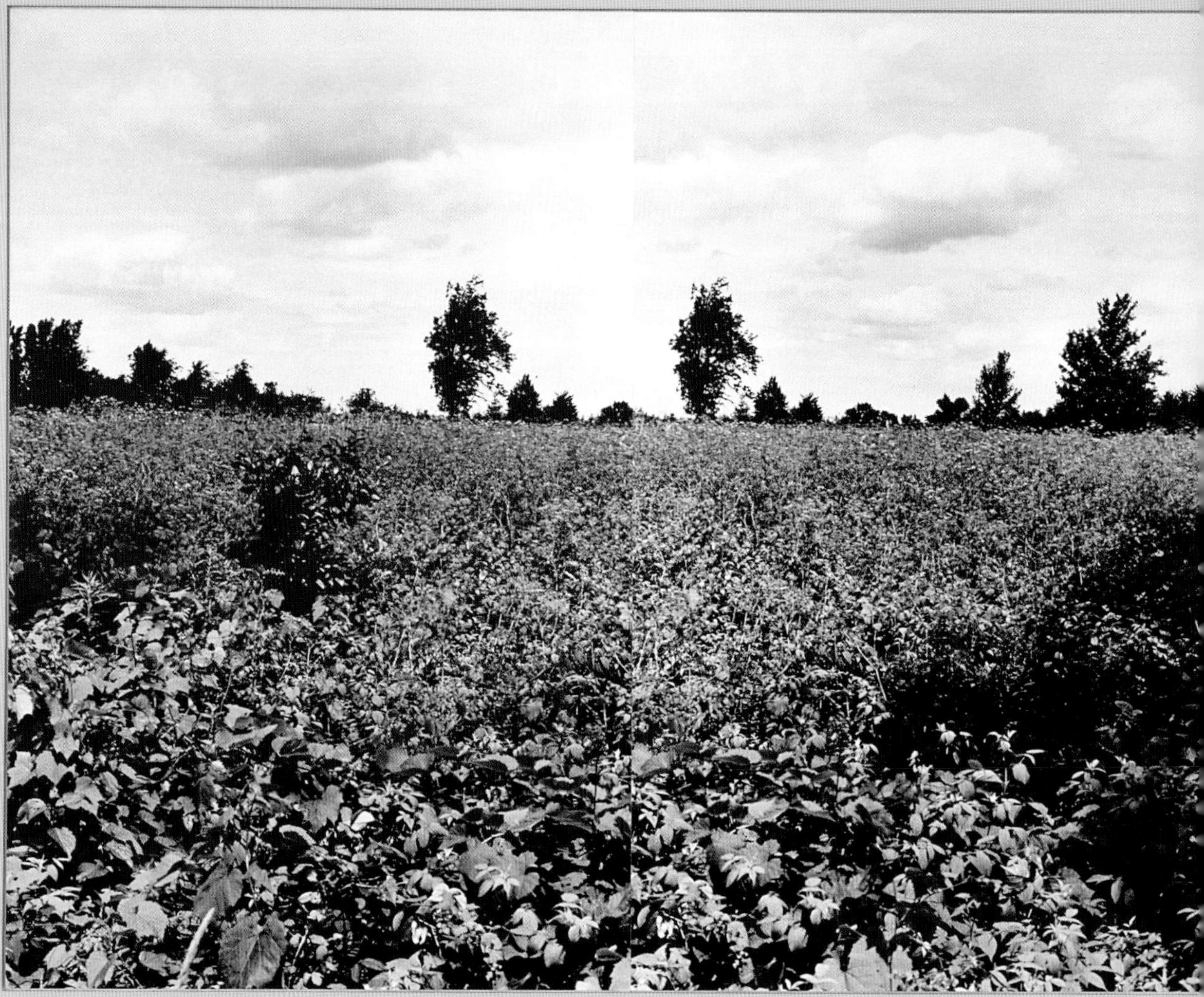

Left: *Pour un oui pour un non*, 2000, edition 2/2, gelatin silver print mounted on plexiglas, with aluminum frame, 275 × 366 × 7 cm, courtesy Galerie René Blouin, Montreal (photo Richard-Max Tremblay), cat. no. 3 Right: *June*, 1999, edition 1/2, gelatin silver print mounted on panel, with aluminum frame, 216 × 292 × 7 cm, The Bailey Collection, Toronto, courtesy Jack Shainman, New York (photo Richard-Max Tremblay), cat. no. 2

Geneviève Cadieux

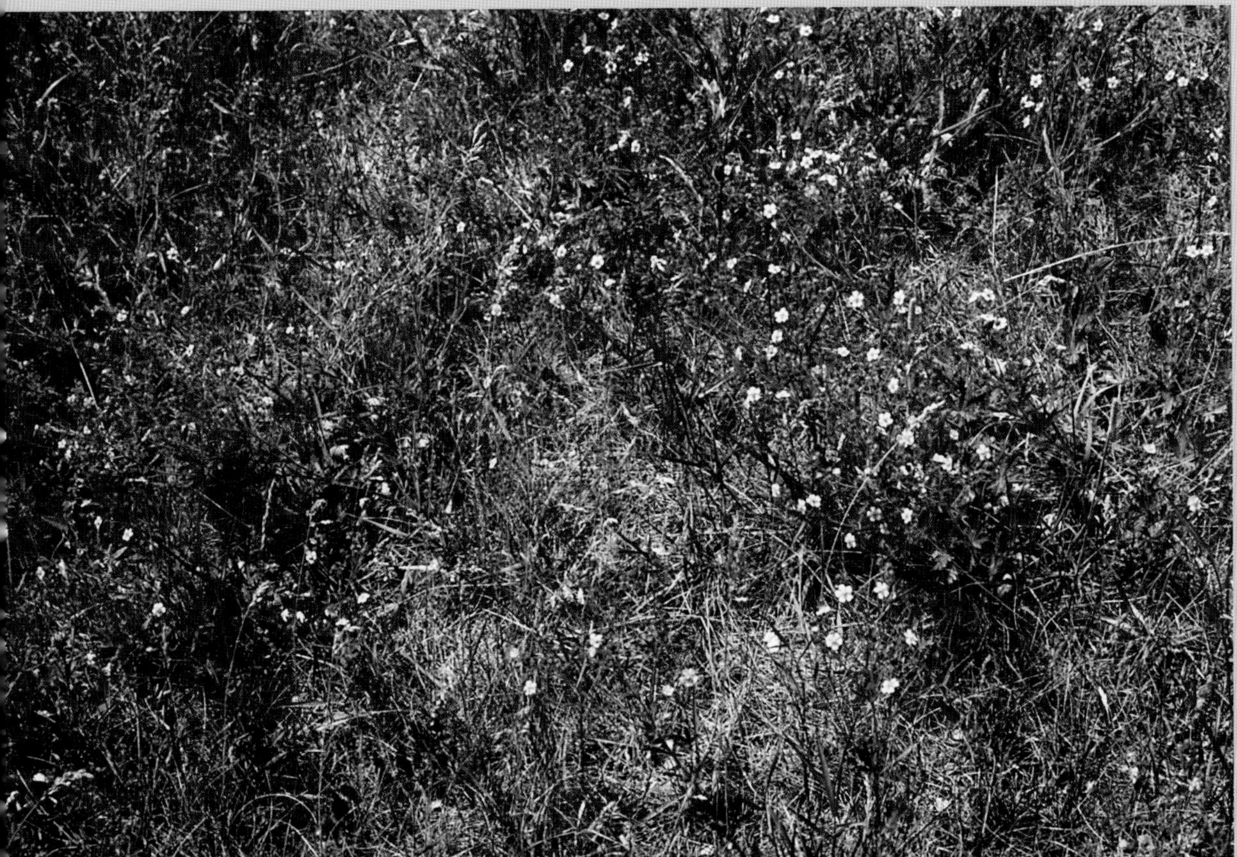

Tears, 1995, edition 2/2, chromogenic print mounted on plexiglas, with aluminum frame, 182.5 × 277 × 7 cm, courtesy Galerie René Blouin, Montreal (photo Richard-Max Tremblay), cat. no. 1

> *The whole task of art is to* express the inexpressible, *to extract from the impoverished and powerful worldly language of the passions, an* other *word, an* exact *word.*[1]

Geneviève Cadieux's oeuvre, comprising large-scale photographic close-ups and, more recently, video, is so closely associated with the representation of the body that her few landscape images appear out of place at first. Yet these images echo so closely those of her bodily landscapes that perhaps we should see them as similar in intention and meaning, in spite of their initial strangeness.

Of the three works in the exhibition, two, *Pour un oui pour un non* and *June*, are black-and-white photographs, while *Tears*, the earliest, is in colour, although its effect is attenuated by the fact that what we see is an almost monochromatic white field. Although Cadieux's work is primarily executed in colour, in the past she has used black and white for its connotations of distance and absence. One thinks, for example, of *Hear Me with Your Eyes*, in which a larger-than-life black-and-white image of the artist's sister crying or moaning and a close-up of her mouth are contrasted with an almost cinematic colour image of the same woman, her mouth wide open in pain. However, by comparison with these images of silent suffering, the landscape images are mute in the extreme. In fact, at first glance they seem inexpressibly banal. Literally nothing is happening in them.

Well, perhaps not nothing. The two close-ups, of the falling snow in *Tears* and of a field of tiny white flowers in *June*, offer no resting point for the eyes, no single point of focus. Both surfaces are like opaque screens, filters between ourselves and something communicable, knowable. This may be going too far. One recognizes the flowers in *June* and could even identify them, although the title suggests that what is important here is not the particular family they belong to but rather the month in which they bloom. They are precisely, objectively present, but what they are meant to express is a moment in time, the moment when, for some reason, they were noticed. It is this reason that is unknowable. *Tears* offers even fewer indicators. Snow in a snow-filled sky is all whiteness, a

[1] Roland Barthes, *Essais critiques* (Paris: Seuil, 1964), p. 17.

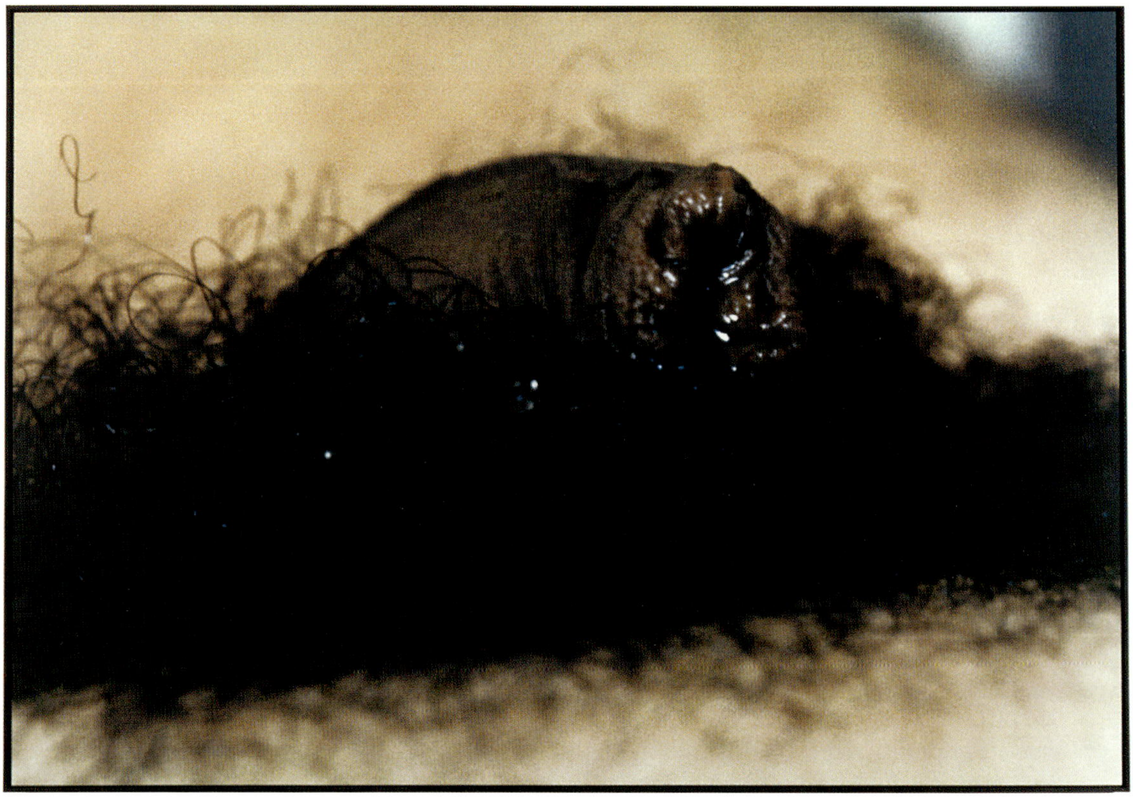

Far from Me, Near to the Distance, 1993, chromogenic prints mounted on plexiglas, with aluminum frame, first element 182.8 × 276.8 cm, second element 182.8 × 267.9 cm, Morris and Helen Belkin Art Gallery, Vancouver (photo Antti Kuivalainen, courtesy Galerie René Blouin, Montreal)

Geneviève Cadieux

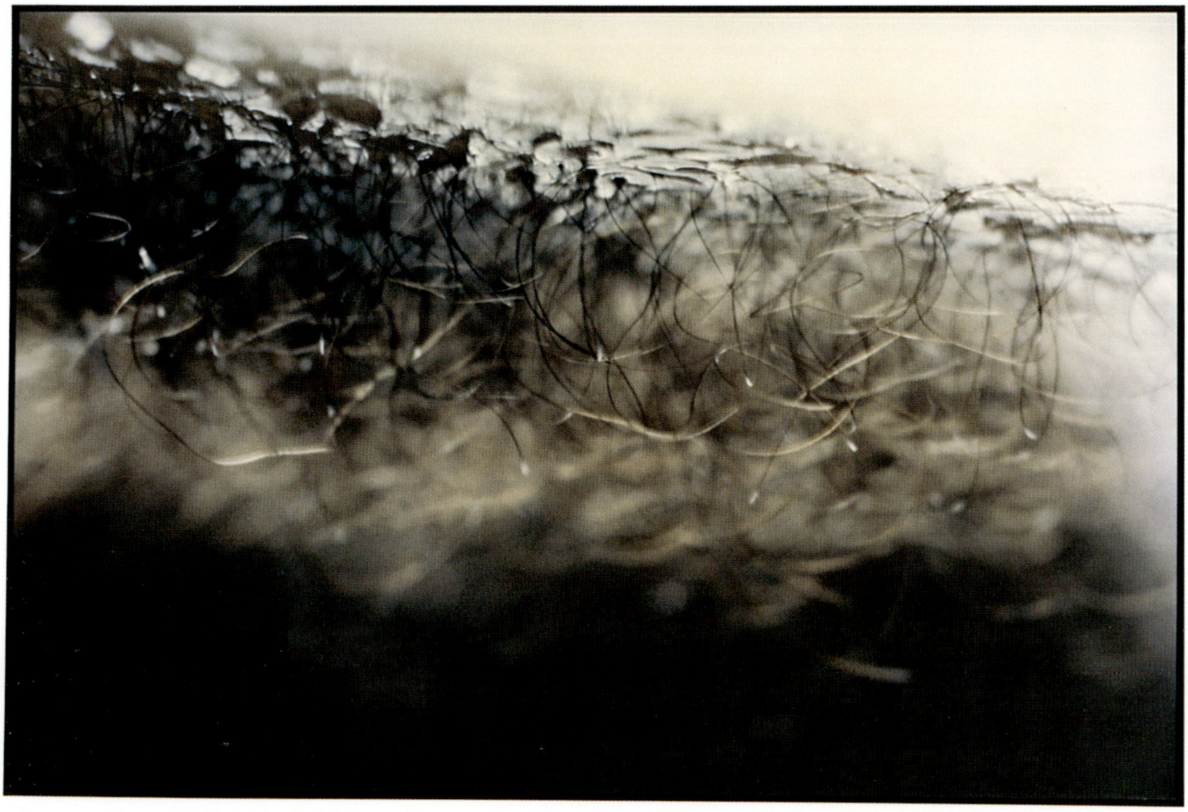

veil through which nothing is visible. The image opens up the abyss of loss. "How like a winter hath my absence been from thee," wrote Shakespeare, claiming with his figure of speech the same image.

The larger and more ambiguously titled *Pour un oui pour un non* is a more complex work. It is the image of a meadow, faintly recognizable as the sort of open yet sheltered space that a pastoral poet might have imagined, ringed with trees to provide an echo for the lover's lament. Yet it is quite ordinary for all that, a landscape which, seen out of the corner of the eye, would go unnoticed, residing in the background of one's memory until something long forgotten called it up. What is remarkable is the seam that runs through the middle, a suture joining not one place but two, or one place displaced, jolting us out of the reverie of wholeness we had begun to imagine. This suture recalls the scar in Cadieux's early works *Memory Gap, an Unexpected Beauty* and *A Cleft in the Bodies' Deep Unison* and invites us to read the landscape as somehow like a body, just as in her other works, such as *Far from Me, Near to the Distance*, we had understood the surface of the body as a landscape. However, the seam both joins and separates, literally doubling and thereby estranging the space of the meadow. Thus it echoes a theme that runs throughout Cadieux's work, of dissociation and rupture.

It is useful to know that the title echoes that of a play by Natalie Sarraute which is about a falling out between two friends over an almost imperceptible intonation of contempt in a few words spoken by one to the other.[2] These words of no great importance betray the abyss that separates the two, an abyss that only widens as they probe their intentions. Sarraute's play, like Cadieux's photographs, underscores the treachery of communication, while at the same time revealing how much may lie in the seemingly unimportant detail or nuance. Like all of Geneviève Cadieux's work, *Pour un oui pour un non* is about nothing, while expressing the irreconcilable, a wordless landscape of feeling.

D.N.

[2] Natalie Sarraute, *Pour un oui ou pour un non* (Paris: Gallimard, 1982).

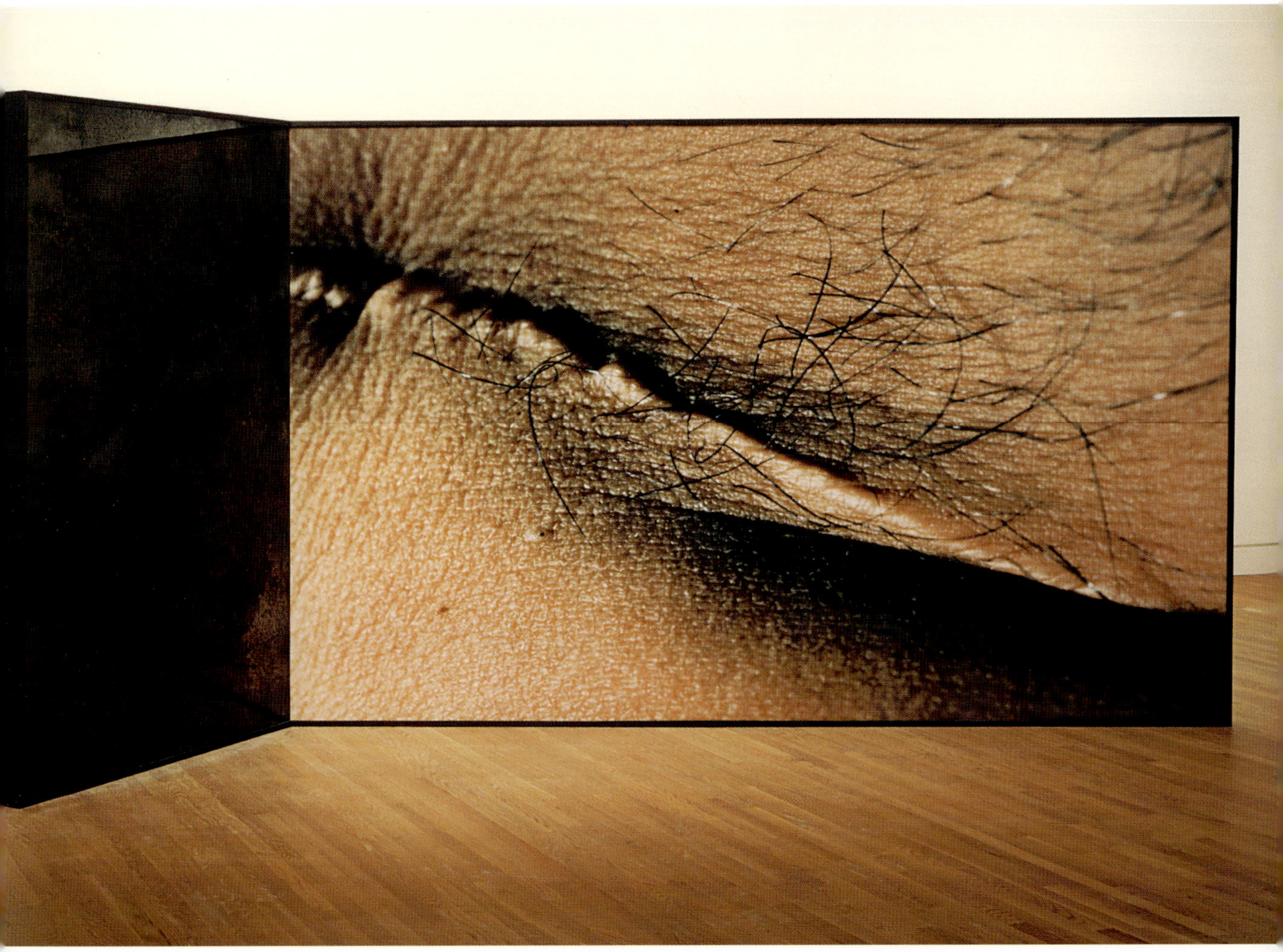

Memory Gap, an Unexpected Beauty, 1988, dye coupler print and mirror on wood, 208 × 472 × 14 cm (assembled), National Gallery of Canada, Ottawa

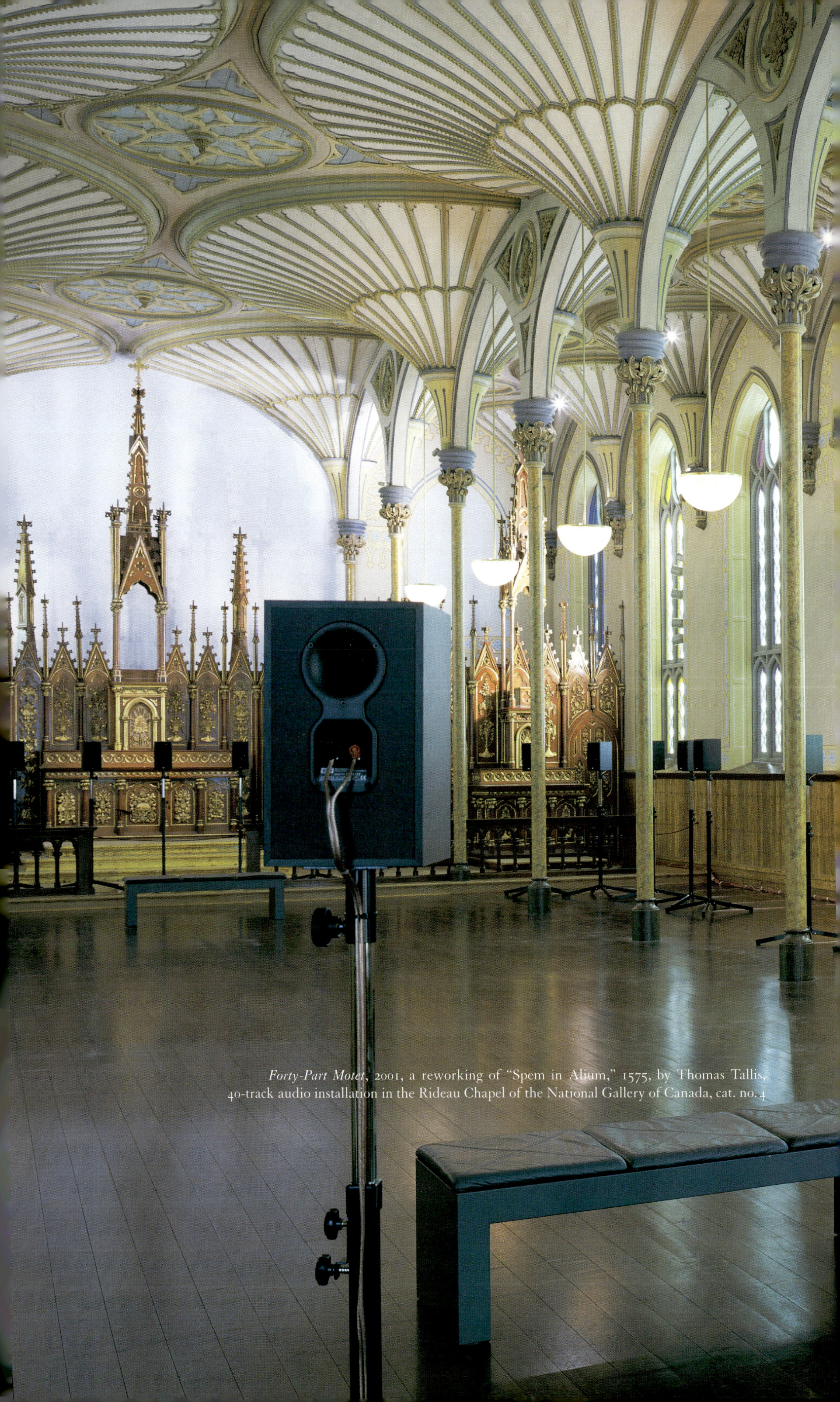

Forty-Part Motet, 2001, a reworking of "Spem in Alium," 1575, by Thomas Tallis, 40-track audio installation in the Rideau Chapel of the National Gallery of Canada, cat. no. 4

Janet Cardiff

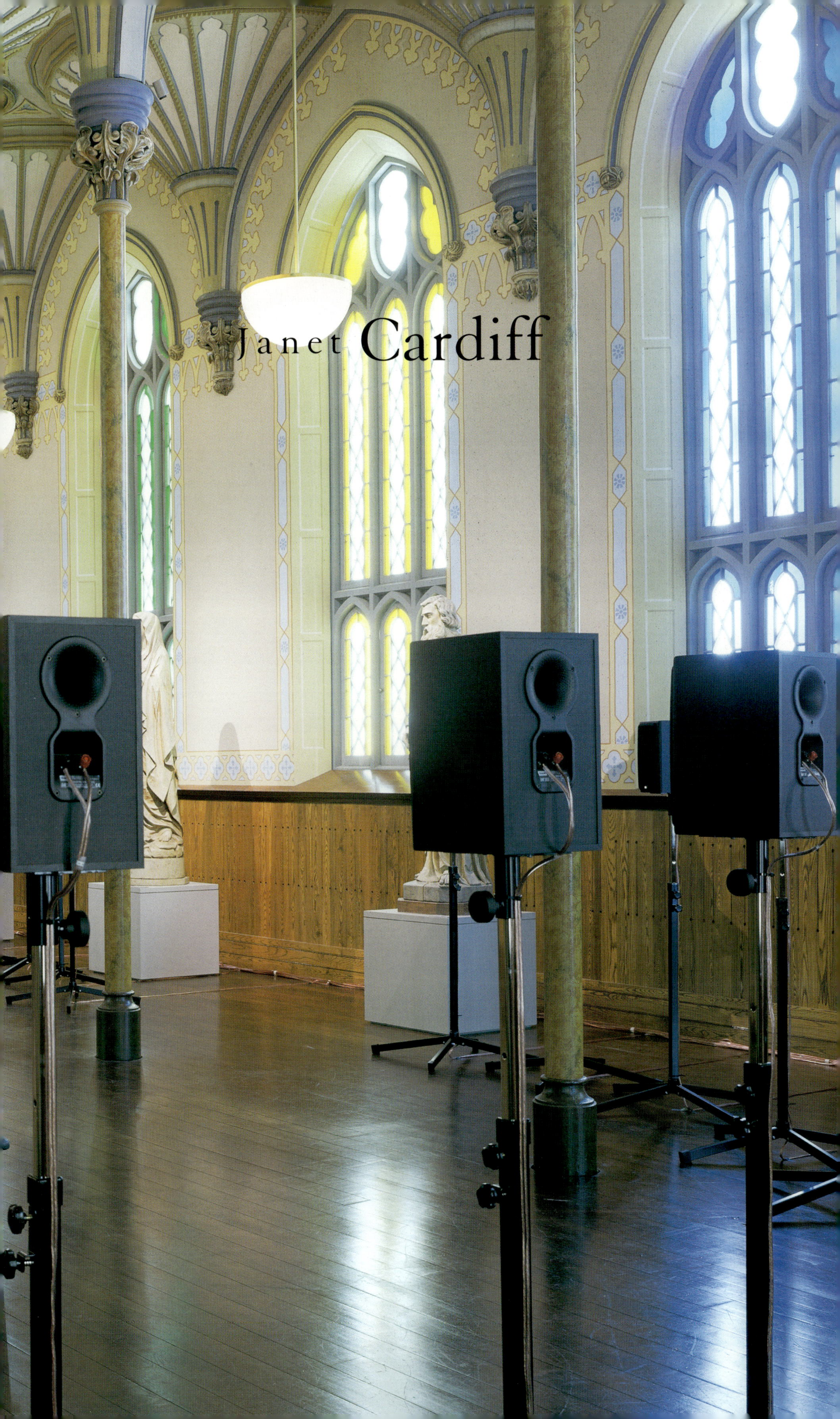

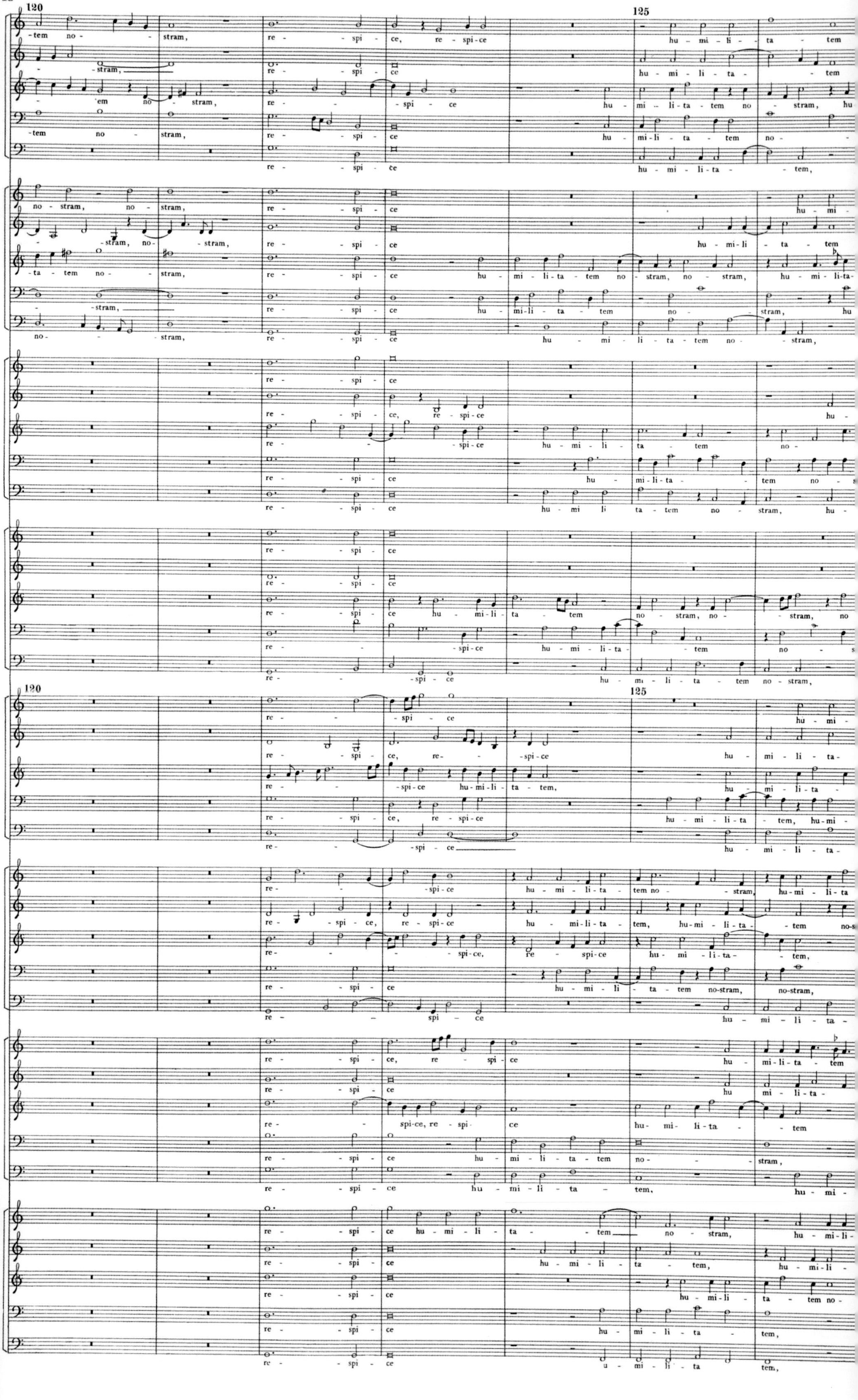
-tem no - stram, re - spi - ce, re - spi - ce hu - mi - li - ta - tem
- stram, re - spi - ce hu - mi - li - ta - tem
-tem no - stram, re - spi - ce hu - mi - li - ta - tem no - stram, hu
-tem no - stram, re - spi - ce hu - mi - li - ta - tem no -
re - spi - ce hu - mi - li - ta - tem,
no - stram, no - stram, re - spi - ce hu - mi -
- stram, no - stram, re - spi - ce hu - mi - li - ta - tem
-ta - tem no - stram, re - spi - ce hu - mi - li - ta - tem no - stram, no - stram, hu - mi - li - ta-
- stram, re - spi - ce hu - mi - li - ta - tem no - stram, hu
no - stram, re - spi - ce hu - mi - li - ta - tem no - stram,
re - spi - ce
re - spi - ce, re - spi - ce hu-
re - spi - ce hu - mi - li - ta - tem no -
re - spi - ce hu - mi - li - ta - tem no - s
re - spi - ce hu - mi li ta - tem no - stram, hu -
re - spi - ce
re - spi - ce
re - spi - ce hu - mi - li - ta - tem no - stram, no - stram, no
re - spi - ce hu - mi - li - ta - tem no - s
re - spi - ce hu - mi - li - ta - tem no - stram,
re - spi - ce hu - mi -
re - spi - ce, re - spi - ce hu - mi - li - ta-
re - spi - ce hu - mi - li - ta - tem, hu - mi - li - ta -
re - spi - ce, re - spi - ce hu - mi - li - ta - tem, hu - mi -
re - spi - ce hu - mi - li - ta-
re - spi - ce hu - mi - li - ta - tem no - stram, hu - mi - li - ta
re - spi - ce, re - spi - ce hu - mi - li - ta - tem, hu - mi - li - ta - tem no - s
re - spi - ce, re - spi - ce hu - mi - li - ta - tem,
re - spi - ce hu - mi - li - ta - tem no - stram, no - stram,
re - spi - ce hu - mi - li - ta -
re - spi - ce, re - spi - ce hu - mi - li - ta - tem
re - spi - ce hu mi - li - ta -
re - spi - ce, re - spi - ce hu - mi - li - ta - tem
re - spi - ce hu - mi - li - ta - tem no - stram,
re - spi - ce hu - mi - li - ta - tem, hu - mi -
re - spi - ce hu - mi - li - ta - tem no - stram, hu - mi - li -
re - spi - ce hu - mi - li - ta - tem, hu - mi - li -
re - spi - ce hu - mi - li - ta - tem no-
re - spi - ce hu - mi - li - ta - tem,
re - spi - ce u - mi - li - ta tem,

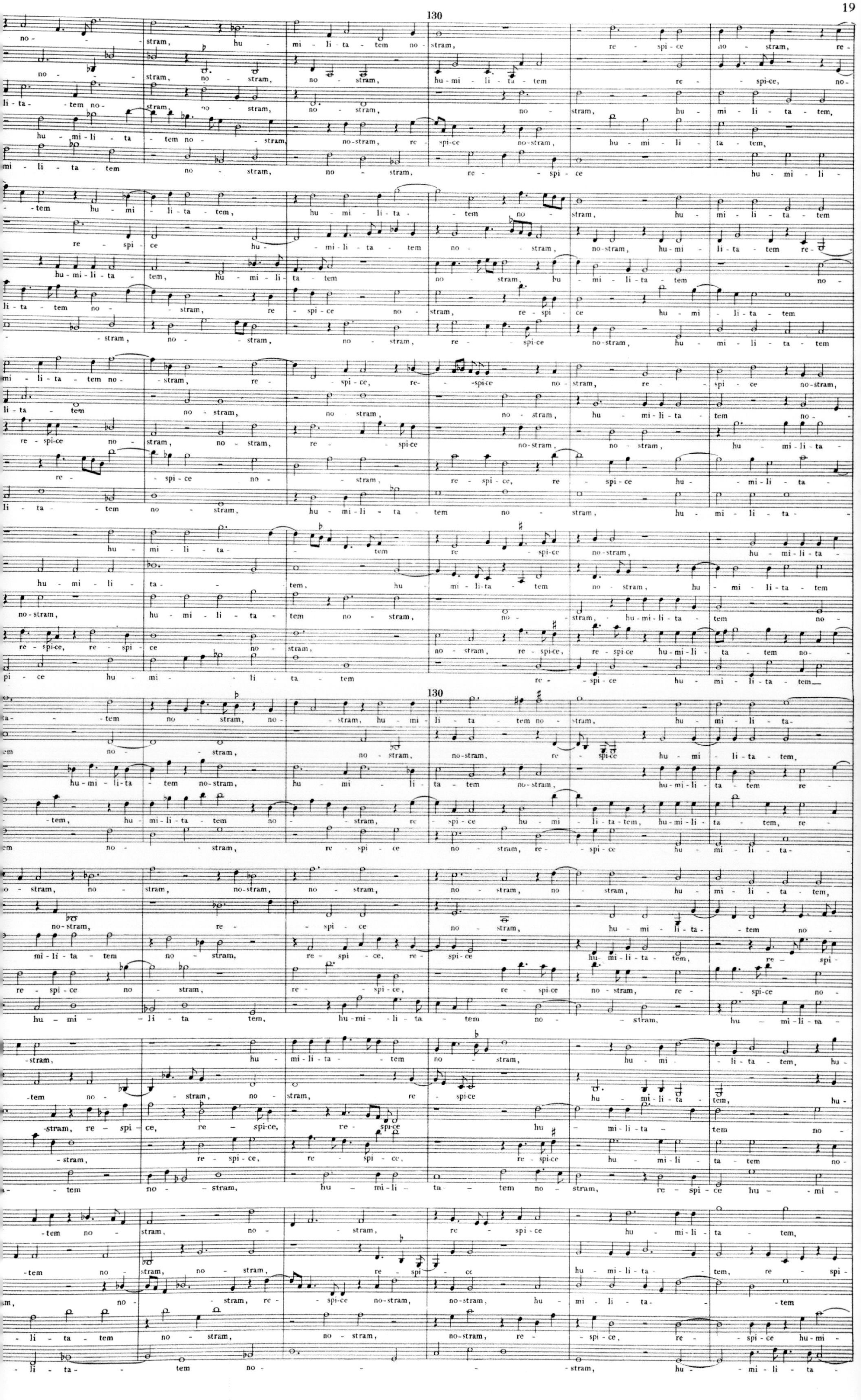
130
no - stram, hu - mi - li - ta - tem no - stram, re - spi - ce no - stram, re -
no - stram, no - stram, no - stram, hu - mi - li - ta - tem re - spi-ce, no-
li - ta - tem no - stram, no - stram, no - stram, no - stram, hu - mi - li - ta - tem,
hu - mi - li - ta - tem no - stram, no-stram, re - spi-ce no-stram, hu - mi - li - ta - tem,
mi - li - ta - tem no - stram, no - stram, re - spi - ce hu - mi - li -
- tem hu - mi - li - ta - tem, hu - mi - li - ta - - tem no - stram, hu - mi - li - ta - tem
re - spi - ce hu - - mi - li - ta - tem no - stram, no-stram, hu - mi - li - ta - tem re -
hu - mi - li - ta - tem, hu - mi - li - ta - tem no - stram, hu - mi - li - ta - tem no -
li - ta - tem no - stram, re - spi - ce no - stram, re - spi - ce hu - mi - li - ta - tem
- stram, no - stram, no - stram, re - spi-ce no-stram, hu - mi - li - ta - tem
mi - li - ta - tem no - stram, re - spi - ce, re - spi-ce no - stram, re - spi - ce no-stram,
li - ta - tem no - stram, no - stram, no - stram, hu - mi - li - ta - tem no -
re - spi-ce no - stram, no - stram, re - spi-ce no-stram, no - stram, hu - mi - li - ta -
re - spi - ce no - stram, re - spi - ce, re - spi - ce hu - mi - li - ta -
li - ta - tem no - stram, hu - mi - li - ta - tem no - stram, hu - mi - li - ta -
hu - mi - li - ta - tem re - spi-ce no-stram, hu - mi - li - ta -
hu - mi - li - ta - tem, hu - mi - li-ta - tem no - stram, hu - mi - li - ta - tem
no-stram, hu - mi - li - ta - tem no - stram, no - stram, hu-mi-li - ta - tem no -
re - spi-ce, re - spi - ce no - stram, no - stram, re - spi-ce, re - spi-ce hu - mi - li - ta - tem no-
pi - ce hu - mi - li - ta - tem re - spi - ce hu - mi - li - ta - tem
130
ta - tem no - stram, no - stram, hu - mi - li - ta - tem no - stram, hu - mi - li - ta-
em no - stram, no - stram, no-stram, re - spi-ce hu - mi - li - ta - tem,
hu - mi - li - ta - tem no-stram, hu - mi - li - ta - tem no-stram, hu-mi-li - ta - tem re -
- tem, hu - mi - li - ta - tem no - stram, re - spi - ce hu - mi - li - ta - tem, hu - mi - li - ta - tem, re -
em no - stram, re - spi - ce no - stram, re - spi - ce hu - mi - li - ta-
o - stram, no - stram, no-stram, no - stram, no - stram, no - stram, hu - mi - li - ta - tem,
no-stram, re - spi - ce no - stram, hu - mi - li - ta - tem no -
mi - li - ta - tem no - stram, re - spi - ce, re - spi-ce hu - mi - li - ta - tem, re - spi -
re - spi - ce no - stram, re - spi - ce, re - spi-ce no - stram, re - spi-ce no -
hu - mi - li - ta - tem, hu - mi - li - ta - tem no - stram, hu - mi-li - ta
- stram, hu - mi - li - ta - tem no - stram, hu - mi - li - ta - tem, hu -
- tem no - stram, no - stram, re - spi-ce hu - mi - li - ta - tem, hu -
- stram, re - spi - ce, re - spi-ce, re - spi-ce hu - mi - li - ta - tem no -
- stram, re - spi - ce, re - spi - ce, re - spi-ce hu - mi - li - ta - tem no -
- tem no - stram, hu - mi - li - ta - tem no - stram, re - spi - ce hu - mi -
- tem no - stram, no - stram, re - spi - ce hu - mi - li - ta - tem,
- tem no - stram, no - stram, re - spi - ce hu - mi - li - ta - tem, re - spi -
m, no - stram, re - spi-ce no-stram, no-stram, hu - mi - li - ta - - tem
- li - ta - tem no - stram, no - stram, no-stram, re - spi - ce, re - spi - ce hu - mi -
- li - ta - tem no - stram, hu - mi - li - ta -

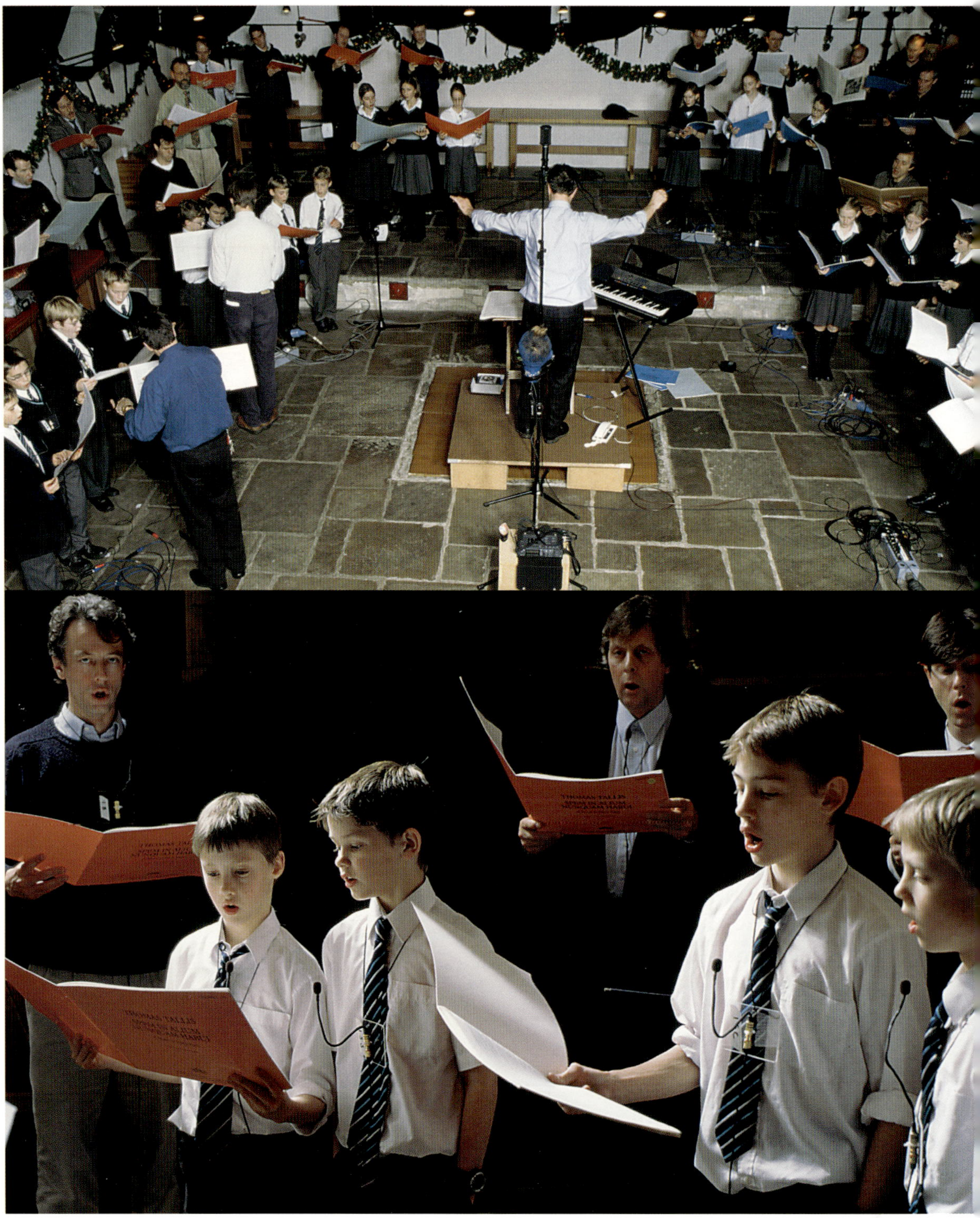

Recording session with members of the Salisbury Cathedral Choir, 5 December 2000 (photo Hugo Glendinning)

Pages 64–65: section of the score for Thomas Tallis's *Spem in Alium Nunquam Habui*, 1575 (Oxford: Oxford University Press, 1966).

Janet Cardiff

Janet Cardiff's art takes a variety of forms, but its one constant is sound used in a particularly three-dimensional way. Whether a given work is an installation or one of the audio walks for which she has become known, the effect is to alter the prior sense of the space one inhabits. This is because of the demand her art makes that one move along a predetermined trajectory, as in the audio walks, or randomly from one point to another in an installation. Thus the visitor becomes an active participant in a performance for one or several players (depending on the logic of the given piece). The usual visual experience of a work of art recedes into the background of Cardiff's largely narrative art, while auditory clues, to which we are usually less sensitive, take on a new importance. This heightened reliance on the sense of hearing, together with the complex tapestry of sounds she weaves, is one of the reasons for the strong effect her work has on the participant.

Cardiff has acknowledged a theatrical intention in her audio walks, likening their effect to that of a movie soundtrack playing in one's head. Others have compared following her walks to "dreaming another's dreams."[1] Both of these analogies are pertinent. The first captures the extraordinary intimacy of the experience and its collage-like, non-linear structure, while the second emphasizes its fictional quality. Cardiff frequently uses references from *film noir* or the detective story, so that the walks sometimes have a period feel, lending a curious sense of déjà vu to the present moment. In recent works, she has introduced a cinematic reference in miniature. In *Muriel Lake Incident*, realized in collaboration with George Bures Miller and shown at the Istanbul Biennale in 1999 and at the Tate Modern in 2000, she frames the visual effects within the proscenium arch of a tiny theatre. In her walk for the Carnegie International in 1999, titled *In Real Time*, she introduces a hand-held digital camera, used like a surveillance device. In both she accords a new importance to watching, although the position of the spectator shifts, between them, from the watcher to the watched.

[1] Kitty Scott, "I want you to walk with me," in James Lingwood and Michael Morris, *Janet Cardiff: The Missing Voice (case study b)* (London: Artangel, 1999), p. 15.

In her work for this exhibition, *Forty-Part Motet*, based on *Spem in Alium* by the sixteenth-century English composer Thomas Tallis, Cardiff returns to the investigation of aural and physical space and to the installation format of earlier works like *Whispering Room* (1992). What sets this new work[2] apart from the others is her use of a single musical composition—one of the most complex pieces of polyphonic choral music ever written—rather than a scripted montage of found material. Cardiff was given a recording of Tallis's music by a singer who had listened to one of her works and understood the relationship of Tallis's spatial use of sound to her walks. In her recreation of the motet, recorded with forty microphones and played back on forty speakers mounted on stands throughout the Rideau Chapel in the National Gallery, Cardiff breaks apart the aural space which an audience in a concert would normally perceive from only a single position. As she explains:

Some believe that Tallis originally composed this 40-part motet in a very spatial way—designed for a chapel with 8 alcoves for the 8 different choirs to sing around the central core so that the voices would move around the audience. Most people experience this piece now in their livingroom in front of only two speakers, the spatial construction lost in the mix. Even in a live concert the audience is separated from the individual voices. Only the performers are able to hear the person standing next to them singing a different harmony. I wanted to be able to experience this piece of music in a more intimate and physical way, to hear it from the viewpoint of a singer, to be able to "climb inside" the music, connecting with the separate voices. As with Whispering Room *I am also interested in how sound may construct a space in a sculptural way and how the audience may choose a path through this physical yet virtual space.*[3]

Forty-Part Motet was originally intended to evoke a space of plenitude, where each voice joins with thirty-nine others to sing praise to God the all-merciful and all-powerful. The music transports the listener to a paradisiacal space, a second Garden of Eden, in which difference is resolved in a harmonious whole (explicitly expressed in the complex harmonies of the music). In separating the voices and opening the space to the trajectories of the visitors who move through it at will,

[2] *Forty-Part Motet* was recorded by SoundMoves. It was produced by Field together with the Arts Council of England, the Salisbury Festival and Salisbury Cathedral Choir, Baltic, Now Festival, and The New Art Gallery Walsall. Loudspeakers were provided by B&W Loudspeakers (www.bwspeakers.com). Additional production assistance for the North American presentation was provided by the National Gallery of Canada. [3] Janet Cardiff, email to the author, 11 October 2000.

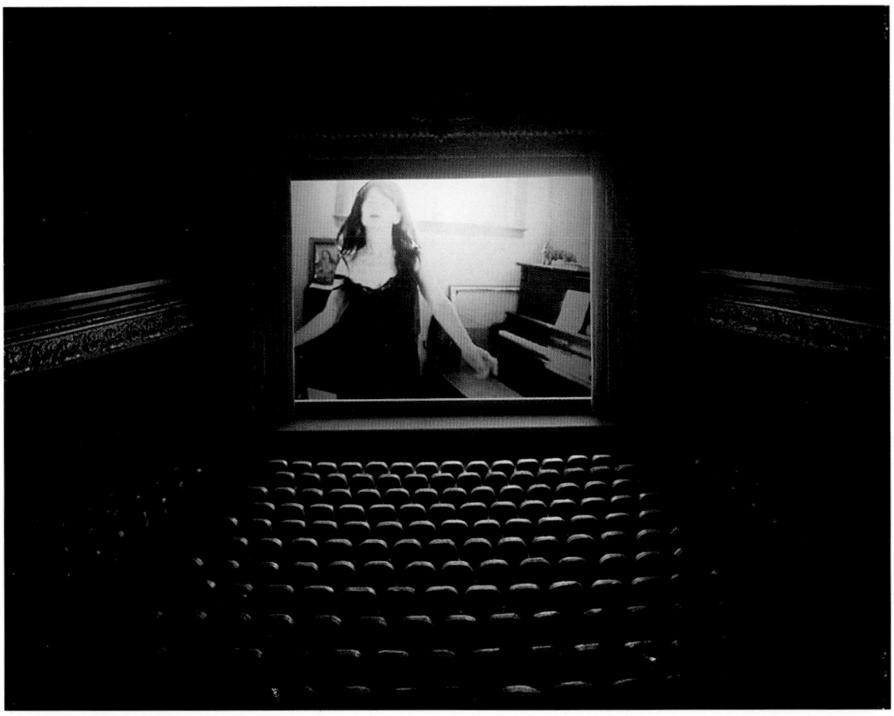

Cardiff interjects a modern consciousness of the individual. Her interest in the modalities of subjective experience is at odds with the religious sentiment of the music. However, her intuition of the similarities between its polyphony and her own spatialized use of sound is accurate, and it is interesting to note that such complex sonorities were eventually rejected as too worldly for sacred music. Now, the ineffable beauty of the music, which each person will perceive differently according to the path chosen, transports the listeners to a place that is all the sweeter for being provisional and temporary rather than eternal.

D.N.

Janet Cardiff, in collaboration with George Bures Miller, *Muriel Lake Incident*, 1999, wood, audio-video projection, and steel, 184.2 x 229.2 x 157.5 cm (photo courtesy of the artist and Luhring Augustine, New York)

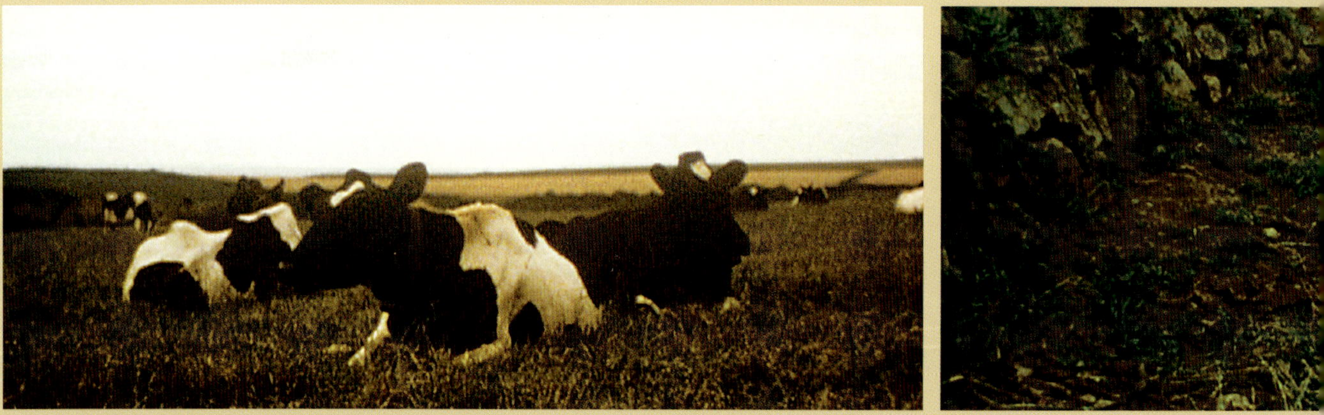

Banewl, 1999, 16 mm colour anamorphic film with optical sound, 63 minutes, courtesy of the artist, Frith Street Gallery, London, and Marian Goodman Gallery, New York and Paris, cat. no. 5

Tacita Dean

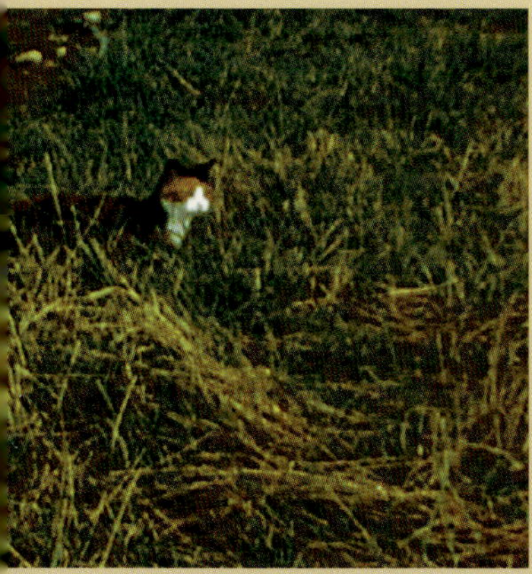
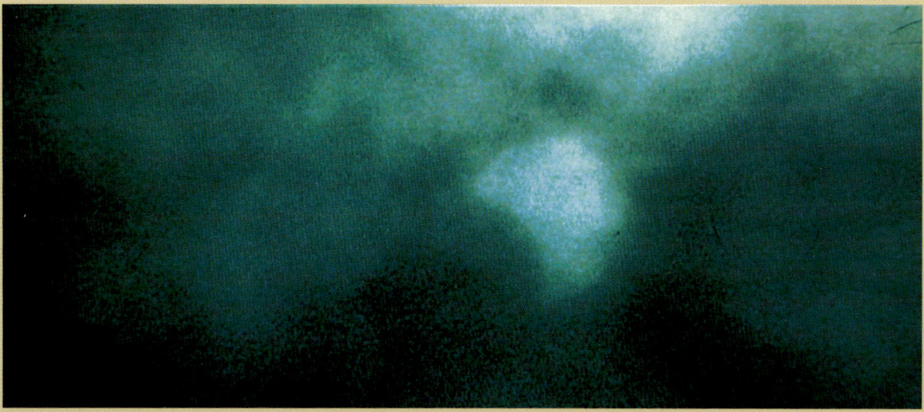

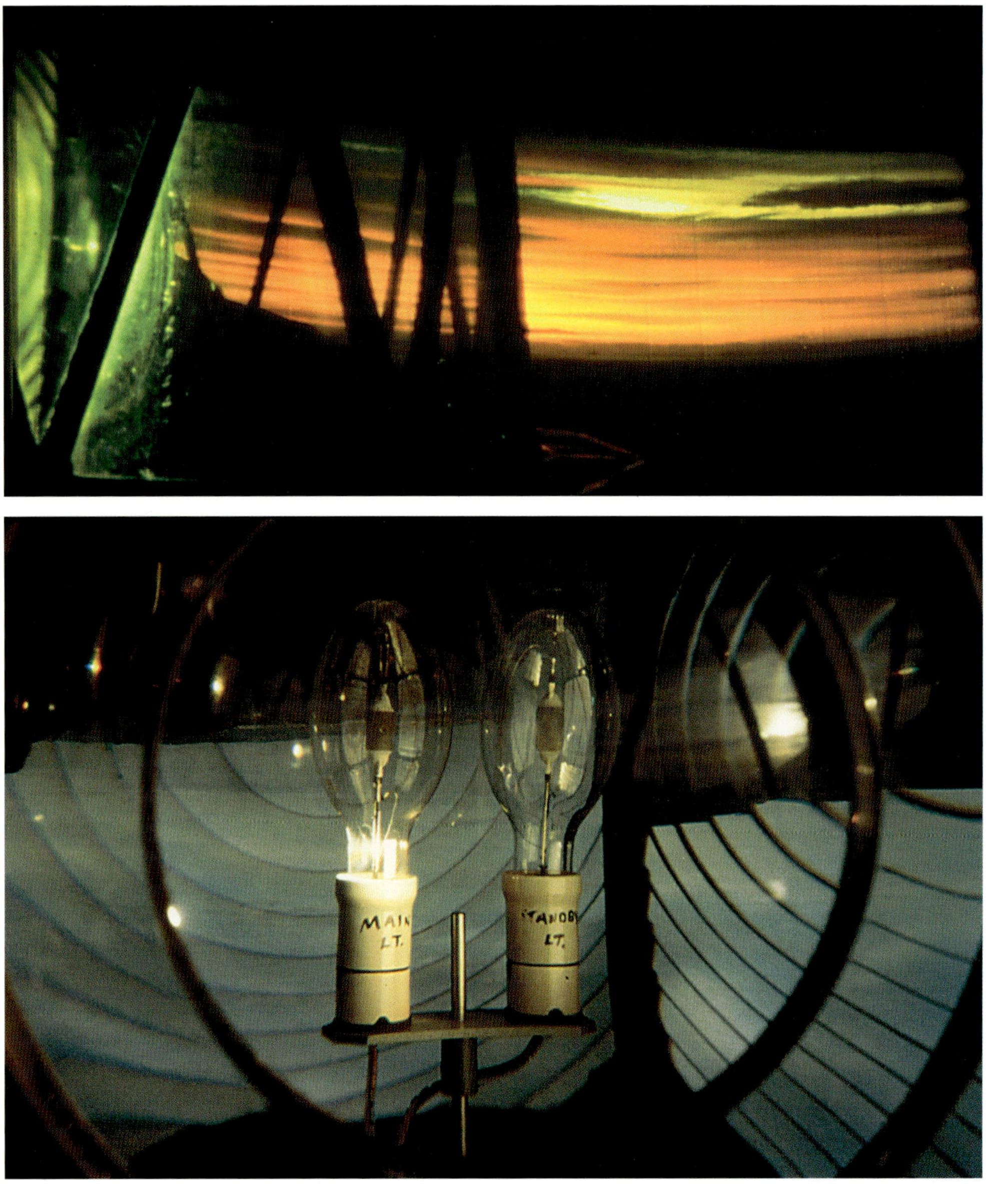

Disappearance at Sea (Cinemascope), 1996, 16 mm colour anamorphic film with optical sound, 14 minutes (photo courtesy of the artist, Frith Street Gallery, London, and Marian Goodman Gallery, New York and Paris)

The clouds had given the day a strange intensity. We hadn't seen the sun's corona nor the diamond ring effect, and Dick hadn't found any crescent suns pinholed beneath the trees. What we had was the place: the ground and the sky; the animals and the birds, and Banewl, the farm itself. The eclipse was about waiting for darkness to happen and then equally for the return of a normal sun. The clouds allowed us to experience this coincidence of cosmic time and scale on our terms and in our human time, measuring it against the movements of animals and the fine detailing of our natural world.[1]

The pastoral mood and arcadian setting of *Banewl* are somewhat unusual in Tacita Dean's work, which encompasses installation, sound works, drawing, and photography, as well as film. She is drawn to stories of unusual human determination and of belief in unlikely fate or luck, and her works often imply a quest or involve an actual journey. The most exemplary of these is the constellation of works made in response to the story of Donald Crowhurst, whose doomed attempt to sail solo around the world occasioned much media attention and is now almost forgotten.[2] In her first two films inspired by Crowhurst's story, *Disappearance at Sea* and *Disappearance at Sea II*, there is no reference to his fateful journey. Instead, a lighthouse beacon, surveying the surrounding land and sea, and the movement of the setting sun stand in for the human drama, which is in essence the search for an epic dimension transcending everyday life. In her book, named after Crowhurst's craft, *Teignmouth Electron*, Dean recounts the story in her own words, pairing it with an account of her investigations and related stories. Her research has the quality of a personal odyssey, and its own epic dimension is realized with the making of the last film, for which she travelled to the Caribbean island of Cayman

[1] Tacita Dean, "Banewl," in *Tacita Dean: Selected Works from 1994–2000* (Basel: Museum für Gegenwartskunst, 2000), p. 52. [2] Donald Crowhurst, an amateur yachtsman, set sail in a trimaran from Teignmouth in Devon in 1969, one of nine sailors competing in a solo, non-stop, round-the-world race sponsored by the *Sunday Times*. Inexperienced and ill-prepared, he was mid-way into the Atlantic when he realized that he could not complete the race. Instead of continuing or calling for help, he broke off radio contact and began to fake his position, keeping two sets of logbooks, until eventually he lost track of time and no longer knew where he was. Overwhelmed, he jumped overboard. His abandoned boat was found ten days later, floating several hundred kilometres off the British coast.

Brac. There she finally found the derelict hull of Crowhurst's trimaran, recovered from the ocean only to be abandoned in paradise.

Dean travelled to the Cornish coast to make *Banewl*, and the bucolic landscape where the film is set is never far from the sea. Yet it is a world removed from the relics of Cayman Brac. It is a relatively long film for her, and slow, as befits a film whose subject, even more than the solar eclipse, is about waiting. Above the clouds, the BBC's Hercules plane can be heard filming a rare celestial drama, while on the ground, where Dean and her crew wait, the clouds break only after the few minutes of total darkness when the earth's shadow blots out the sun. Instead of the sun, there is everything earthly. Swallows swoop and dart nervously in the sky; cows move slowly in the meadow, lowing occasionally and lying down when full darkness comes, obedient to the waning light no matter what the hour; and the cock crows as day breaks again, an almost comical welcoming of the light's return. Three different scales of time intersect in *Banewl*: cosmic, human, and animal, and as we watch the film our linear sense of time, which demands drama and purpose, slowly yields and gives way to the lovingly detailed rhythms of the natural world. This is the unhurried twilight of the pastoral, when natural and human time briefly merge and lend themselves to reverie.

The spell of the moment is broken soon enough; the sun bursts through the clouds, gloriously but anti-climactically, and our sense of anticipation cheated returns too. However, something else sustains the film: a sense of the extraordinary quality of light even in its more ordinary moments. Dean's film shares this sense with the works of nineteenth-century painters like Constable and Turner, who both insisted that the source of their unusual effects lay in the finely tuned observation of nature. Oddly, the pastoral *Banewl* and the elegiac Crowhurst saga turn out to have more in common than is first apparent—a feeling for nature and its rhythms, against which the human quest is measured. Although in her more recent films Dean allows nature to tell the tale rather than introduce narrative, her scenarios turn on intersections of the ordinary and the extraordinary, hope and disillusion, truth and concealment, worthy of the most eloquent of storytellers.

D.N.

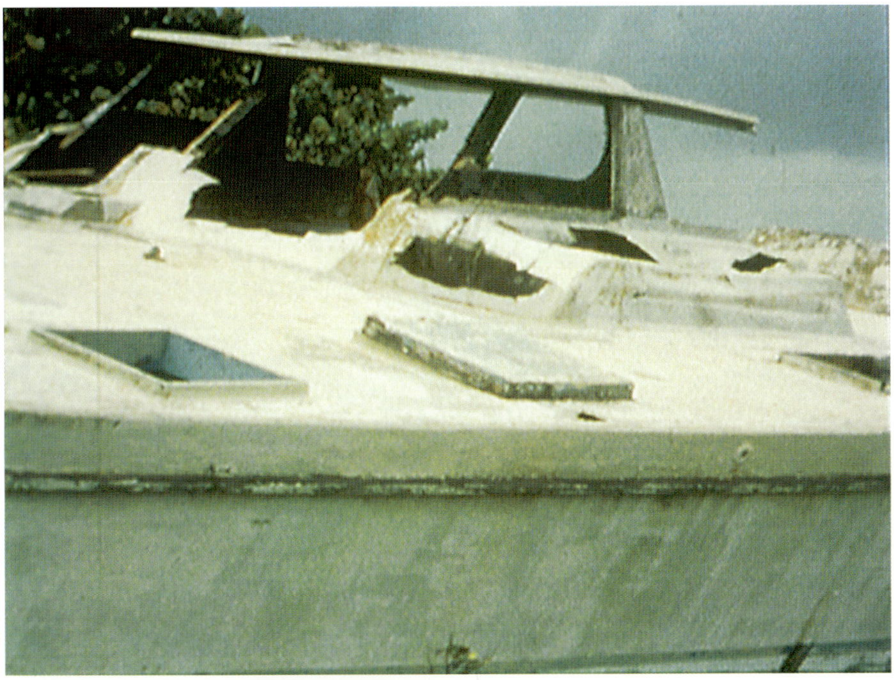

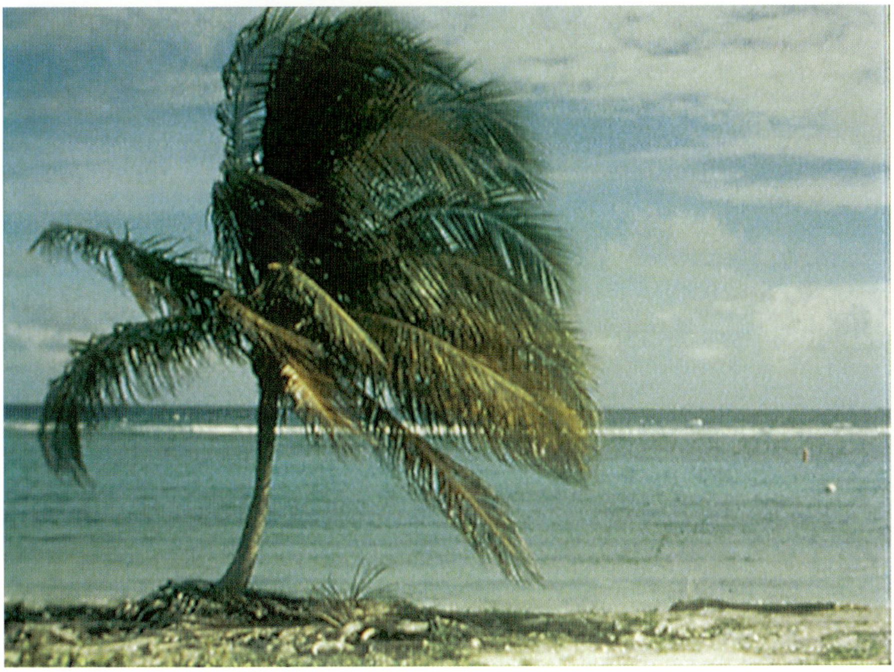

Teignmouth Electron, 1999, 16 mm colour film with optical sound, 7 minutes (photo courtesy of the artist, Frith Street Gallery, London, and Marian Goodman Gallery, New York and Paris)

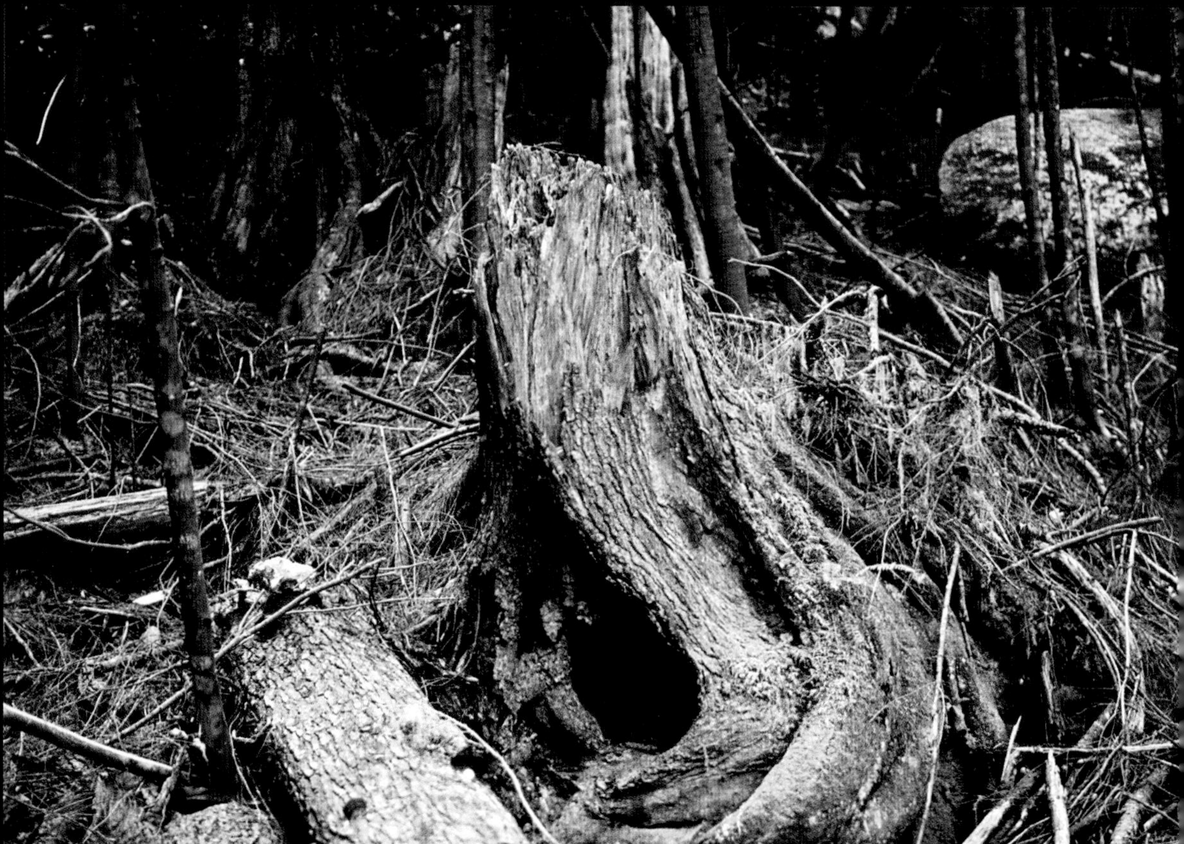

Liz Magor

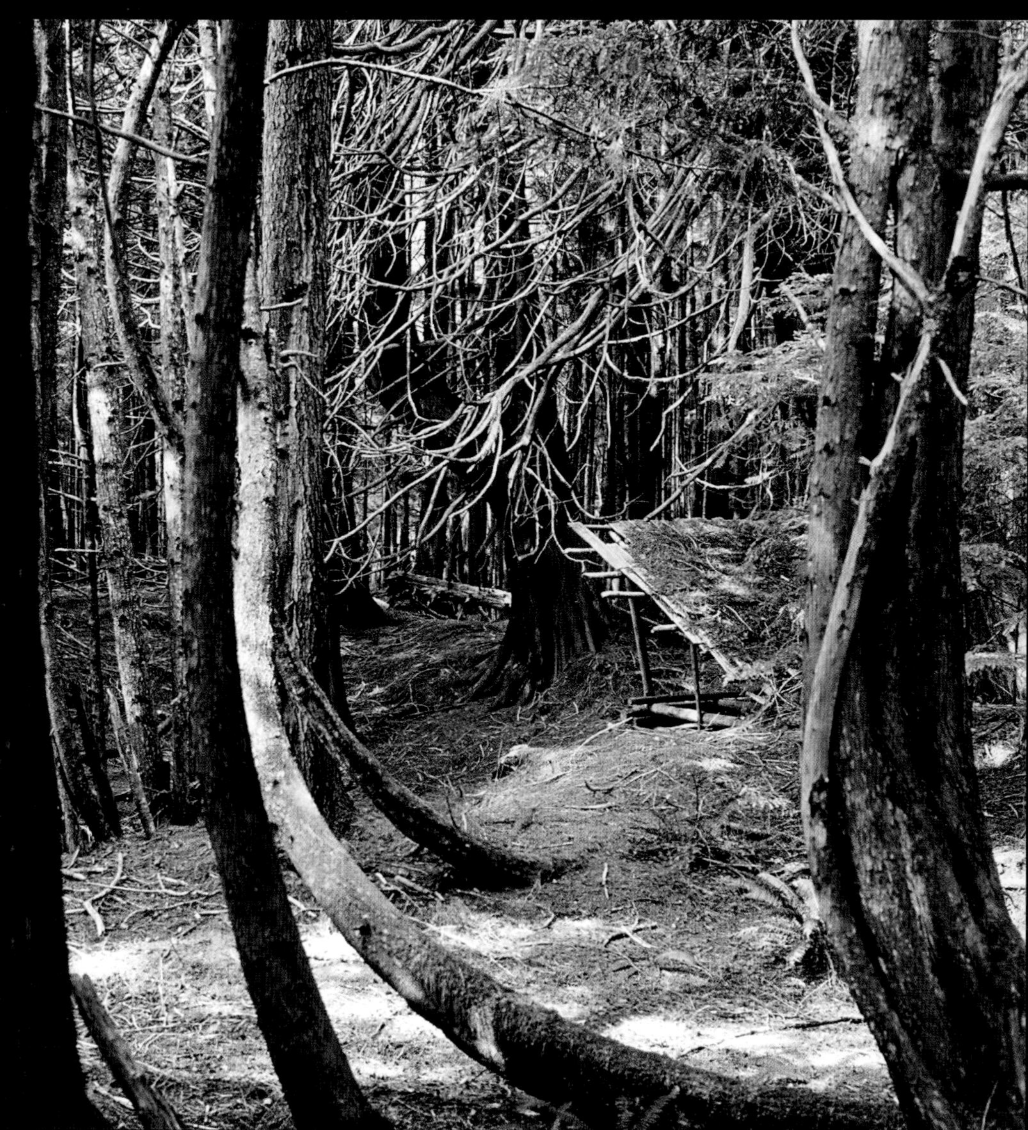

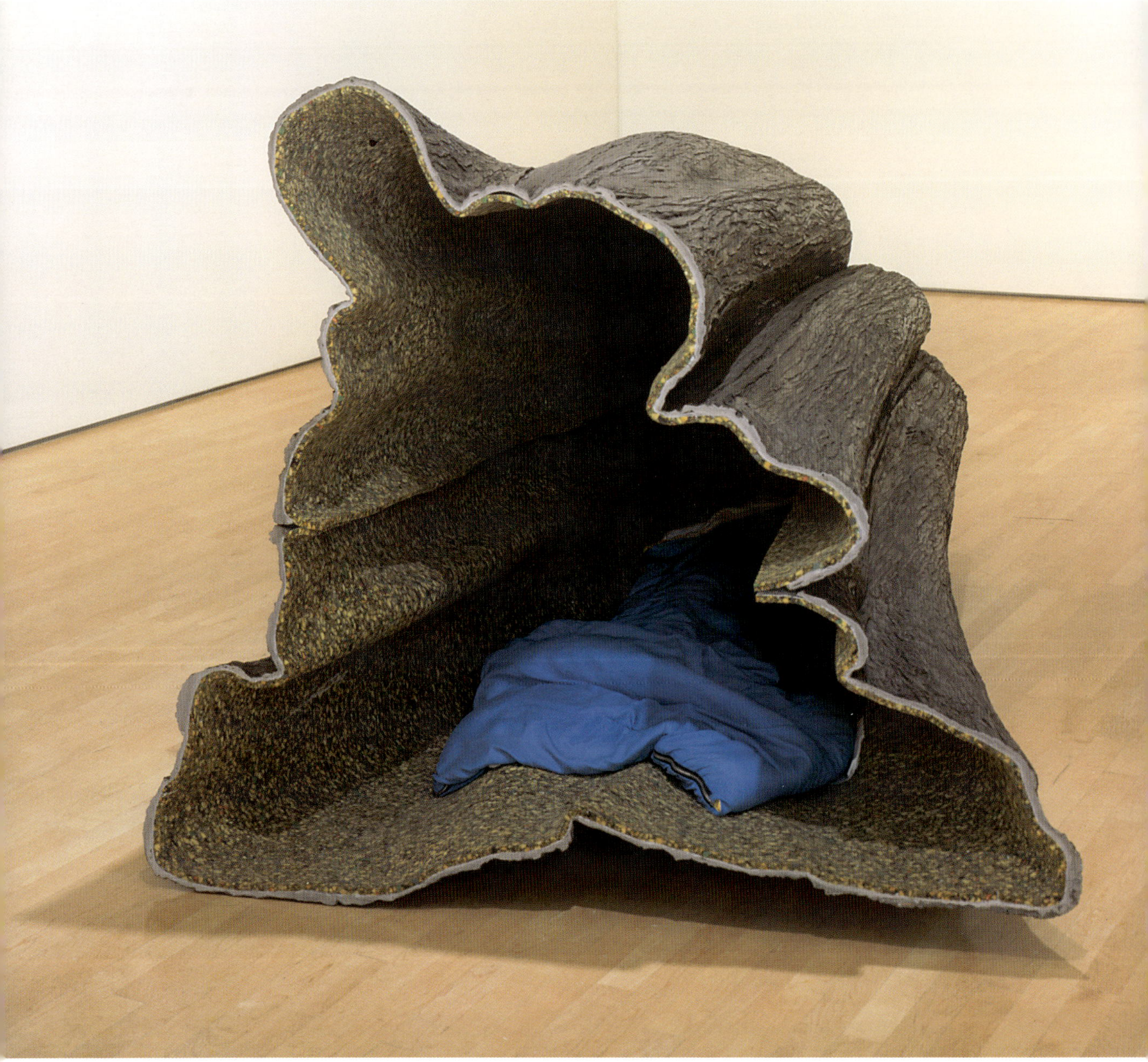

Hollow, 1998–1999, polymerized alpha gypsum, fabric, and foam, 182.8 x 106.7 x 121.9 cm, National Gallery of Canada, Ottawa, cat. no. 6

Pages 76–77: two images from *Deep Woods*, 1999, edition 1/3, 8 gelatin silver prints, selenium-toned, 25.4 x 28 cm each (5 prints), 12.7 x 16.5 cm each (3 prints), National Gallery of Canada, Ottawa

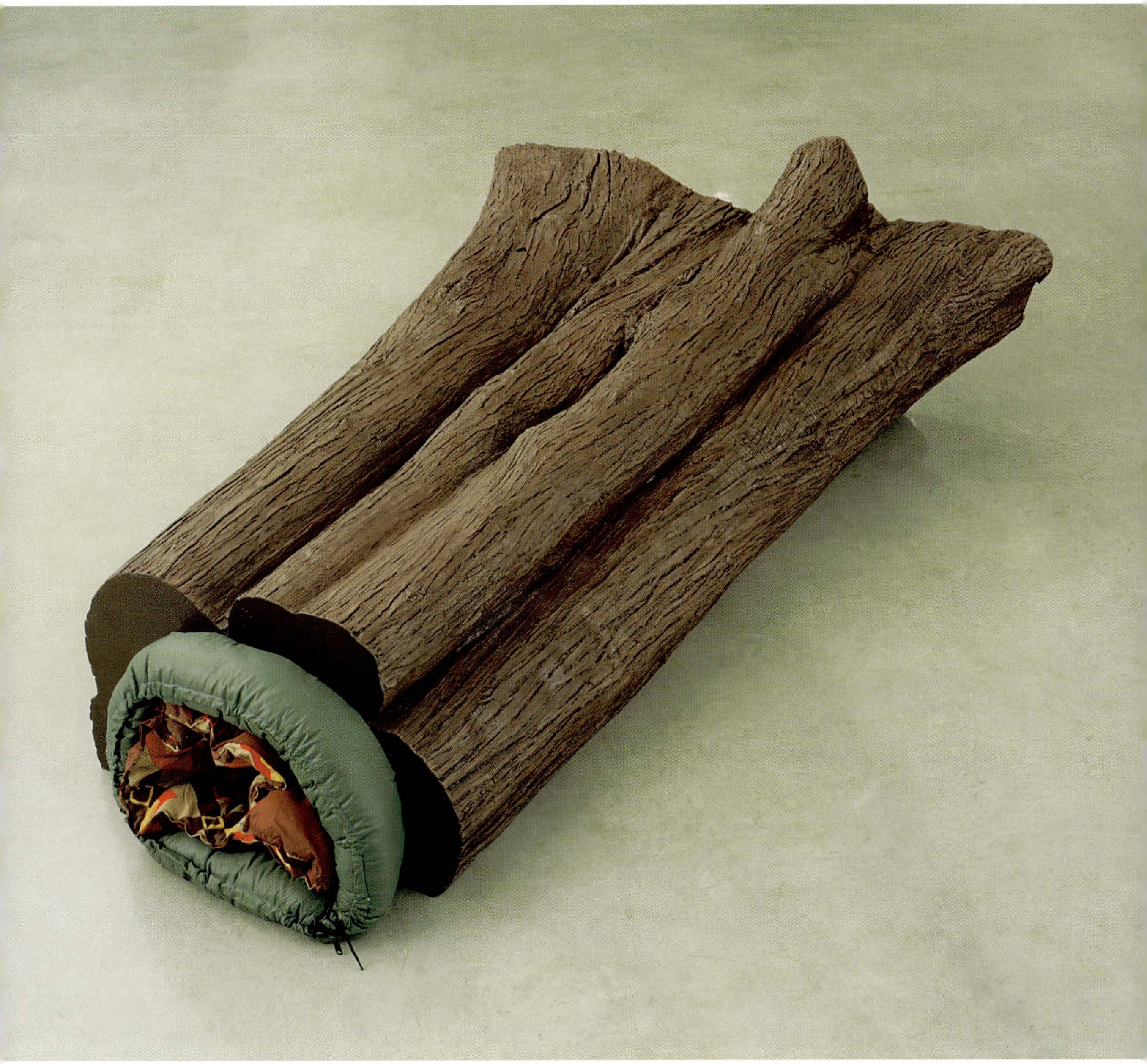

Burrow, 1999, polymerized alpha gypsum and fabric, 58 x 173 x 137 cm, Vancouver Art Gallery, Vancouver (photo Barrie Jones), cat. no. 7

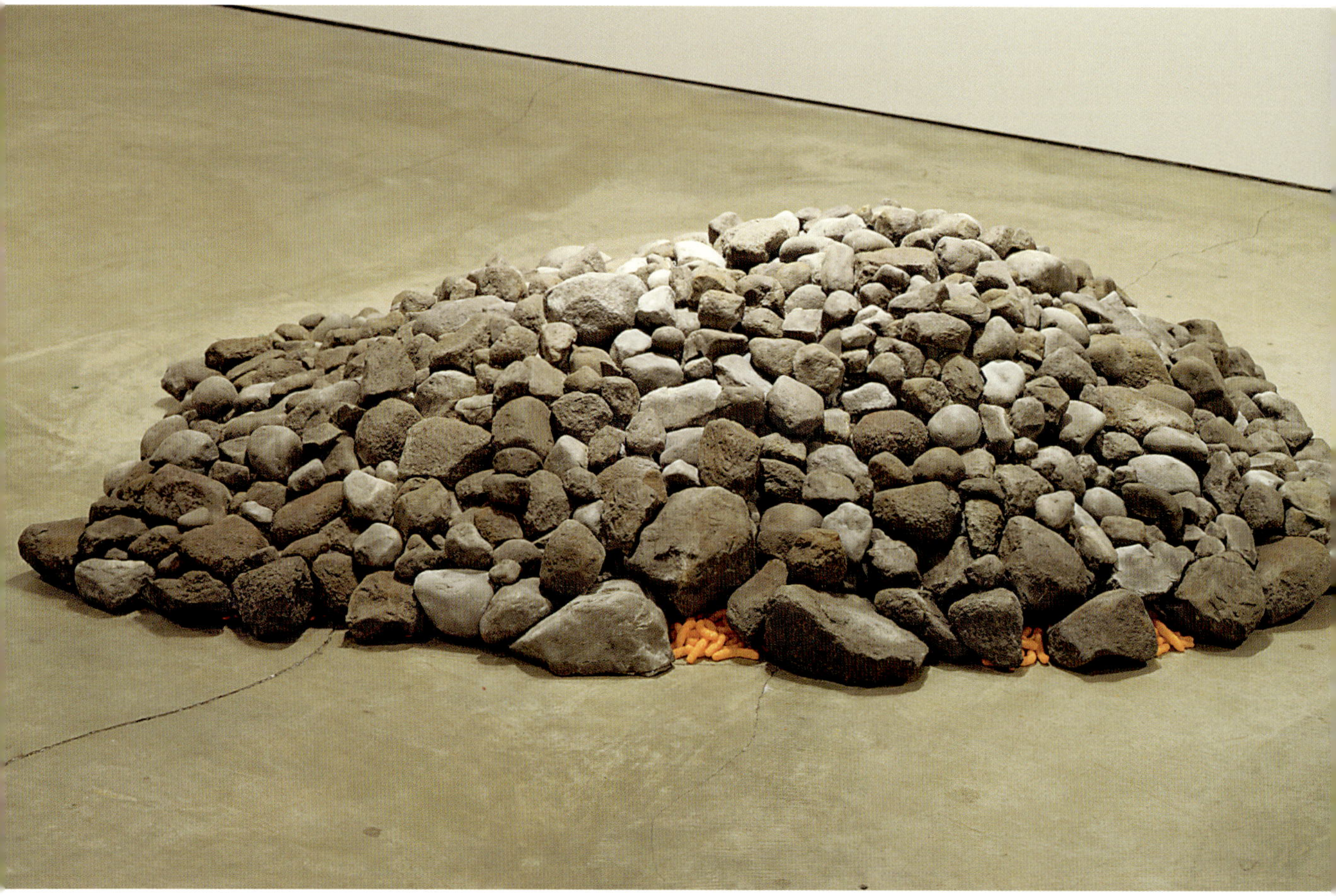

Chee-to, 2000, plaster, resin, and food, 183 x 244 x 61 cm, Art Gallery of Ontario, Toronto (photo Kim Clarke, courtesy Susan Hobbs Gallery, Toronto), cat. no. 8

Liz Magor

Toward the end of the 1980s, Liz Magor made a tiny replica of a cabin and situated it in a field of snow that was made of cotton batting and dotted with a few miniature fir trees. This little object, which was seen through the window of an office or store room in a disused factory, contrasted oddly with the surrounding traces of manufacturing activity. It looked as remote and unreachable as a sentimental greeting card, and was perhaps the closest Magor could get to materializing an image from the collective imagination. Several years later she returned to the motif of the cabin. This time it was full-scale and situated in the Toronto Sculpture Garden on a busy city street.[1] However anomalous, this cabin was no image from the imagination but the real thing, fully equipped for survival in the bush. In fact, the weapons collected inside—a compendium of arms from across the ages—went well beyond the essentials, transforming the cabin into an emblem of the fortified dwelling, a last line of defence against the society of others.

The idea of withdrawal and refuge that both these works embody is further explored in the group of recent sculptures included in the present exhibition. In a related series of black-and-white photographs, taken in the forest interior, animal burrows and hollow trees are juxtaposed with various rudimentary shelters built by human hand and since abandoned. Fairy tales and legends support the connection. The forest harbours evil and is a place of trial for the innocent, but it is also the refuge and home of outlaws such as Robin Hood who contest the established order of society. In this regard, it is interesting to note that a WANTED poster for a real-life fugitive, described by police as an anti-social loner who had "fled on foot into the mountain wilderness with his black Lab dog," was the impetus for the log sculptures entitled *Hollow* and *Burrow*.[2] Both were cast from a mould made from the trunk of a living cedar tree on Cortes Island, where the artist lives. *Hollow* is open at one end, and even seems to invite entry, whereas *Burrow* is shut as tight as a turtle's shell against intrusion. Both contain sleeping bags, provocatively raising the idea of refuge. Where does one hide in the woods? What sort of shelter does the real wilderness offer? As Magor observes:

[1] This piece, entitled *Messenger*, was on view for several months in 1996. [2] Nancy Tousley, "Into the Woods," in *Liz Magor* (Toronto and Vancouver: Art Gallery of York University, Toronto, and Contemporary Art Gallery, Vancouver), p. 38.

These... sculptures exploit the belief that nature is the source of our most ideal and authentic refuge. Taking the form of hollow logs and tree trunks — the child's dream of perfect shelter — they offer the image of a natural hideout. But they also suggest the condition of last resort: for the fugitive, the misanthropist, and the disenfranchised.[3]

In *Chee-to* and *Stores* Magor turns to the problem of supplies; it's not enough just to find a place to sleep. A cache allows for mobility: hide the food there and come back for it later, when the coast is clear. *Chee-to* is a kind of cairn, a landmark that might be found in the open, erected sometime past by people cannier in the ways of nature and knowledgeable about wild things also scavenging for food. Like the logs, it is a careful replica, a plausible sign of the natural world. *Stores*, on the other hand, speaks of life on the streets, another kind of wilderness. Both belong to a world where food comes in plastic bags from the grocery store and orange-coloured puffs of air and corn make a good snack. In this world, nature is a fiction, a place of the past.

The unconcealed artifice of Magor's sculptures is an indication of her underlying interest in "how certain images pass for (and perhaps preclude) the authentic in spite of their obvious fakeness."[4] *Hollow*'s realism is undone by the dappled foam that lines its interior. The Chee-tos lying underneath the cairn, bought from the grocery store, are insubstantial substitutes for food. The plywood and drywall hiding the bags of real potatoes and carrots are simulations of the original detritus. The cabin in the Sculpture Garden was transported from its site in the woods and re-assembled in the city by a firm specializing in such moves. Nothing is what it first appears to be. Magor explores the desire for the real and authentic, which is equated with simplicity. An industry has grown up around this sophisticated urge. Even the patently fake tokens of authenticity culled from the past and marketed by Ralph Lauren and Martha Stewart enjoy remarkable success. Magor locates her sculptures on the fringes of this modern Arcadia. Doubly encoded, they play off the visual ironies of real and fake while below the surface they probe the tensions between real homelessness and its delusive middle-class twin.

D.N.

[3] Liz Magor, exhibition statement, Equinox Gallery, Vancouver, 1999. [4] Liz Magor, email to the author, 11 October 2000.

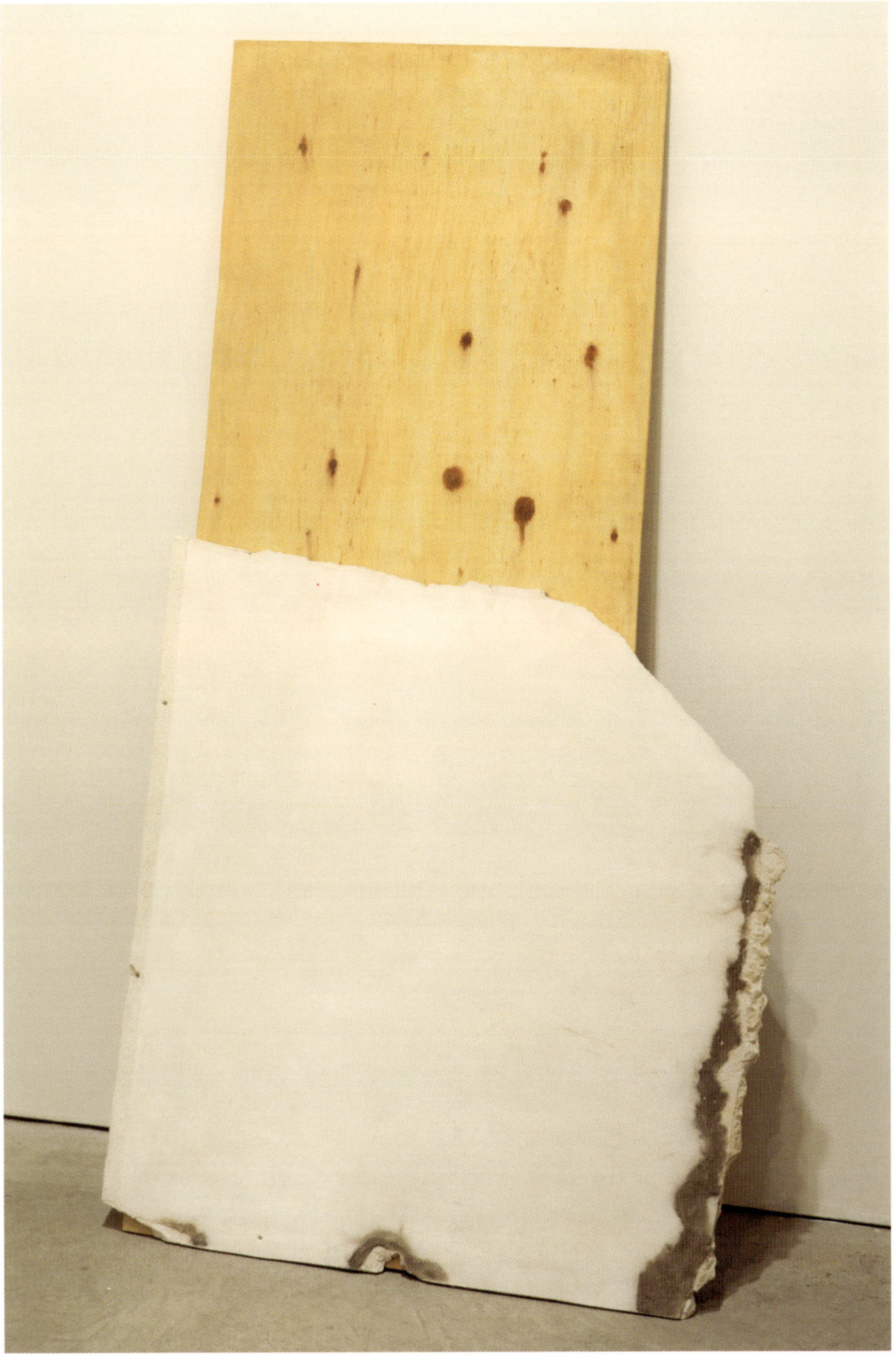

Stores, 2000, plaster, resin, and food, 155 x 81 x 36 cm, courtesy Susan Hobbs Gallery, Toronto (photo Isaac Applebaum), cat. no. 9

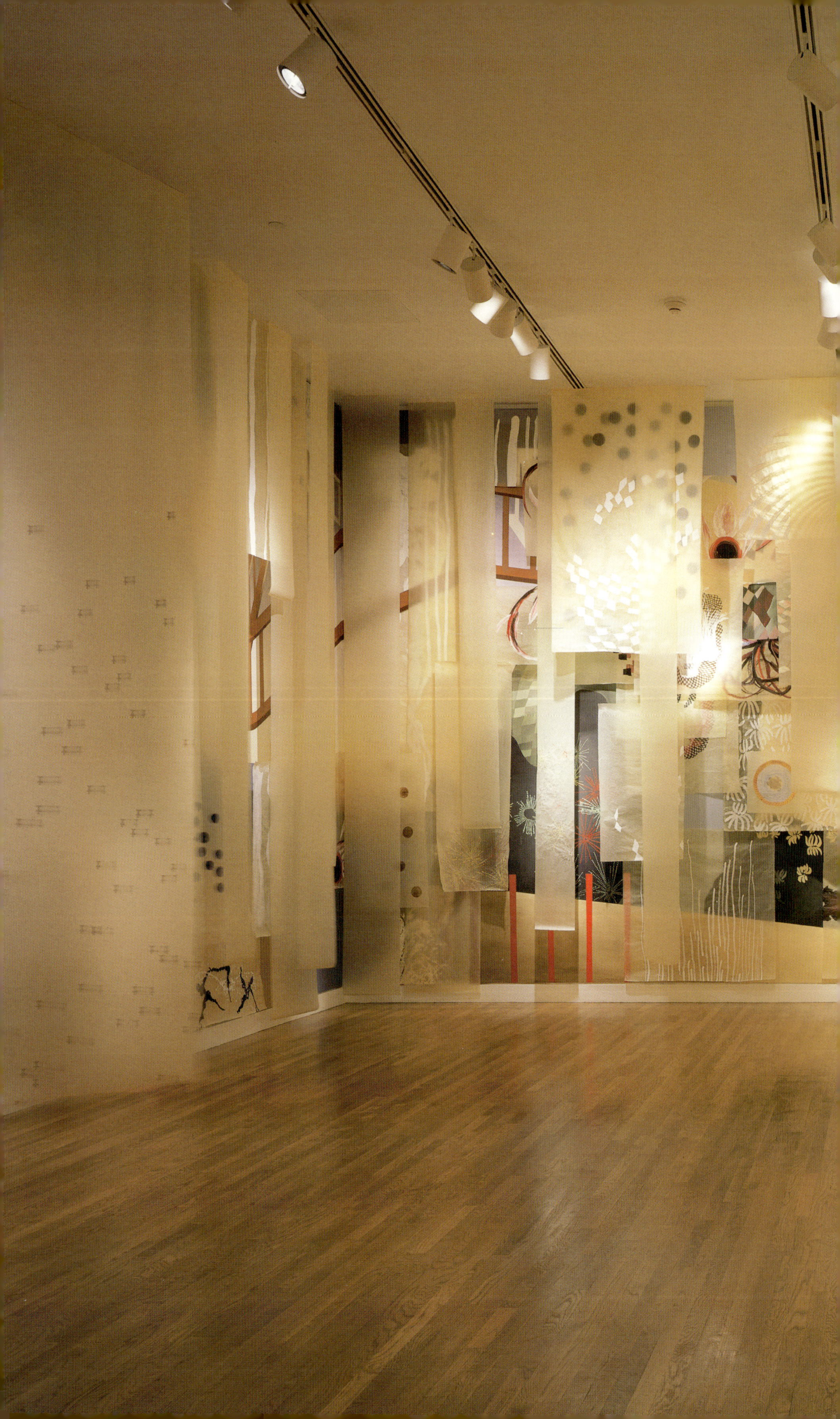

Shahzia Sikander

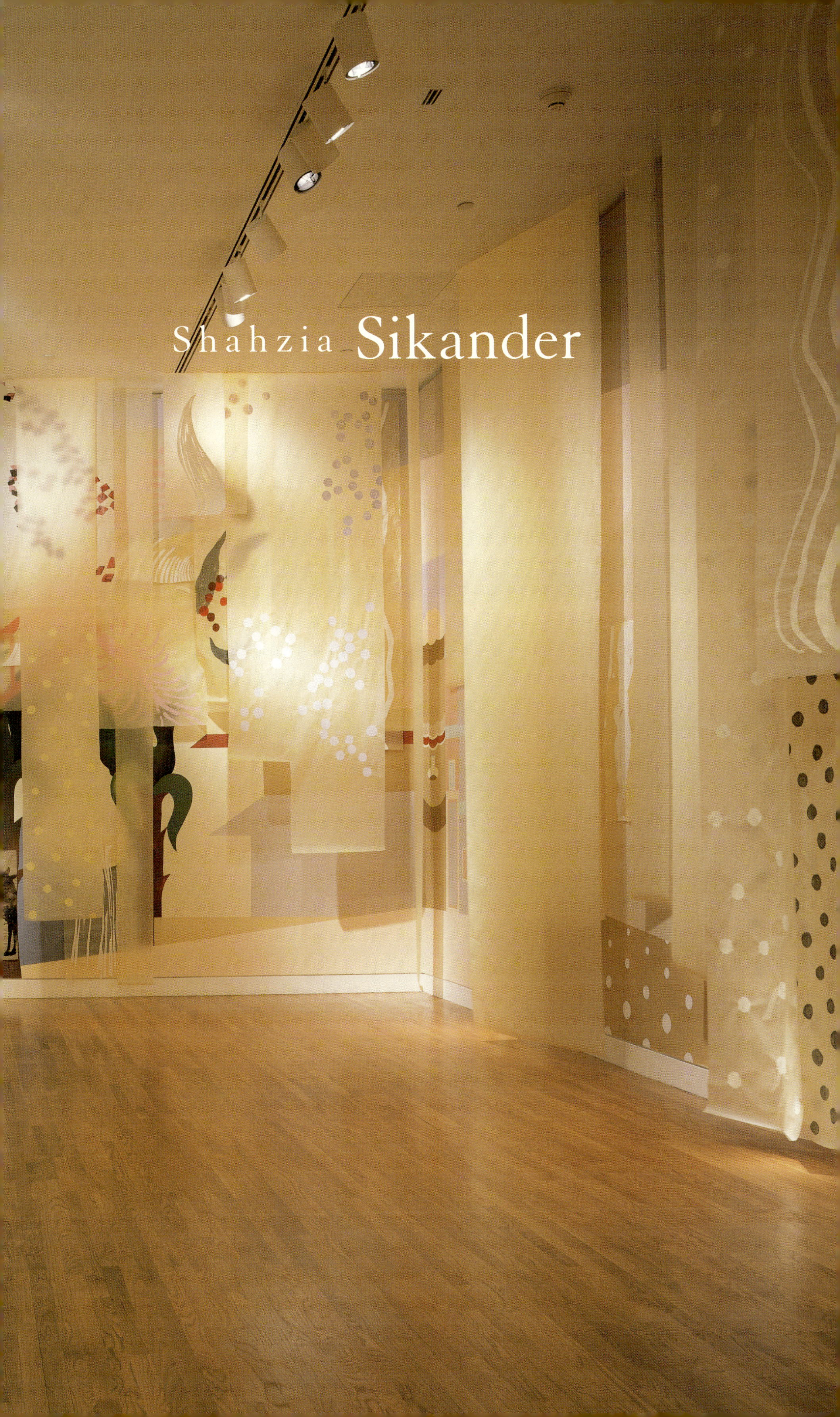

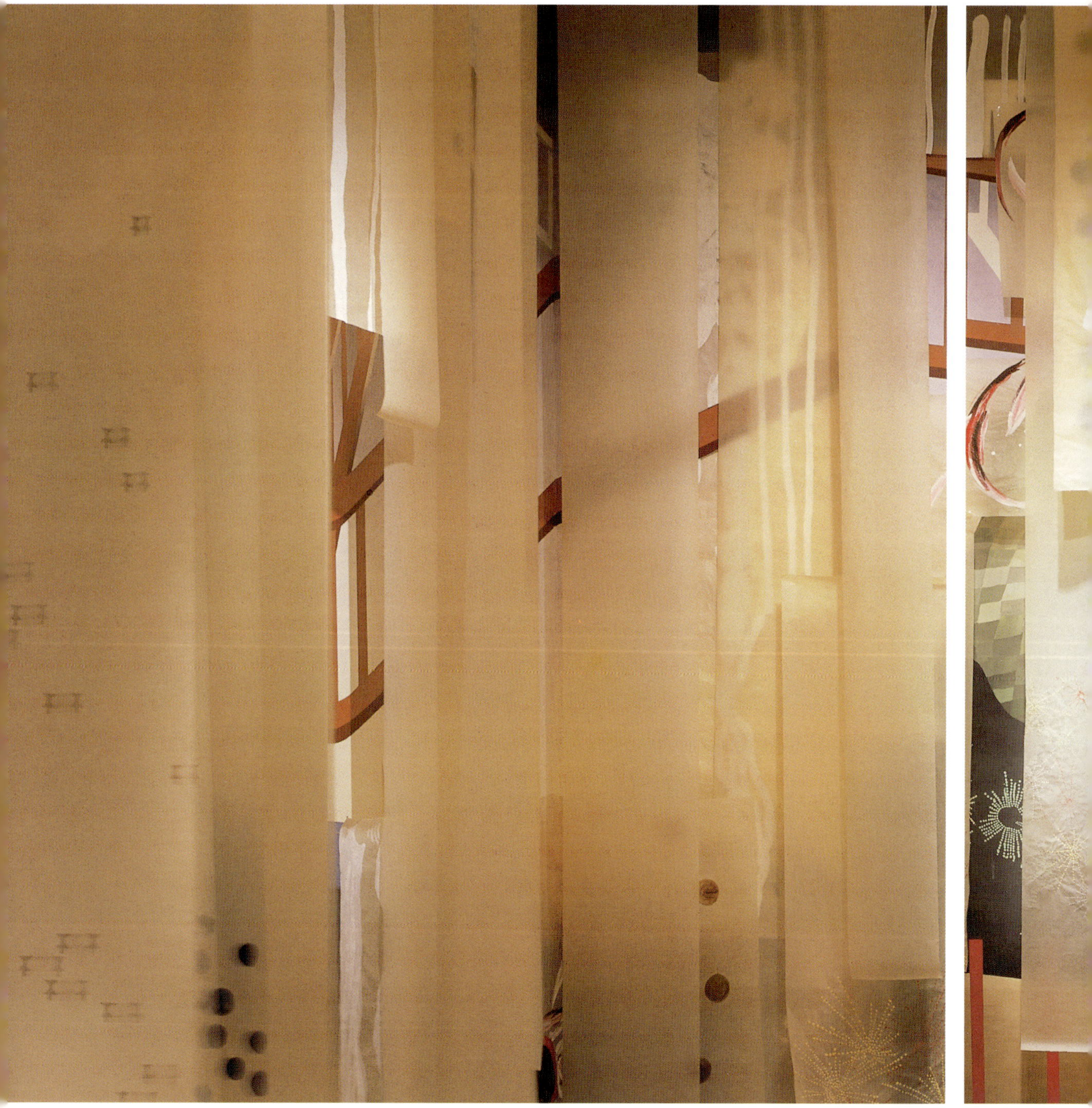

Pages 84–87: *Chaman*, 2000–2001, acrylic, gouache, and ink on tissue paper, installation at the National Gallery of Canada, courtesy of the artist and Deitch Projects, New York, cat. no. 10

Shahzia Sikander

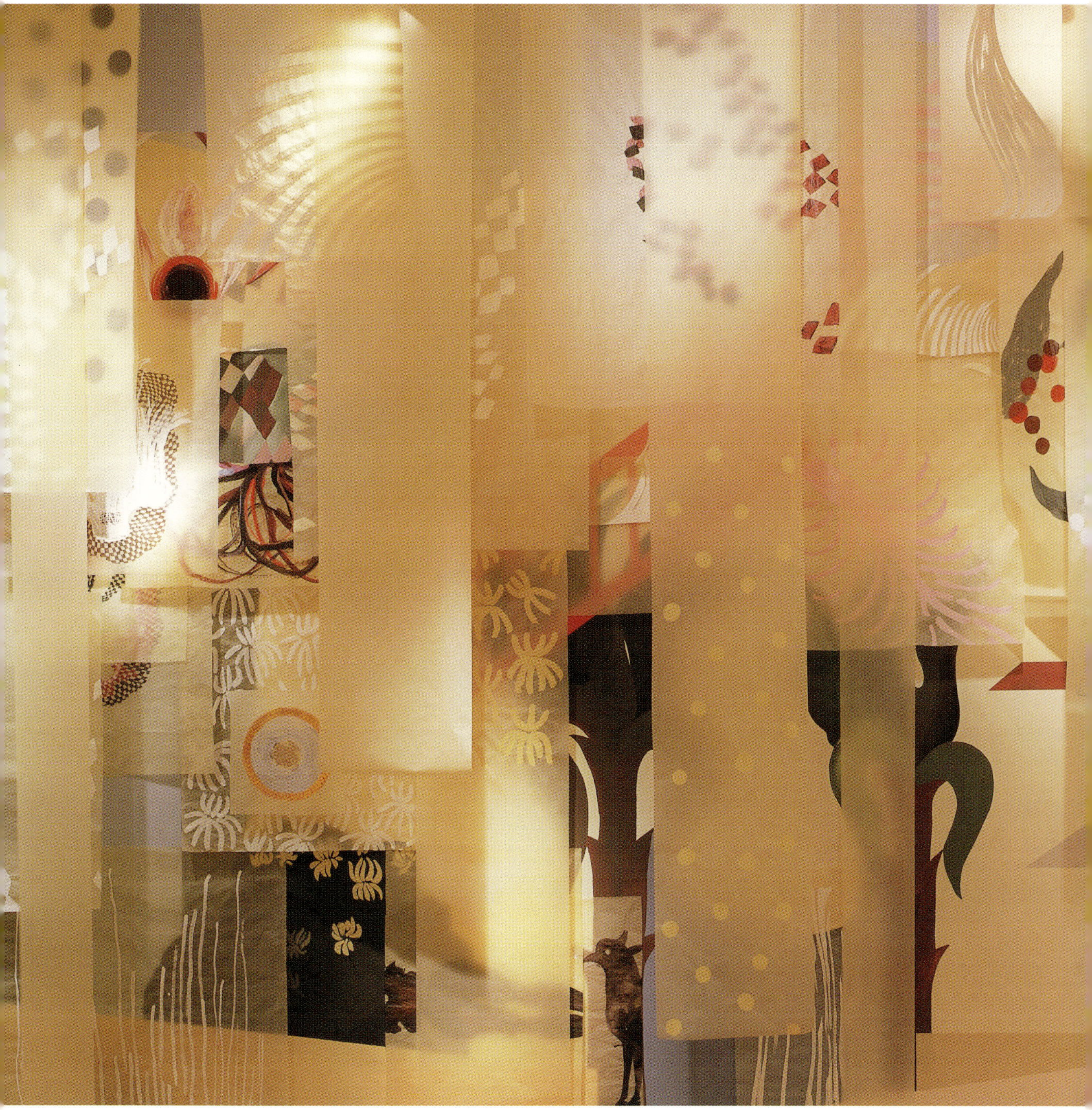

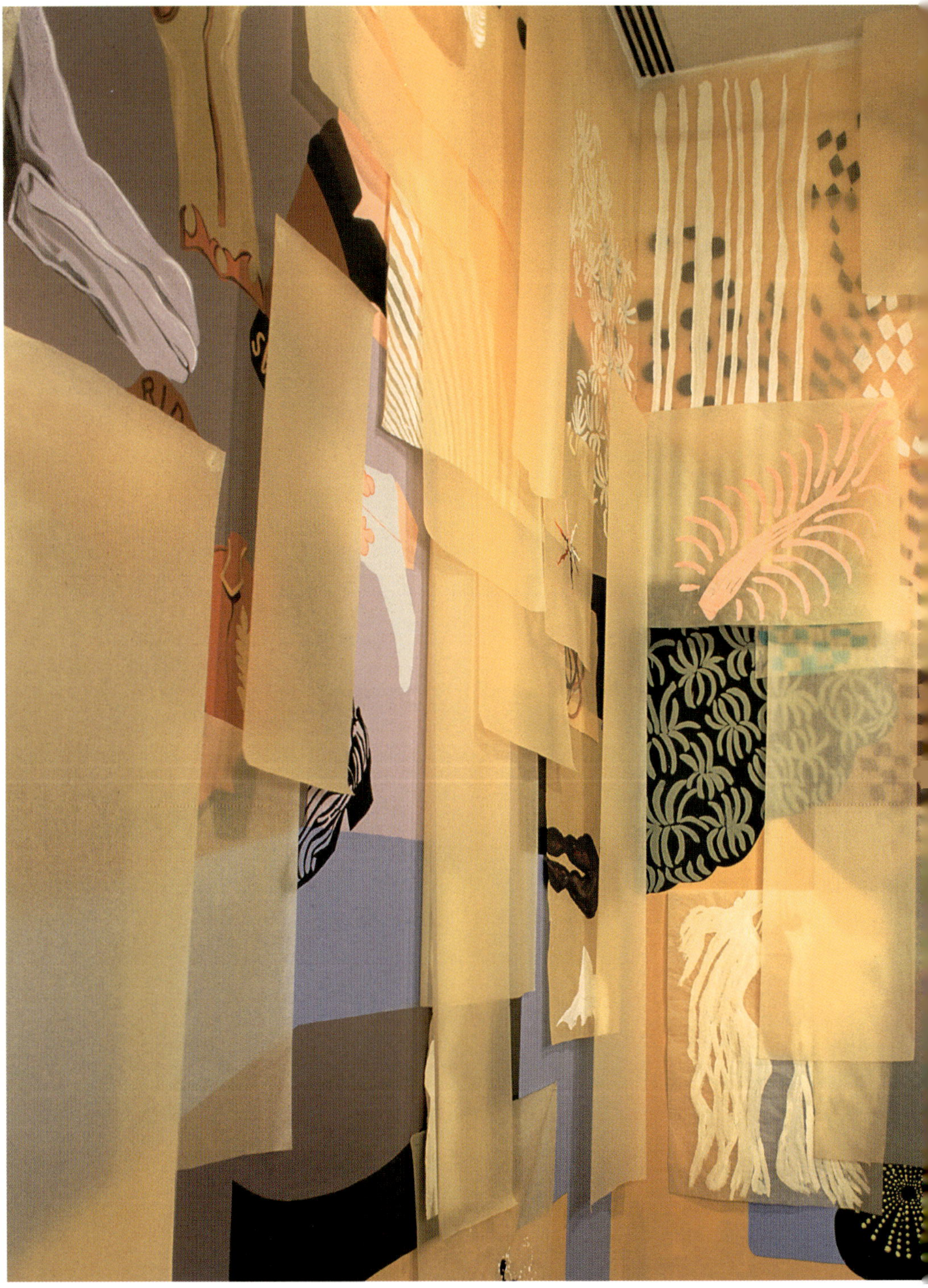

Chaman, 2000, acrylic, gouache, and ink on tissue paper, installation at the Philip Morris branch of the Whitney Museum, New York, courtesy of the artist and Deitch Projects, New York

Shahzia Sikander

The rhetoric of postcolonial studies has made exotic a rather unfashionable word. It does, however, remain a useful category of inquiry... as a way of understanding that which is immune to translation, that which is received intact and is allowed to exist without an equivalent.[1]

Shahzia Sikander operates as an artist in a space of hybridity. In her work the promiscuous association of different codes of representation—Hindu and Islamic, figurative and abstract, photographic and painterly—stands in odd contrast to the rigorous material discipline of miniature painting, the oldest figurative painting tradition of the Middle East and the Indian sub-continent, that grounds her artistic practice. Subjects such as the court, the hunting scene, and the garden, which traditionally had their own space and formal conventions, frame unlikely apparitions in her paintings: portraits of real people, or images such as that of an acrobat in a striped leotard which have personal or iconic meaning for her. Nor is this hybridity a simple matter of bringing Eastern traditions into the West. A figure that appears again and again in her work is a voluptuous, many-armed goddess from the Hindu pantheon, laden with weapons, whose form is veiled with the chador often worn by Muslim women. The veil that would usually be interpreted as a symbol of oppression in the West is here a mask, both mysterious and empowering. It is a recurring and ambiguous motif in her work, a symbol perhaps of the core of untranslatability in all poetic and personal languages.

One of Sikander's earliest images is that of a scroll in which she depicts a continuous and ever-changing architectural space. A white-clad figure moves through this space, which suggests now privacy and modernity, now a more communal and traditional space of shared activities, and emerges at the other end to paint a portrait of herself. The doubling of the artist's figure, both observer and observed, is a specifically self-conscious pose communicating an awareness of multiple realities. Later, this multiplicity is given a more sophisticated and less narrative form, when it is translated into the discontinuous operations of collage.

[1] Faisal Devji, "Translated Pleasures," in *Shahzia Sikander* (Chicago: The Renaissance Society, 1998), p. 11.

Layering and veiling are omnipresent in Sikander's recent work, wedding a modernist understanding of the visual power of the stylistic ruptures of collage with a much older preference for the seductive evasions of the indirect utterances. At the same time, a loose and gestural vocabulary emerges and is overlaid upon the more strictly stylized images of the miniature, as if two languages, one primal and direct, the other full of elaborate poetry, commingled in a new and unfamiliar tongue.

The miniature paintings in this exhibition and the mural work entitled *Chaman* share the theme of the garden, understood as a place where different realities are reconciled. In *Chaman* Sikander has created an enclosure, veiled by layers of tissue paper that hang, overlapping, from the walls. The room feels like a walled garden, secure from intrusion. Compositional hierarchies are abolished from these walls, resulting in a profusion of images that break down distinctions between the animate and the inanimate realms, producing a sensation of imaginative release inviting reflection. *Chaman*, which means "garden" in Urdu, was first created for the Philip Morris branch of the Whitney Museum in New York, where it was shown between April and July 2000. In the second version of the work, made for the National Gallery of Canada, Sikander has constructed an almost theatrical space, its entrance framed by floating sheets of tissue paper that hang at an angle to the walls. The imagery of the room builds up gradually. It is sparer and more abstract on the side walls and denser on the end wall, inviting and drawing the viewer into the space. Within, the atmosphere created by the pastel colours and the layers of tissue paper is warm and sensual. Echoing motifs in the miniature paintings, repeated geometric designs alternate with the curved outlines of a woman's figure, while painted floral and architectural forms play off one another on the walls. The contrast suggests the complex, hybrid character of the garden, a place not only of sensual repose but intended also for contemplation.

Sikander often refers to her experience of leaving Pakistan to study and take up residence in the United States as a pleasing dislocation. Trained as a miniaturist—an anachronistic and idiosyncratic choice within the context of her schooling—she learned not only a discipline and a technique but a conceptual means of encoding reality into images that were meant to be read like poetry. Instead of repeating the conventions, she has translated them into a fluid and hybrid prose that links cultural tradition with the space of lived experience.

D.N.

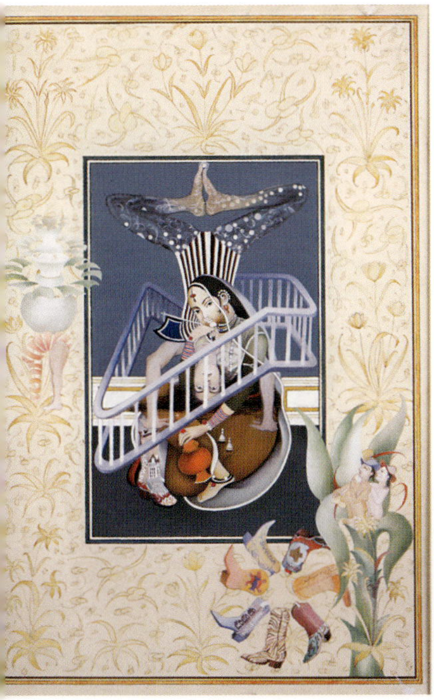

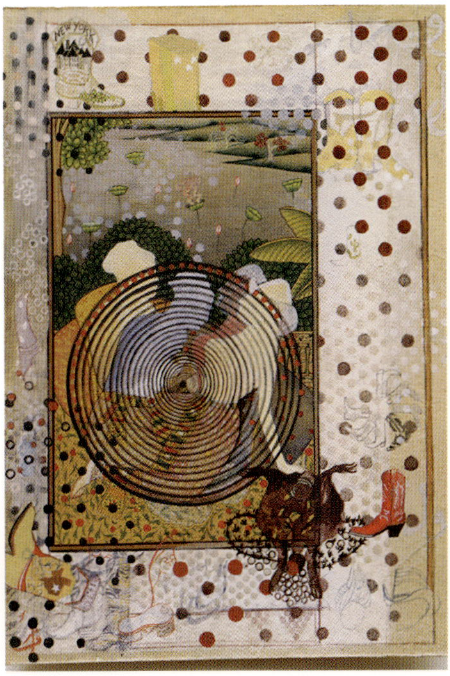

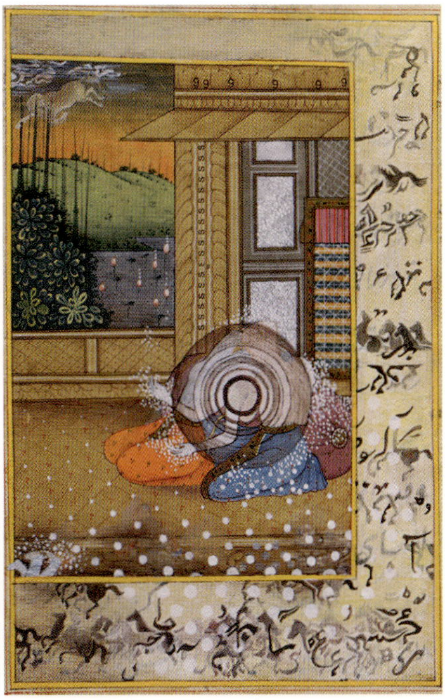

Elusive Realities, 2000, vegetable colour, dry pigment, watercolour, and tea on handmade wasli paper, 27.9 × 18.7 cm, The Speyer Family Collection, courtesy Deitch Projects, New York, cat. no. 11 *Riding the Ridden*, 2000, vegetable colour, dry pigment, watercolour, and tea on handmade wasli paper, 20.3 × 13.7 cm, Collection of Niva Grill Angel, New York, courtesy Deitch Projects, New York, cat. no. 12 *Riding the Written*, 2000, vegetable colour, dry pigment, watercolour, and tea on handmade wasli paper, 20.3 × 14 cm, private collection, London, cat. no. 13

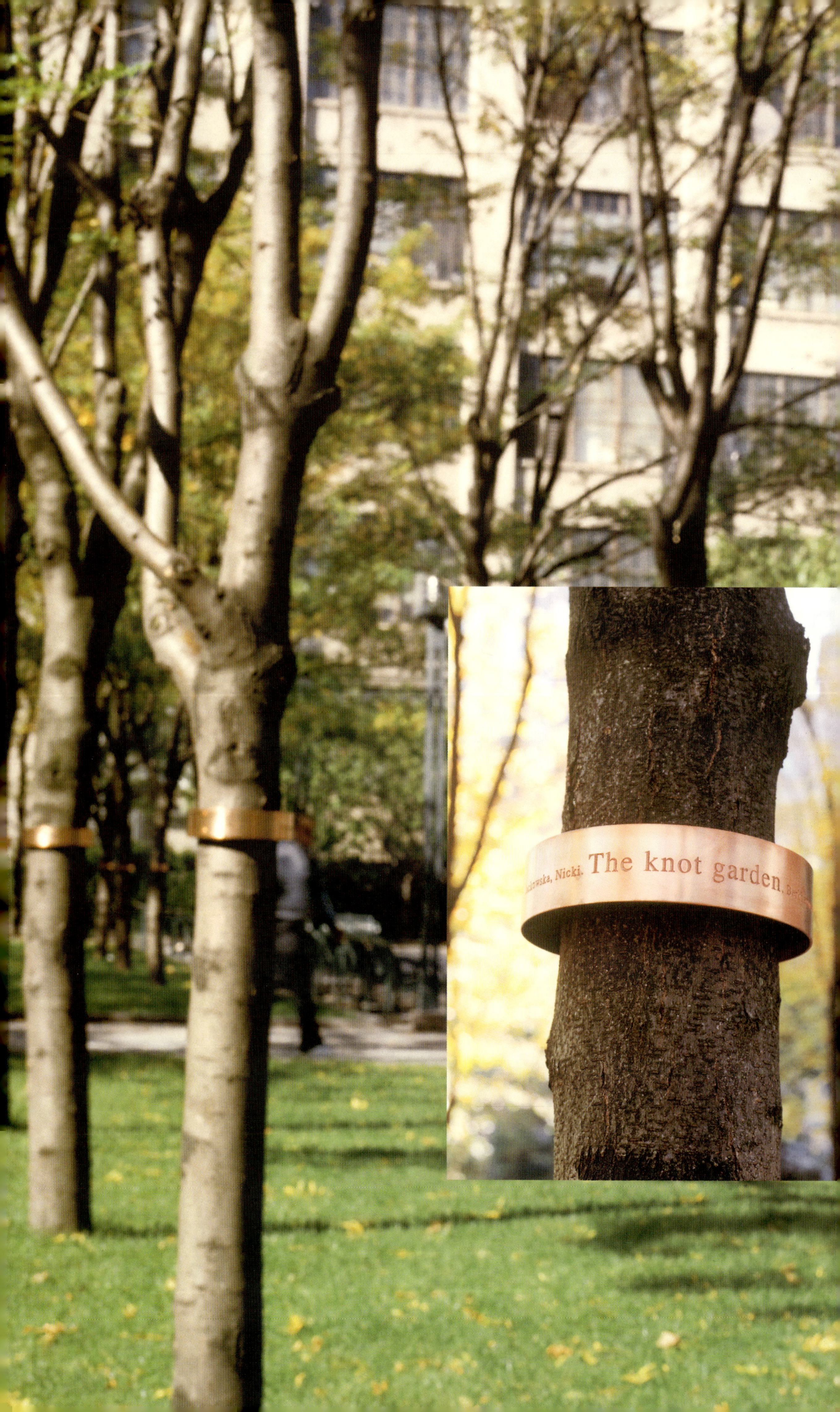
Nicki. The knot garden.

Valeska Soares

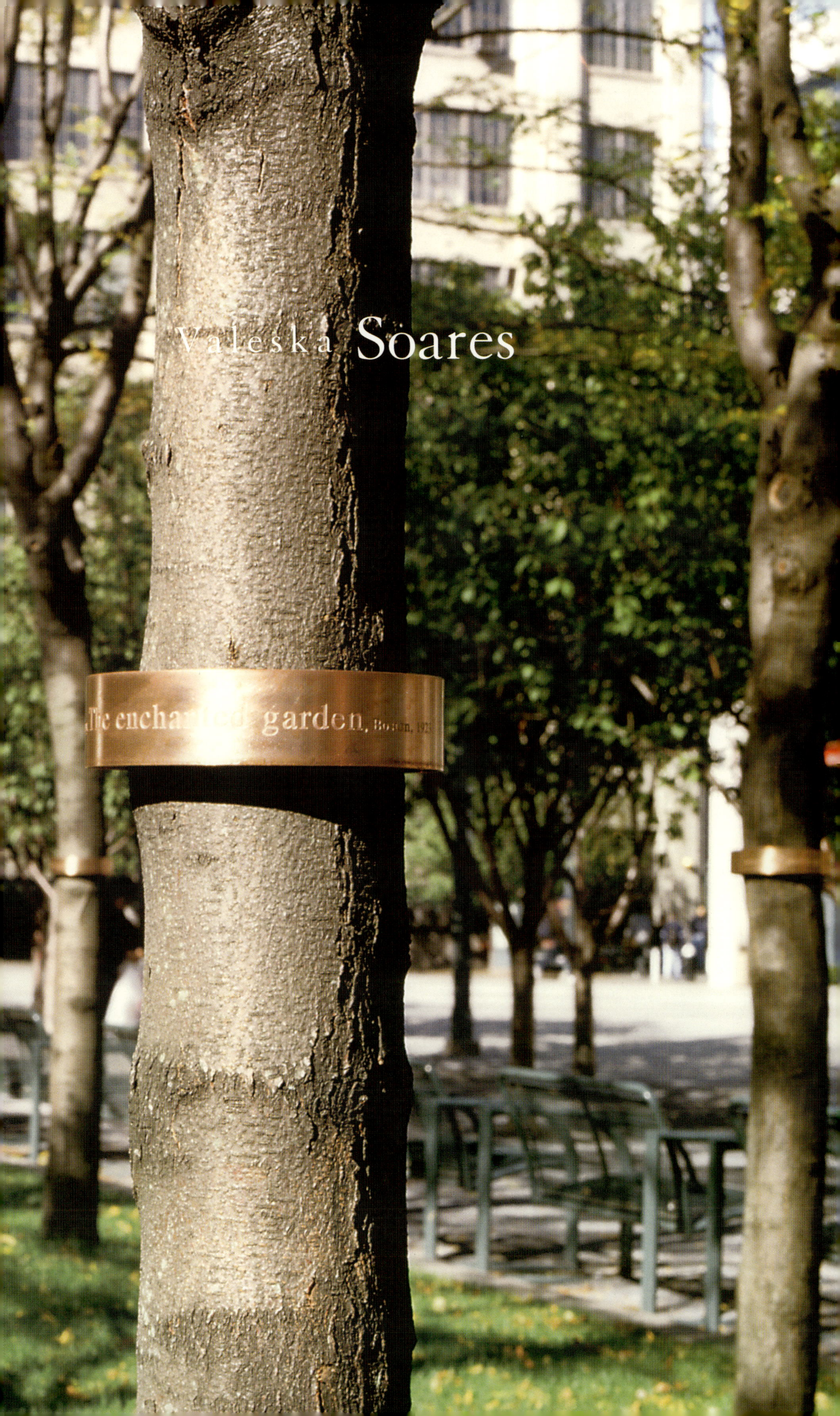

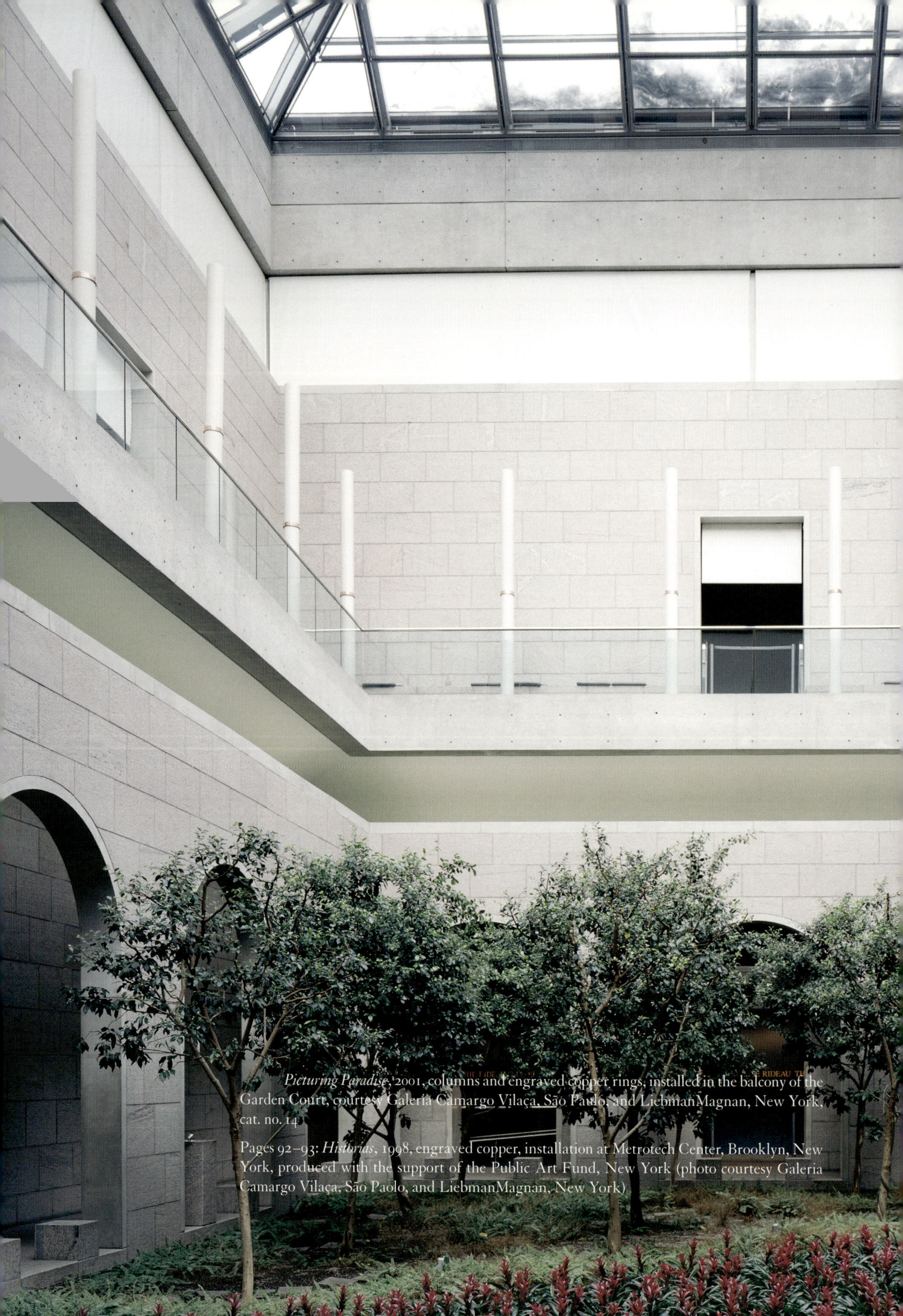

Picturing Paradise, 2001, columns and engraved copper rings, installed in the balcony of the Garden Court, courtesy Galeria Camargo Vilaça, São Paulo, and LiebmanMagnan, New York, cat. no. 14

Pages 92–93: *Historias*, 1998, engraved copper, installation at Metrotech Center, Brooklyn, New York, produced with the support of the Public Art Fund, New York (photo courtesy Galeria Camargo Vilaça, São Paolo, and LiebmanMagnan, New York)

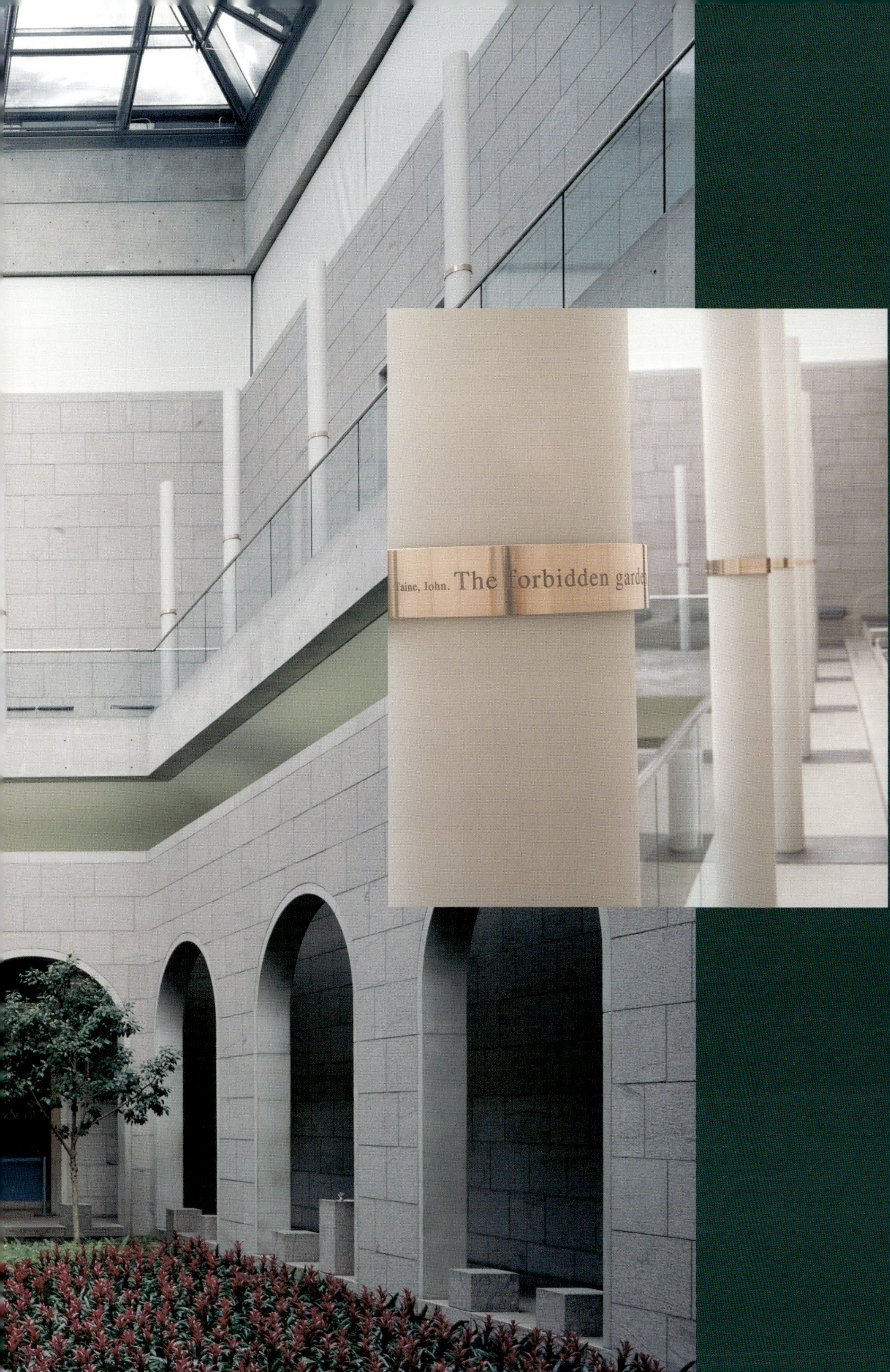
Taine, John. The forbidden

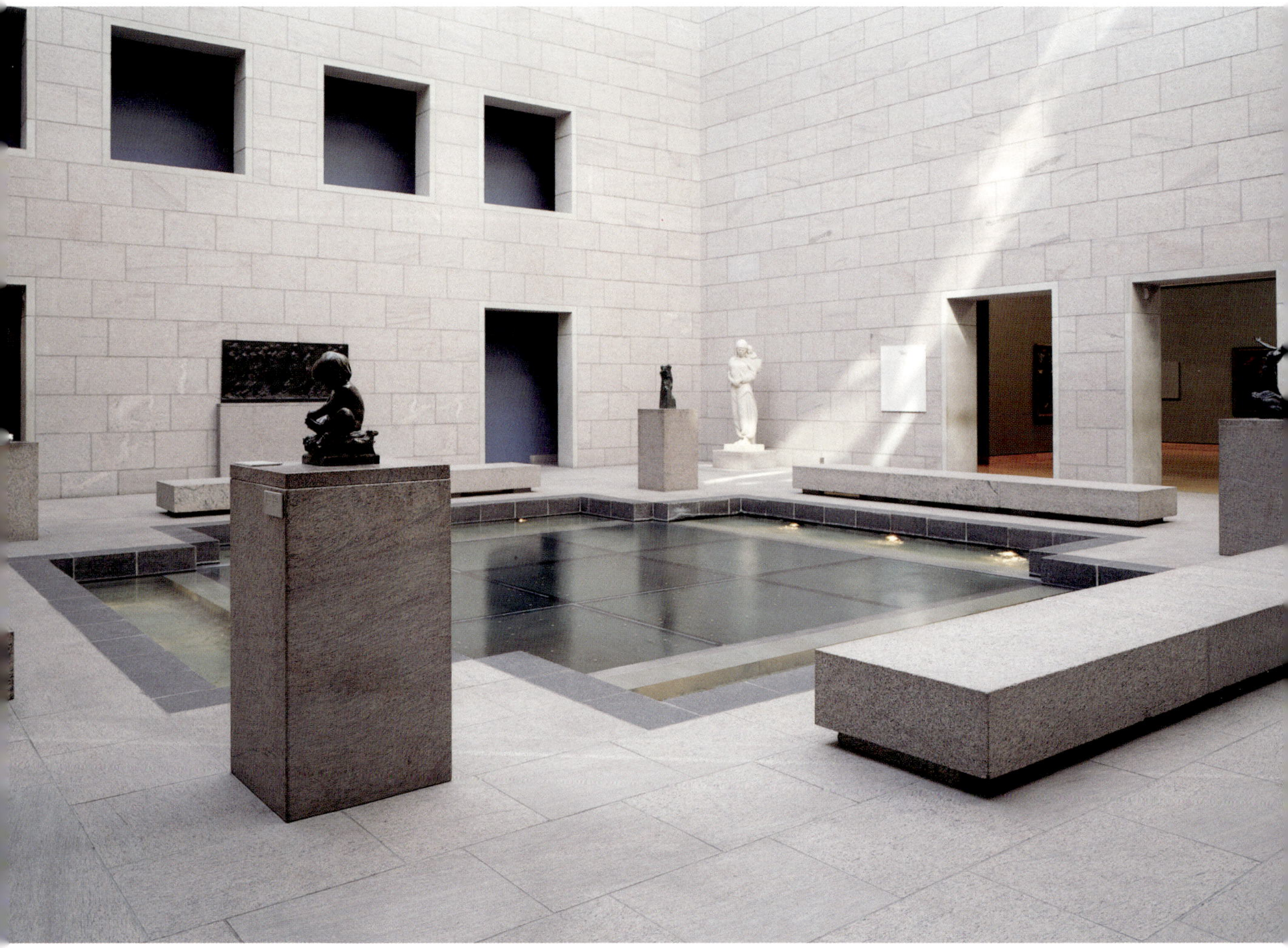

Picturing Paradise, 2001, perfume, installed in the Water Court, courtesy Galeria Camargo Vilaça, São Paulo, and LiebmanMagnan, New York, cat. no. 14

There is a very close correlation between the physical appearance of a constructed landscape and the philosophical thinking of a period. When you read what people wrote about gardens, there is always a correlation with philosophical quests. Garden paths related to the acquisition of wisdom, or to experiences that might only exist subjectively. There has always been this desire to transcribe that into some kind of physical space that related to nature — nature controlled, never nature in its natural state.[1]

Various objects evoke the architecture of the church in Valeska Soares's earlier work—empty niches and rows of benches that bear the imprint of knees. At the same time, the sound of heartbeats, the sweet and slightly sickly odour of wilting roses, and the soft, skin-like smoothness of beeswax lend this space of adoration a sensual atmosphere of human passions and losses. In the Christian faith, human history begins with the fall from grace. The eating of the apple marks not only the acquisition of knowledge but also the original sin and the expulsion from the Garden of Eden into a wild and hostile nature. From the Middle Ages onward, the cloistered garden was conceived as a refuge in the midst of meaningless natural disorder, a meditative space symbolizing the fruitfulness and perfection of paradise. Later, the garden was associated with both intellectual activities and courtly love, drawing on the traditions of the Classical world and Persia. It became a metaphor for earthly life, its paths leading to wisdom or deception.

In Soares's recent work there has been a shift from a religion-tinged iconography of belief and love to the secular motif of the garden. There are at least a couple of reasons for this new subject. Given Soares's training as an architect and her interest in spaces that are in-between—between emotion and reason, for example, or between logic and intoxication—the garden, rationally designed yet sensually experienced, is a ground rich with potential subjective, historical, and even political significance. At the same time, for personal reasons she was obliged to leave behind the small garden she had been cultivating behind her brownstone house in Brooklyn. She mapped the space of this real garden and cast the flower pots into aluminum, beeswax, and porcelain replicas, creating a virtual garden as a *memento* of the loss, in a work that she called *Untitled* (from *Vanishing Point*).

[1] Valeska Soares, in conversation with Vik Muniz, 2000.

Soares's project for the National Gallery is in two parts and uses spaces that were conceived by the building's architect as places of repose from the art-historical trajectories of the galleries. The first is the Water Court, whose central feature is a geometrical pool of water with a Greek cross shape which suggests the four points of the compass. Although it is an area without plants which few visitors would identify as a garden, it contains one of the central features of the classical and medieval garden: moving water, which not only is a source of fertility, but also symbolizes the four rivers of Creation that water the world. Soares adds nothing visible to the space. Her intervention, a perfume solution that wafts through the court, hints at the sensual intoxication associated with the garden in contrast with the rational geometry of the pool, in a gesture that may be understood as an allusion to the formal gardens of the French and Italian Renaissance.

The second part is made up of columns arranged around the perimeter of the balcony of the adjacent Garden Court, a space with a permanent planting of trees and flowers. Each of the columns is girdled with a copper band inscribed with the author, date of publication and title of a book containing the word "garden." First conceived for the Brooklyn Botanical Garden (though, for technical reasons, not realized there), the copper bands originally encircled the trees like specimen labels. They recall the fact that in the first, ambitious botanical gardens embarked on after the discovery of the New World, nature was intended to be read like a book, in which each plant had its meaning in a rational and orderly model of Creation. However, Soares is not interested in simply replicating this religious/scientific model. In her bibliography, the word garden is taken metaphorically—some of the books are romances, others are works of politics or anthropology —so that together the titles offer a historical landscape of Western thought[2] in which the garden, in its manifold identity, lies at the conceptual centre.

Relocating her project to the art gallery, Soares sets up a playfully subversive parallel between her subjective, circular narrative and the linear, encyclopedic reading of art history proposed by the museum. Reading its architecture as a garden, she proposes a poetic transformation of its landscape into an arcadian space where sensual and intellectual reflection are combined.

D.N.

[2] This part of the project is an adaptation of a work called *Historias*. The titles were culled from a bibliography of works in English, French, Italian, Portuguese, and Spanish prepared by the critic and curator Adriano Pedrosa. For the National Gallery, Soares has chosen titles only in English, French, and Portuguese (her mother tongue).

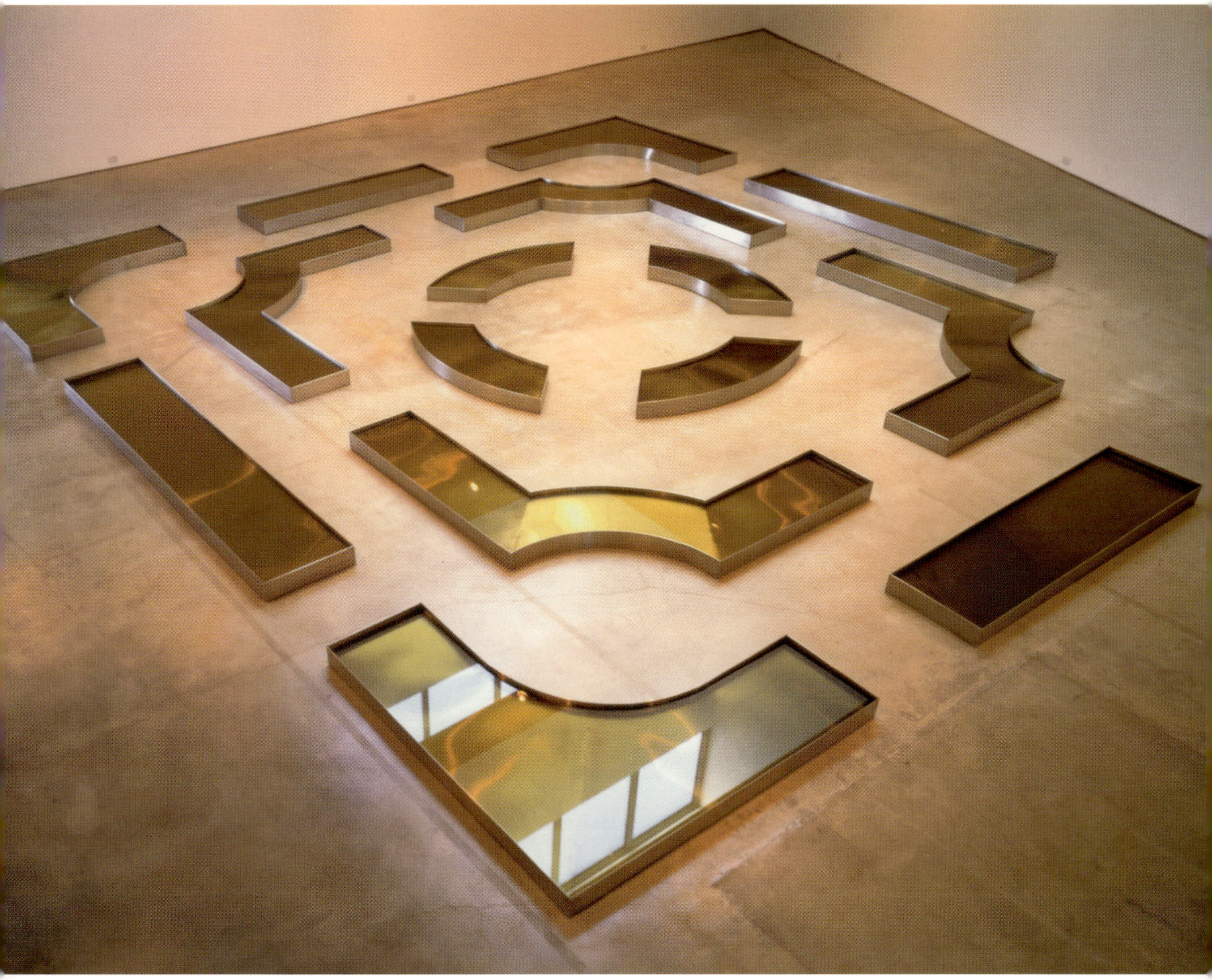

Vanishing Point, 1998, stainless steel tanks and perfume (photo courtesy Galeria Camargo Vilaça, São Paolo, and LiebmanMagnan, New York)

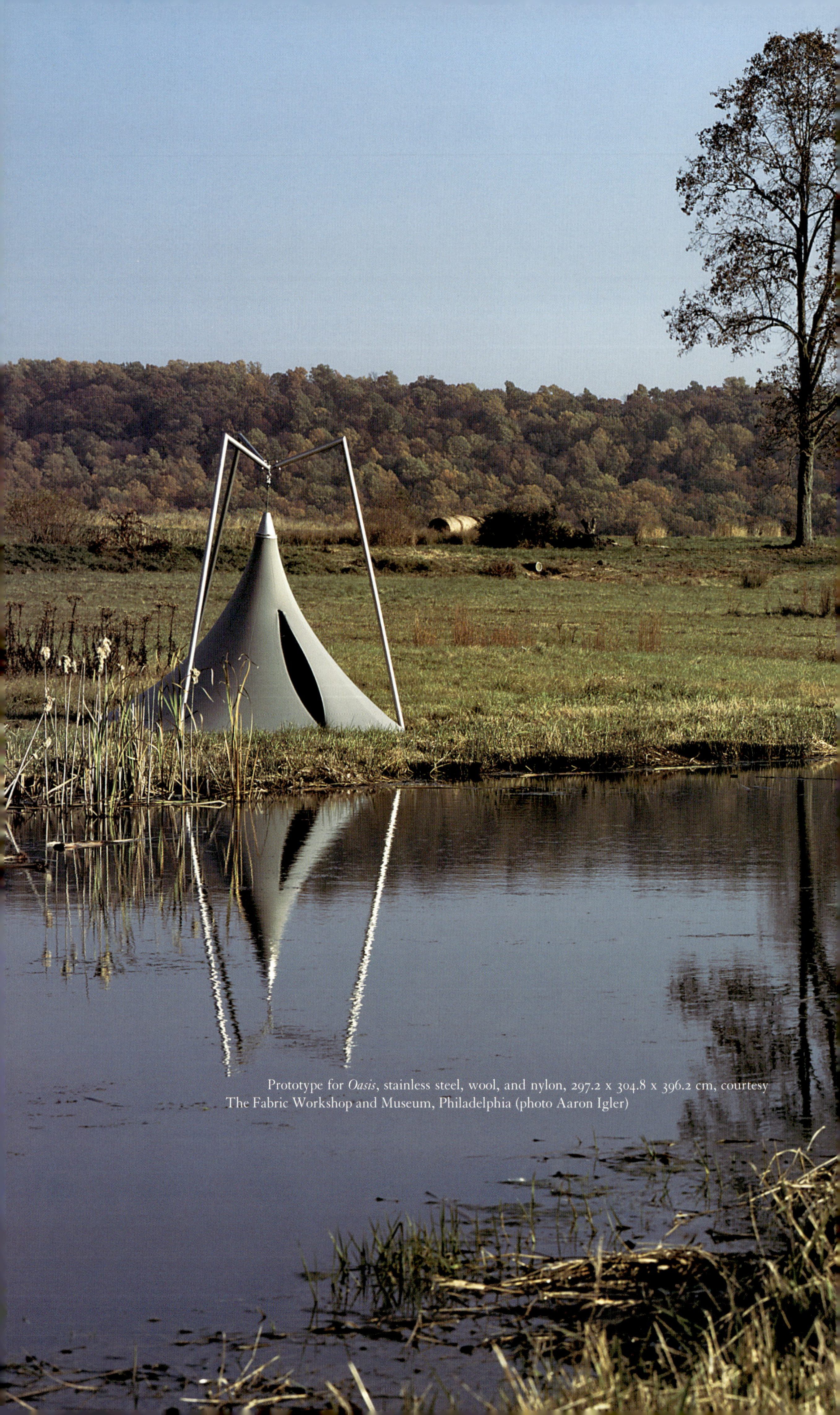

Prototype for *Oasis*, stainless steel, wool, and nylon, 297.2 x 304.8 x 396.2 cm, courtesy The Fabric Workshop and Museum, Philadelphia (photo Aaron Igler)

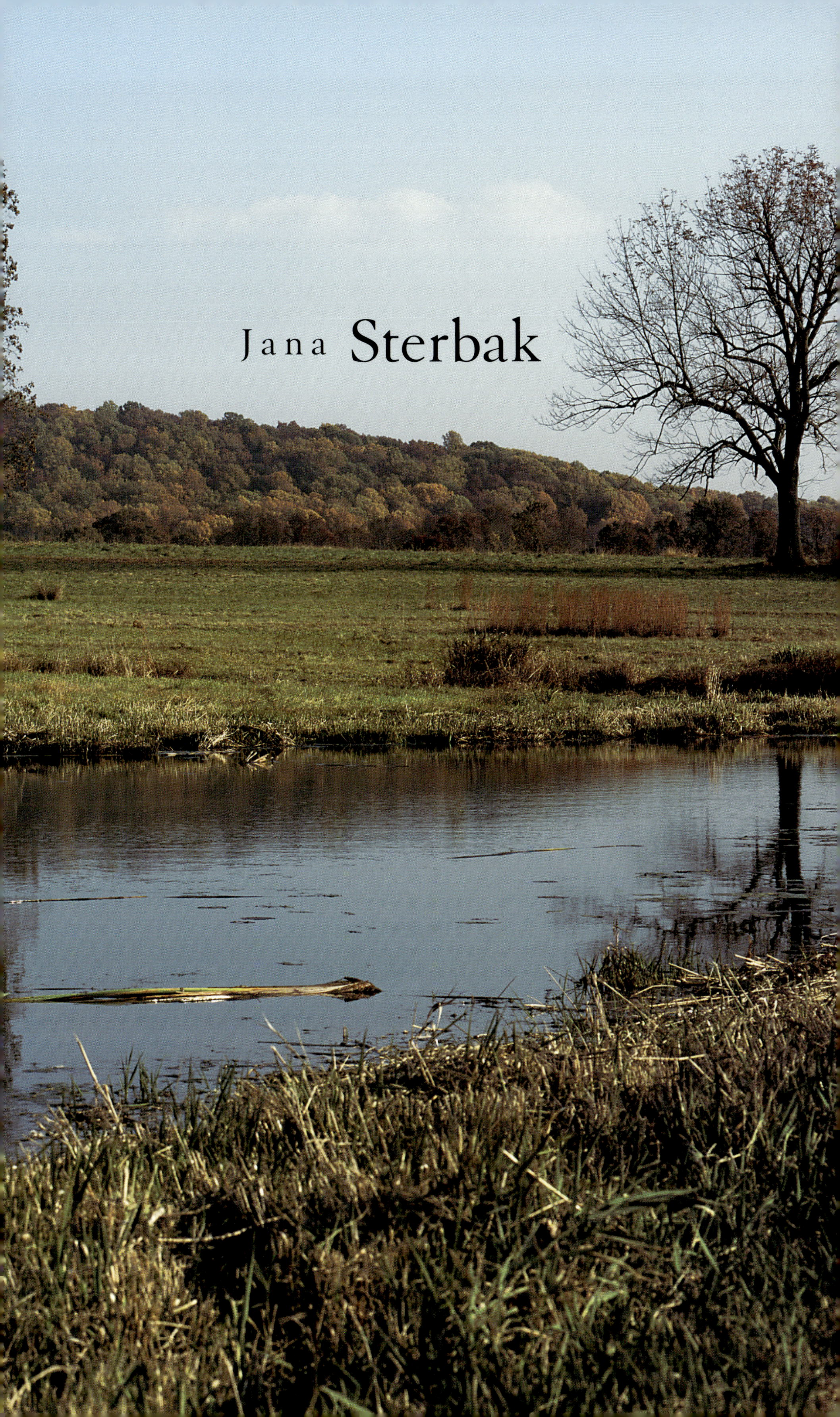
Jana Sterbak

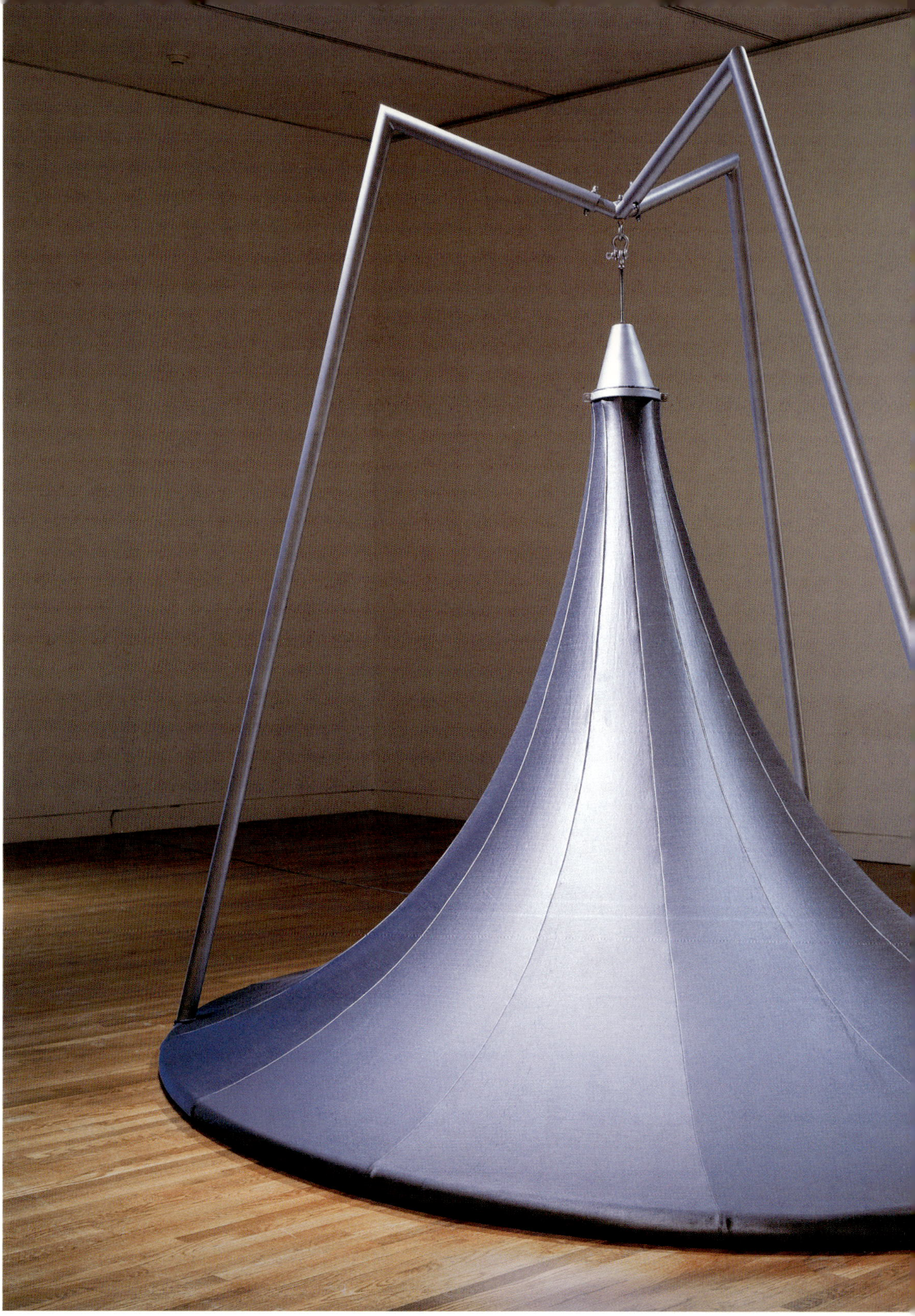

Oasis, 2000, stainless steel, 297.2 × 396.2 × 304.8 cm, anonymous loan, courtesy of the artist and The Fabric Workshop and Museum, Philadelphia, cat. no. 15

Measurements of a portion of the radio frequency spectrum inside the tent (red) and outside the tent (black), courtesy KTL Ottawa Inc.

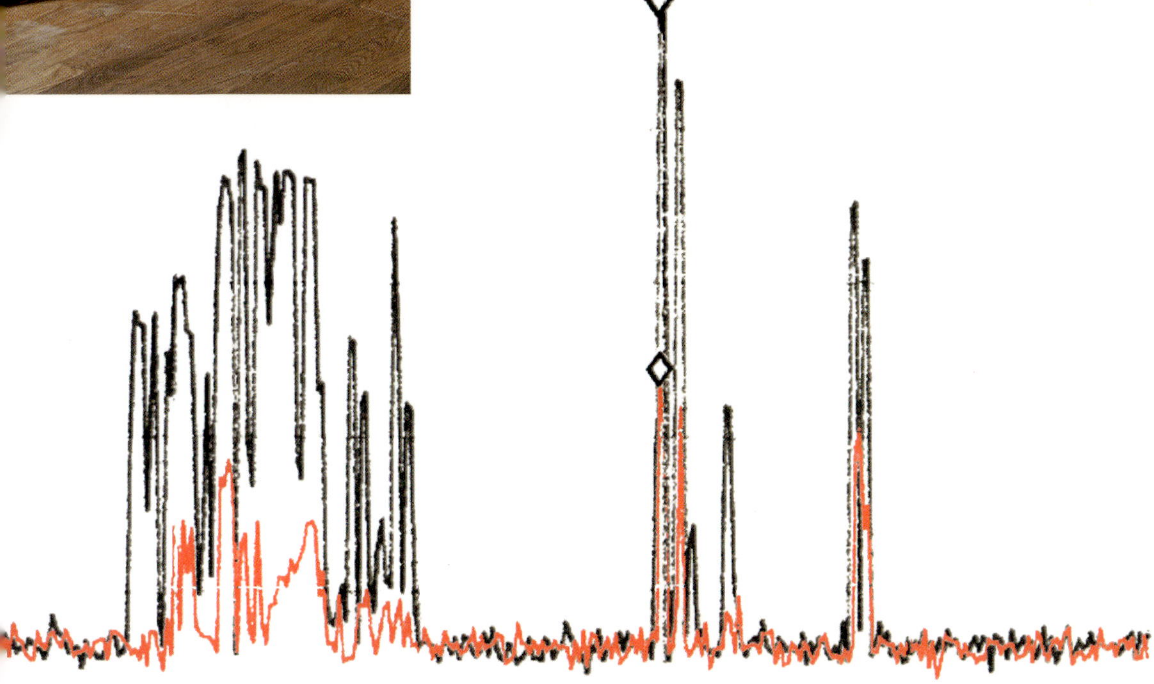

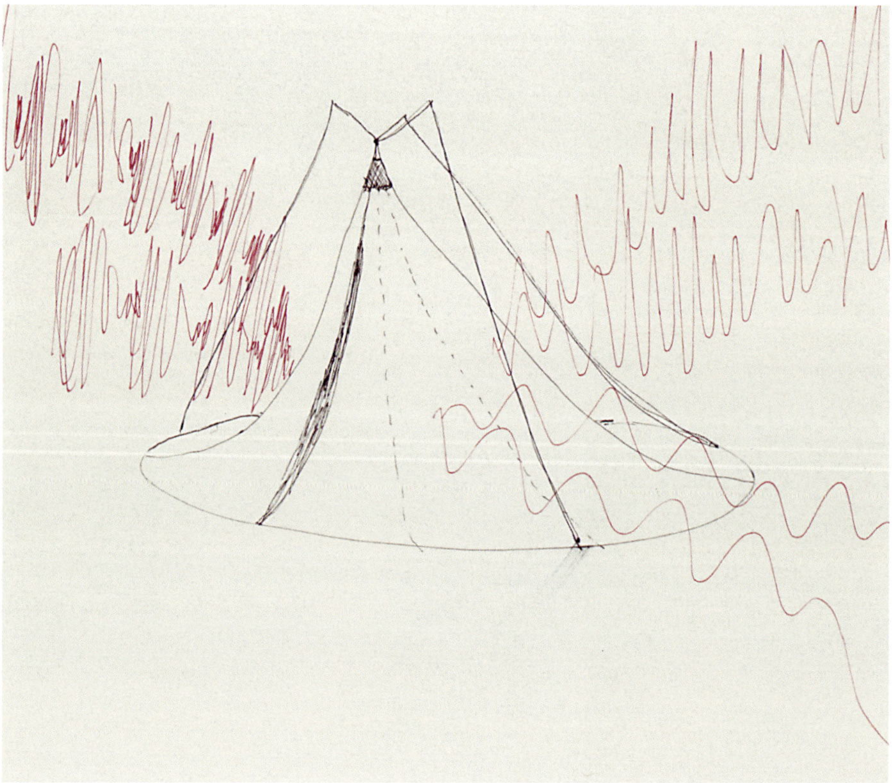

Sketch for *Oasis*, 1998, pen and ink on paper, 21.5 x 28 cm

Jana Sterbak

The space that surrounds a body is already in some condition to affect bodies near it.[1]

Hell is other people.[2]

The truth of the first statement, by William Berkson, may be verified by experiments demonstrating that all matter is united by fields of force, among them the so-called electromagnetic field that governs relations of attraction and repulsion in the physical world. The truth of the second statement, by Jean-Paul Sartre, is poetic and psychological. Although they are contradictory—one is an affirmation of the permeability of all physical boundaries, the other of their spiritual necessity—both are distinctively modern in their implicit rejection of metaphysics as an explanation of being. Their terms provide a conceptual enclosure for Jana Sterbak's art, which is concerned with relations of attraction and repulsion on both the physical and the existential planes. These differences cannot be resolved logically; they can only be short-circuited, as it were, by art. This is why poetic and conceptual tools of double meaning—irony, humour, metaphor—are so important to Sterbak. Although science is the *other* to which she continually returns, her art contains almost as many allusions to magic. Simone de Beauvoir's observation, based on ethnographic studies, holds true for her: "Knowledge and magic are inseparable: a science of the nature of things allows objects to be made use of both according to the rational laws of cause and effect and according to their magical affinities."[3]

Because the individual is the focus of her art, Sterbak's work foregrounds the body and its extensions, especially clothing. However, it would be a mistake to think that for her the body is the locus of identity. Rather, it marks the physical limits of the self, which seeks to extend its influence expressively and technically through a variety of garments. *Oasis* is the most recent of these second skins that both extend and protect the individual.[4] The name *Oasis* suggests that a place of

[1] William Berkson, *Fields of Force: The Development of a World View from Faraday to Einstein* (New York: John Wiley & Sons, 1974), p. 114. [2] Jean-Paul Sartre, *Huis clos*, scene 5, Garcin. [3] Simone de Beauvoir, *The Coming of Age*, translated by Patrick O'Brian (New York: G.P. Putman's Sons, 1972), p. 62. [4] *Oasis* was realized in collaboration with The Fabric Workshop and Museum, Philadelphia, with additional production assistance from the National Gallery of Canada and the Canada Council for the Arts. This is its first exhibition.

solace exists, whether it be a pool of water in the desert or a hut in the woods. The shape of the structure, which can be entered through a mouth-like opening, is part gown, part tepee. The latter was in fact a source for Sterbak, who as a child growing up in Czechoslovakia had heard of Karl May and his followers' tribal impersonations, and who was fascinated with "red" Indians. However, any romantic allusions to a return to nature by roughing it in the woods turn out to be ironically intended in *Oasis*.

As camping equipment, it would be quite a high-tech item. Fabricated of cloth woven out of stainless steel filaments (newly developed in Belgium for industrial applications) and supported by a polished metal exo-skeleton, *Oasis* is based on a nineteenth-century Faraday cage capable of blocking out electromagnetic waves of lower frequencies, including cell phone, television, and radio waves. Given the extent to which the multiplication of such communication devices in the last decade has blurred the boundaries of public and private space, Sterbak's shelter might have a certain commercial potential. As metaphor, its womb-like fastness would be disquieting—implying a spiritual homelessness, or the exacerbated nomadism of the modern world—were its alliance of state-of-the-art materials and archaic appearance not so humorously incongruous.

Sterbak's vision of nature is anti-arcadian. It is impossible to reduce it to a green mirror reflecting human nature; rather it is the force that constrains and ultimately absorbs consciousness, its influence extending through the visible and invisible world. Only technique (formerly magic) and art can thwart it by creating new boundaries for human power. Sterbak concentrates on these liminal defensive structures—sheathes and carapaces for the fragile psyche, the soft, vulnerable body—of the individual subject. Against the stealthy invasion of the Other intimated in early works such as *I can hear you think* (of particular interest in relation to *Oasis* because of its analogy between telepathic communication and electromagnetic force fields) or the parasitical relationship of dependency described in *I Want You to Feel the Way I Do (The Dress)*, she erects thicker, tougher skins—dresses, cages, shelters to protect the individual. Of course this freedom is never realized and each new skin produces new discomforts. Ultimately the only oasis is the creative will to explore and record the absurdities of the predicament.

D.N.

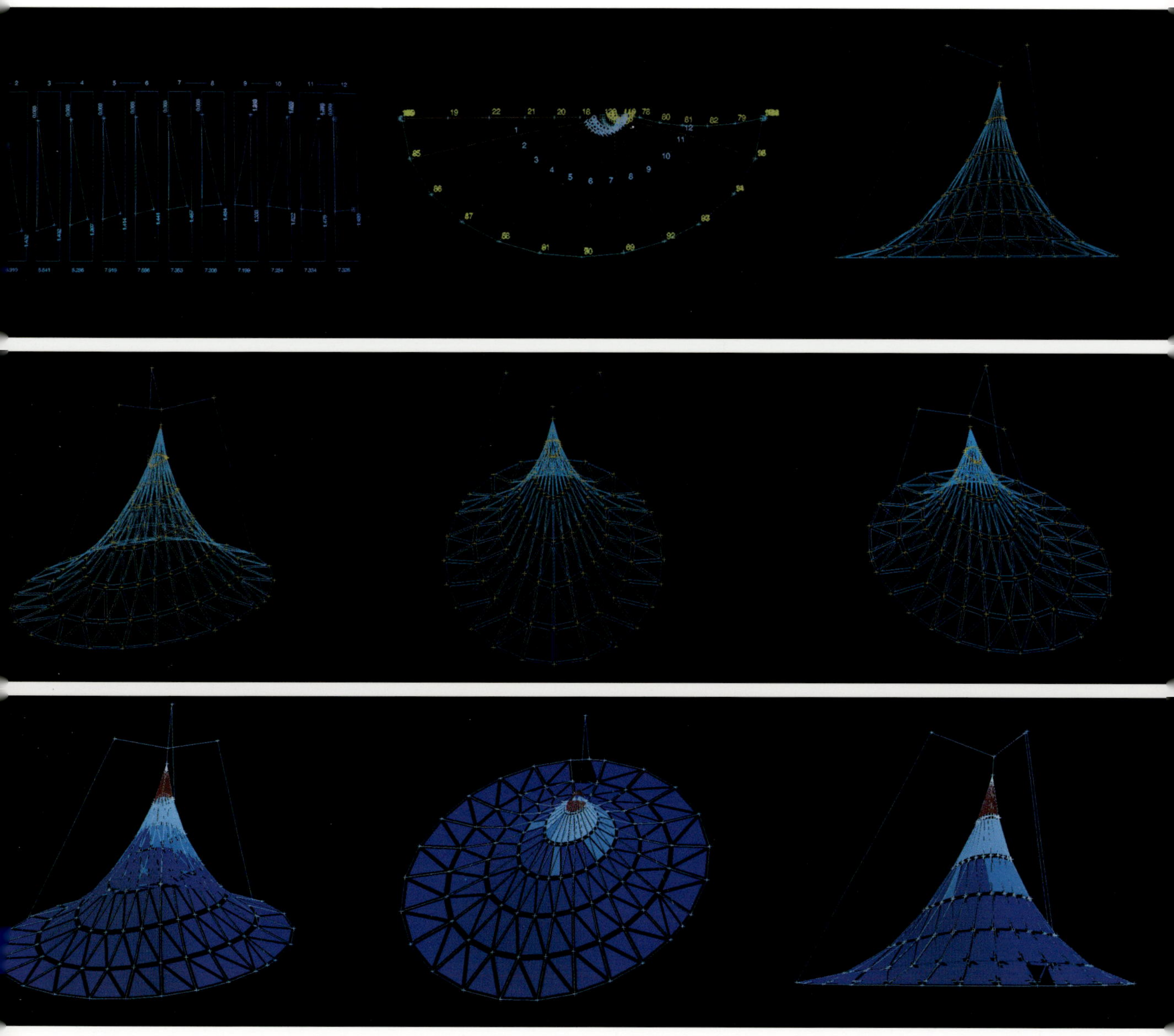

Computer generated form-finding models for *Oasis*, lightweight structural design and engineering consultant FTL Happold, New York (photo Aaron Igler)

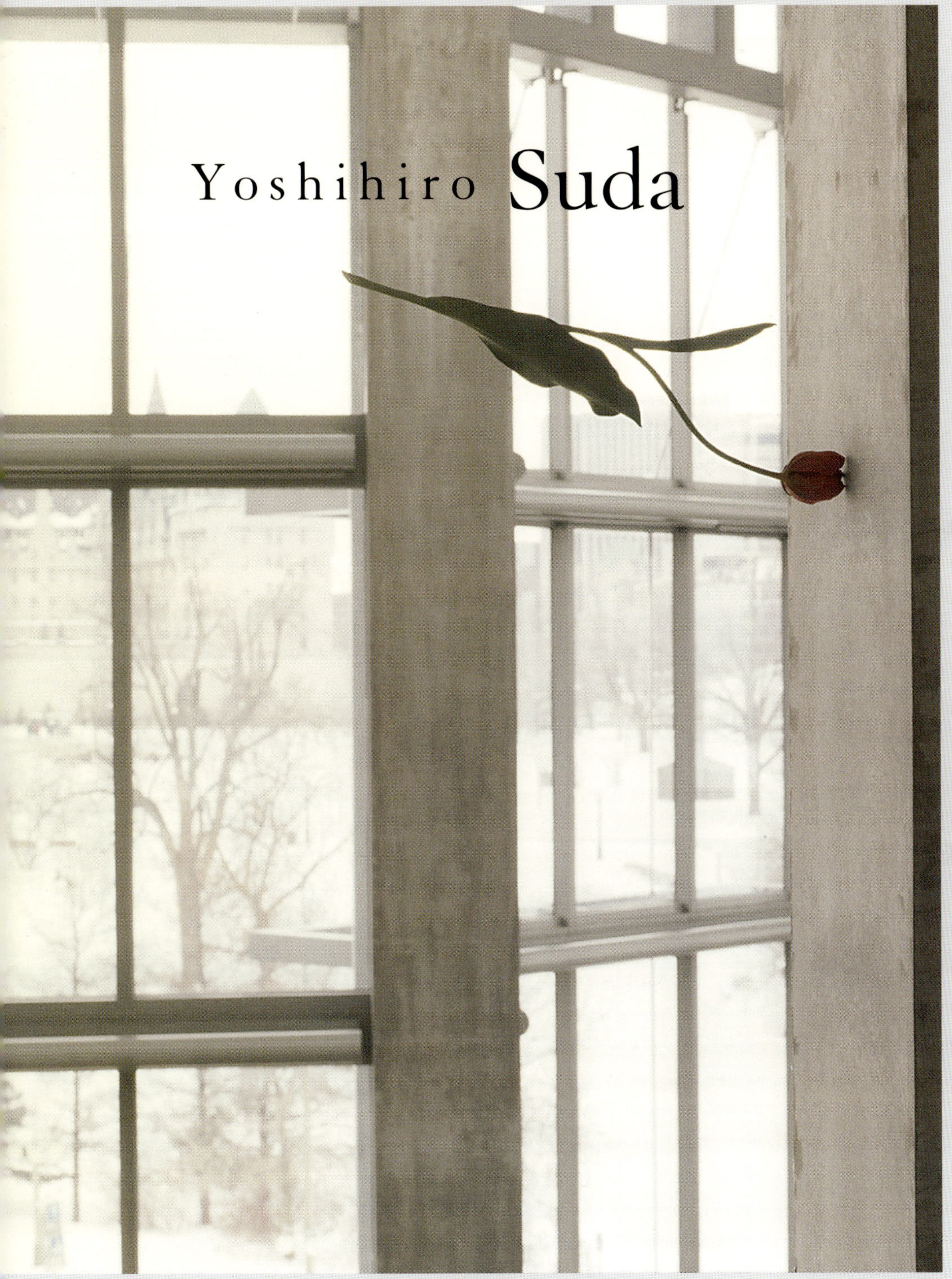
Yoshihiro Suda

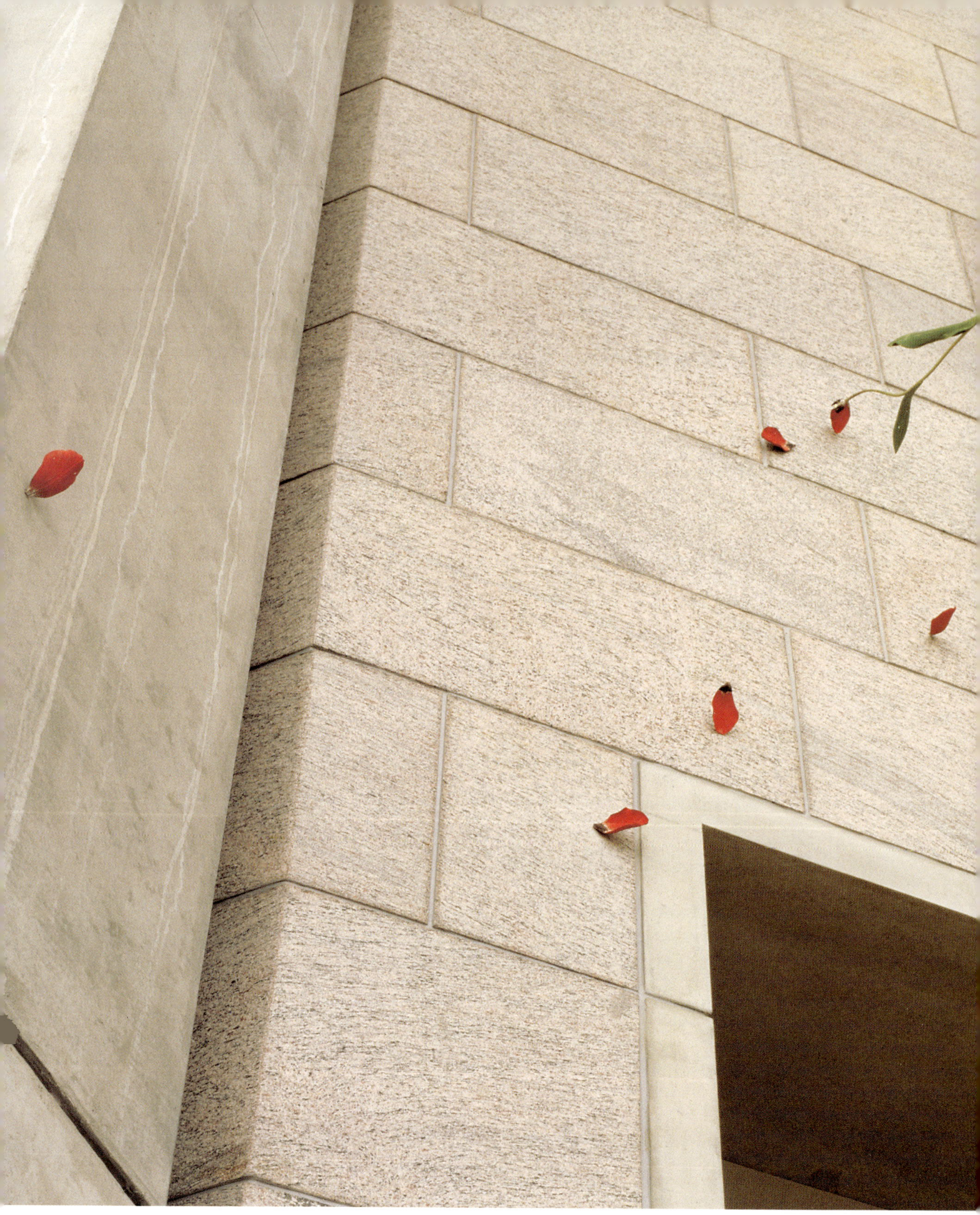

Pages 108–110: *Tulips*, 2001, painted wood, courtesy Gallery Koyanagi, Tokyo, and Galerie René Blouin, Montreal, cat. nos. 16 and 17

When we come upon beautiful things... they act like small tears in the surface of the world that pull us through to some vaster space.[1]

Seldom does one come upon Yoshihiro Suda's minutely detailed carvings of flowers, weeds, twigs, and leaves having anticipated them from a distance. Rather, they surprise us when we were least expecting them. Suda is not only interested in the perfection of detail that confers the startling realism which is the primary material quality of his creation, but in the moment of encounter between observer and object. He stages this encounter to produce different effects, each considered in relation to the intrinsic character of the thing depicted. Thus tiny carvings of weeds may be found pushing up through the floorboards of an apparently empty space just when one was about to conclude that nothing was there. Or a bare twig from a magnolia branch and a few brown leaves swept into a corner may be seen by chance by passers-by glancing into the window of an art gallery. These are things that naturally exist on the periphery of our vision, relegated to the corners of the world by their unimportance. On the other hand, a full-blown lily or magnolia blossom—flowers that normally exist in profusion—is initially concealed, so that its revelation to the eye is all the more absorbing: the single flower seems to fill our field of vision, and its isolation makes it more real, more completely present to us. On another occasion, in a gesture that is almost theatrical, a rose—that most romantic and short-lived of flowers—is arrested as it falls to the ground, its petals already dropping, as if time had stopped just at the moment decay begins.

Suda rarely disguises the everyday qualities of the spaces his objects occupy without filling. Looking at his carved plants, one is also aware of the man-made environment that they have temporarily naturalized, whether this be a room with light streaking through the dirty windows and onto the worn floorboards of a former factory or the cramped but luxurious surroundings of an upscale Tokyo gallery. It is as if the awareness activated by the unexpected discovery of the object he has placed in our path made us more attentive to our own location, yet

[1] Elaine Scarry, *On Beauty and Being Just* (Princeton, NJ: Princeton University Press, 1999), pp. 111–112. Scarry is referring to Simone Weil's essay "Love of the Order of the World," in *Waiting for God*.

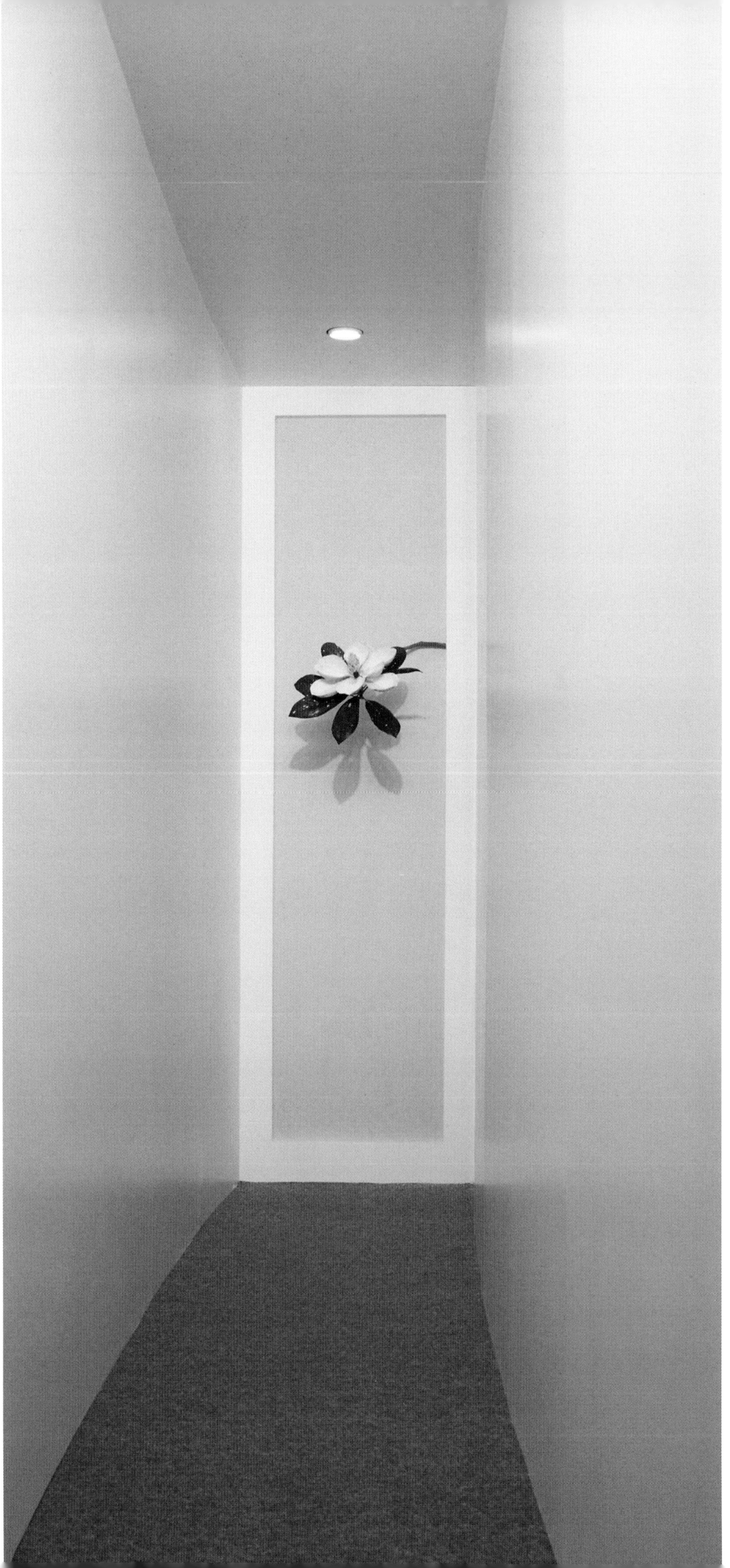

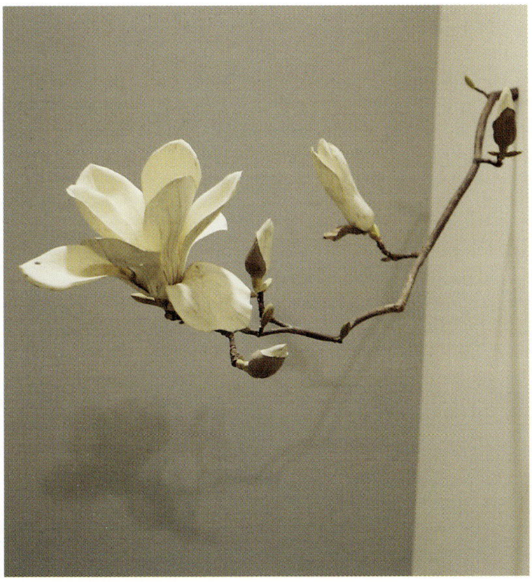

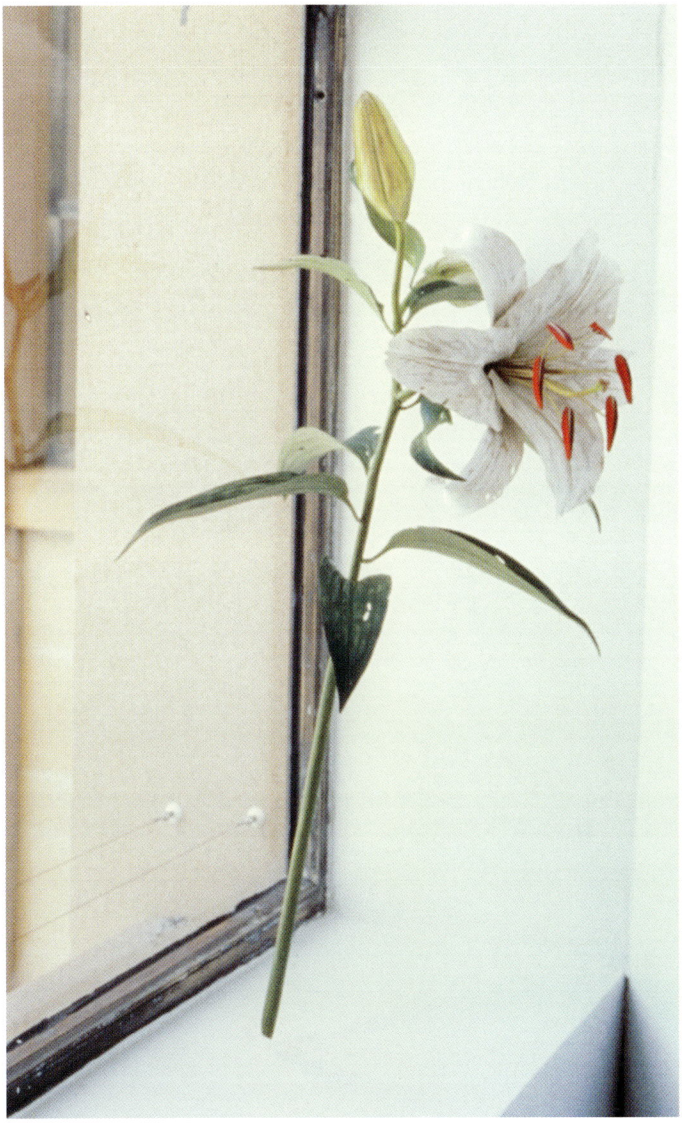

Left: *Magnolia, Flower*, 2000, painted wood, installation at D'Amelio Terras, New York (photo courtesy Gallery Koyanagi, Tokyo) Right: *One Hundred Encounters*, 1998, painted wood, installation at the Biennale of Sydney (photo courtesy Gallery Koyanagi, Tokyo)

Page 112: *Tree of Calm Mountain, Flower*, 1999, painted wood, Chiba City Museum, Japan, installation at Hara Museum of Contemporary Art, Tokyo (photo courtesy Gallery Koyanagi, Tokyo) at the same time displaced us. We stand aside to make room for something new. This experience may be akin to what the Japanese call "Ma." Suda was in the habit of titling each of his exhibits with this word, to draw attention to what existed there in addition to the sculpture. According to Kazuko Aono:

"Ma" is a concept unique to Japanese culture stemming from an age when people did not differentiate between time and space and indicates the mutual relationship between the two. It can be said that [Suda] wants to create a world of expression where the moment of resonance between the "Ma" and the image of the work are trapped forever in the memory of the viewer.[2]

Even though his objects fill the mind, they invite us to look for something beyond them, either something larger or something of the same scale with which they should properly be brought into relation.

Suda's sculpted replicas concentrate on the details of nature's manifold, for its beauty is to be discovered in its particular manifestations. His carvings of plants are faithful to their subjects, yet change them in significant ways. What was previously insignificant is revealed to be exquisitely alive, and what was ephemeral is made permanent, though as fragile as ever, so that its loveliness can remain before the eyes of the beholder as long as desired. The natural world is thus brought into provisional harmony with human nature, in an impulse that may be described as arcadian. Yet this harmony is elusive. The perfection of Suda's flowers makes one aware of the imperfection of the human world, while his references to the life cycle of plants evokes a comparison with human mortality. The sense of perceptual aliveness that the sculptures impart is thus measured against the anticipated extinction of consciousness, making their beauty both sweeter and sadder.

D.N.

[2] Kazuko Aono, *Tree of Calm Mountain*, Hara Documents 6 (Tokyo: Hara Museum of Contemporary Art).

Yoshihiro Suda

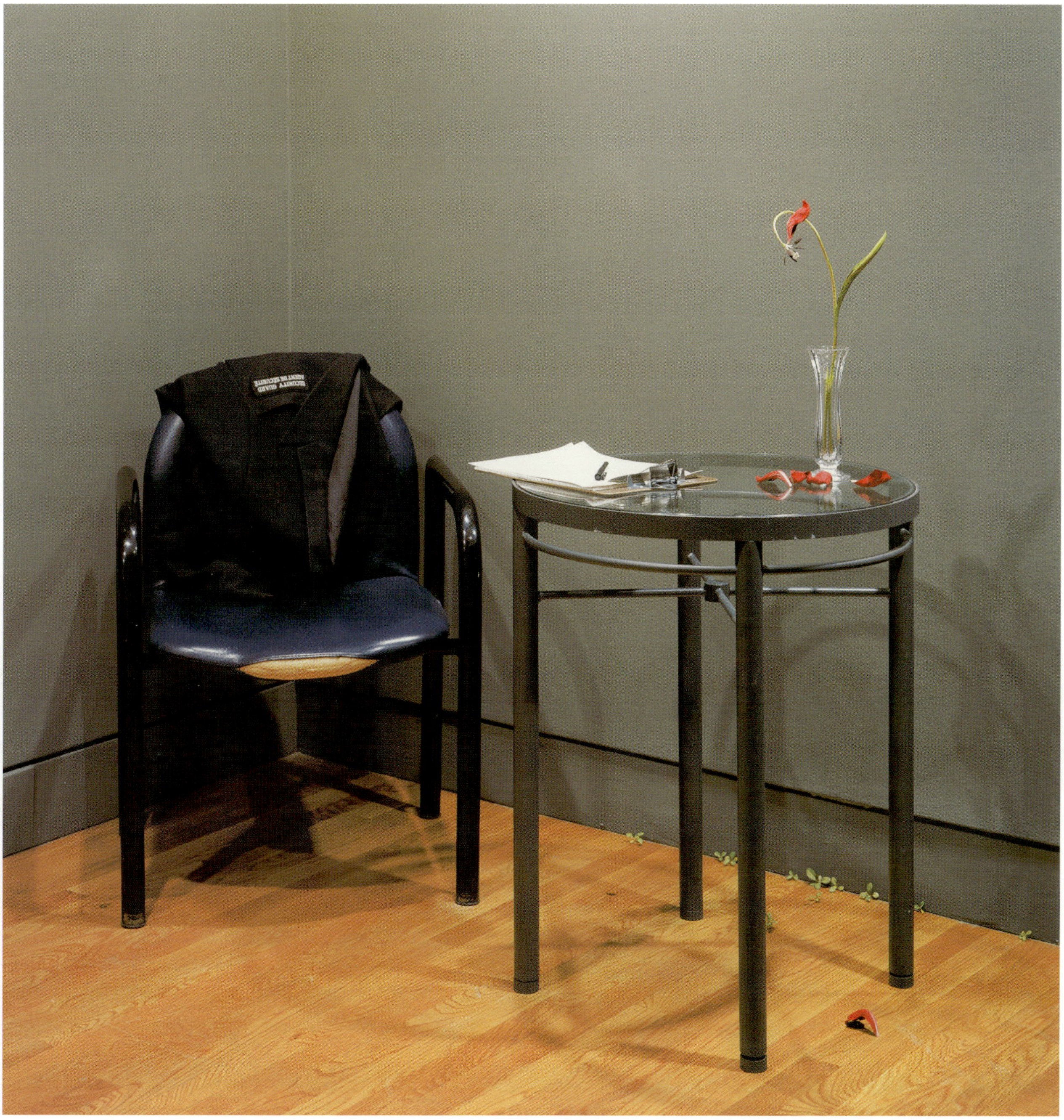

Tulip and Weeds, 2001, painted wood, courtesy Gallery Koyanagi, Tokyo, and Galerie René Blouin, Montreal, cat. no. 18

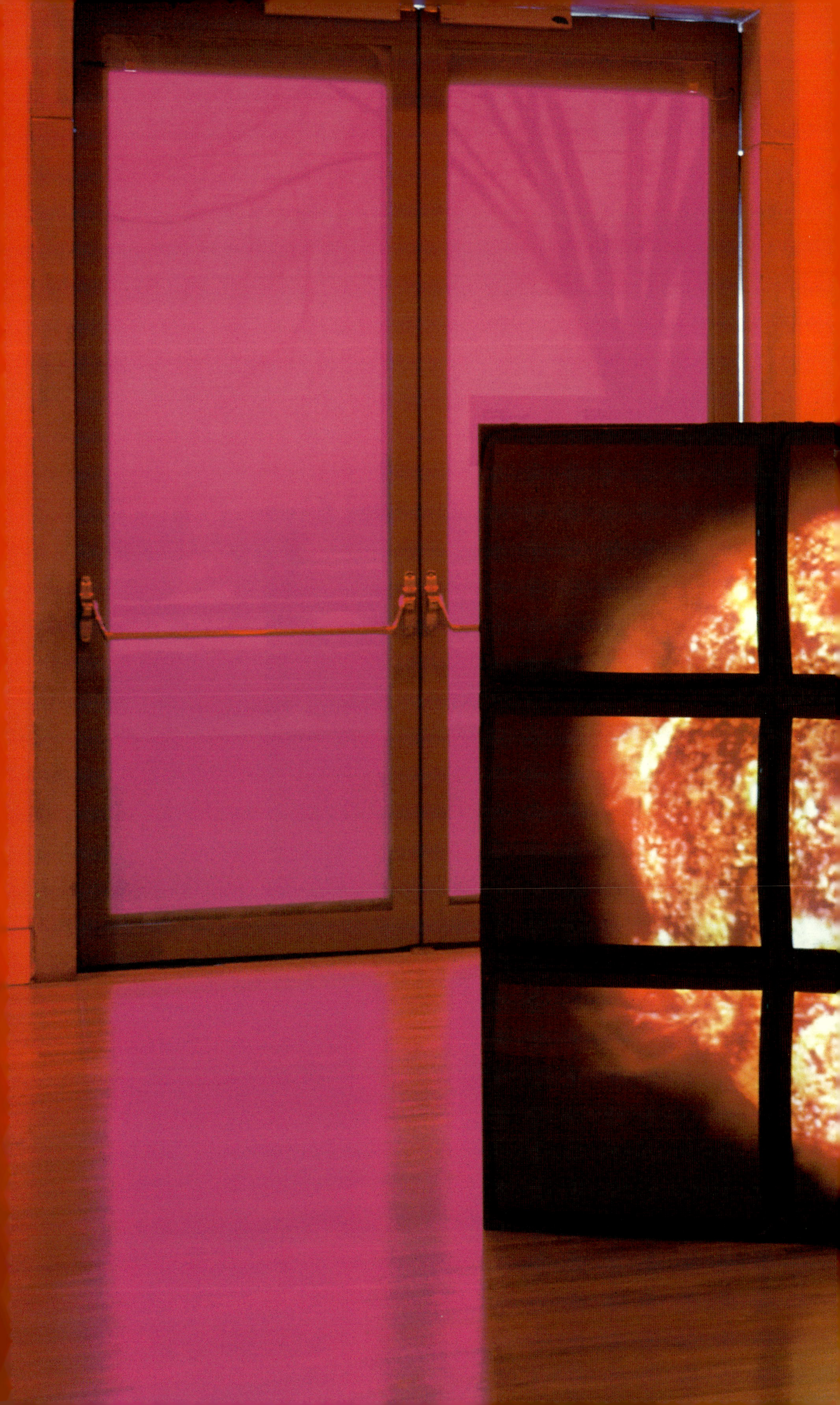

Diana Thater

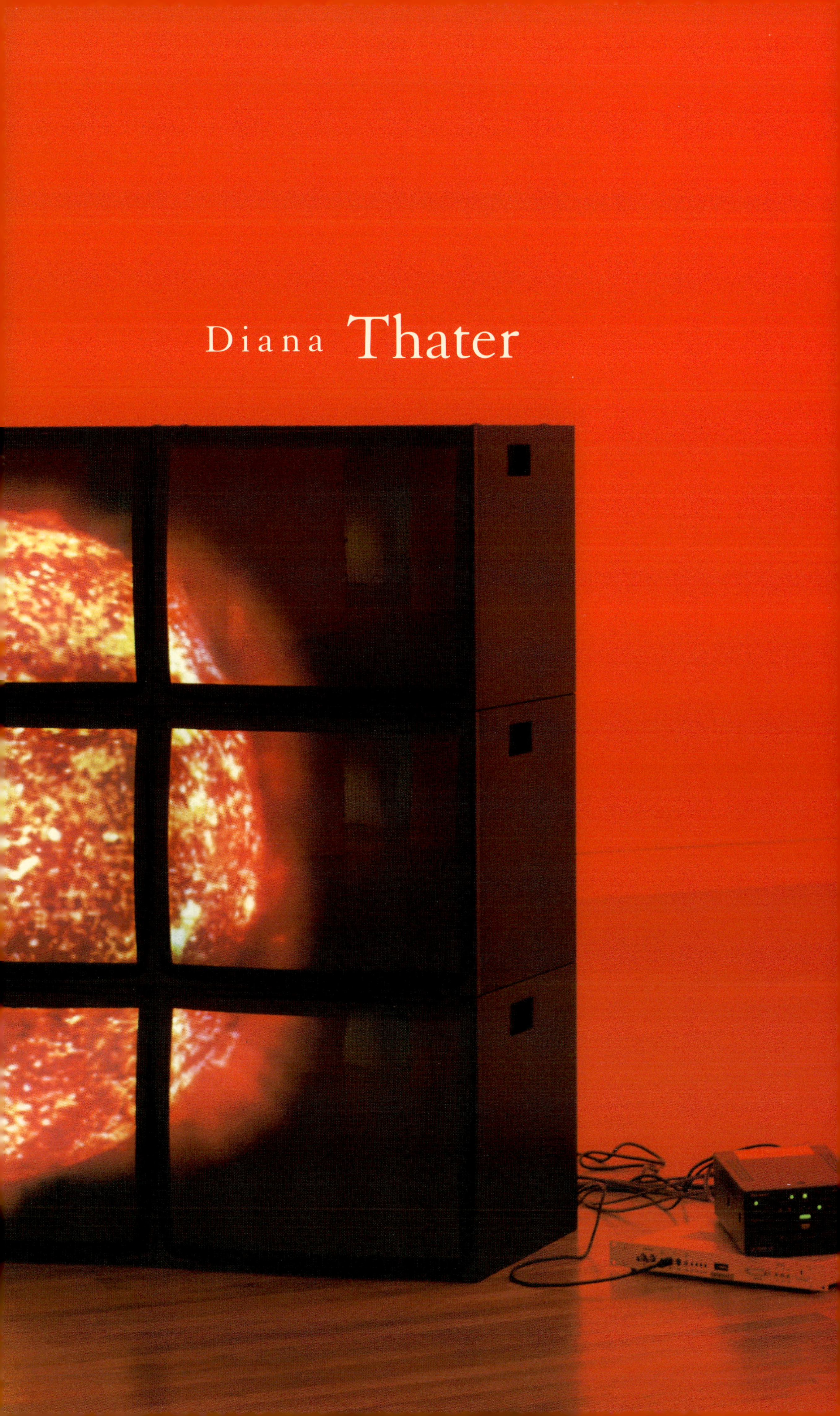

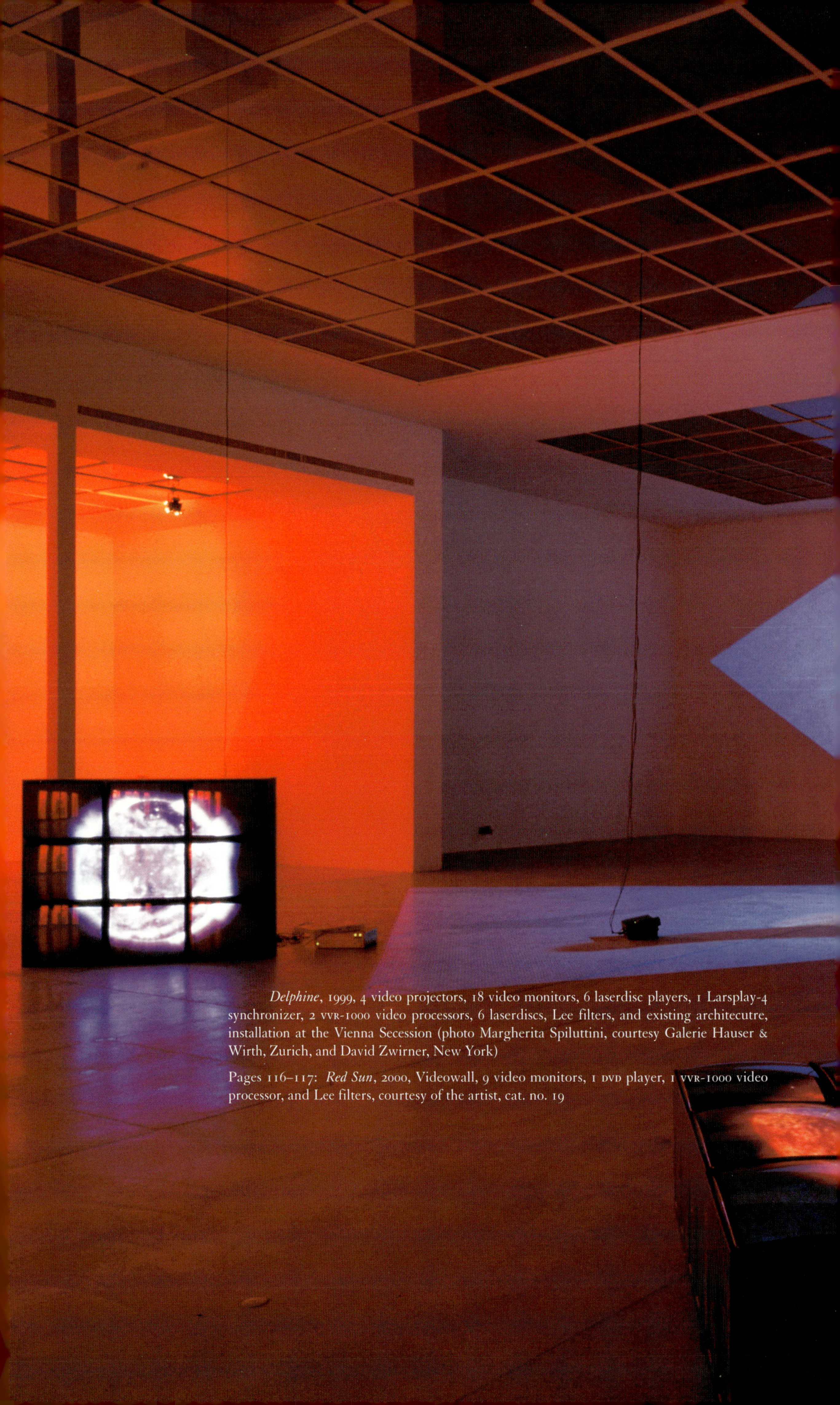

Delphine, 1999, 4 video projectors, 18 video monitors, 6 laserdisc players, 1 Larsplay-4 synchronizer, 2 VVR-1000 video processors, 6 laserdiscs, Lee filters, and existing architecutre, installation at the Vienna Secession (photo Margherita Spiluttini, courtesy Galerie Hauser & Wirth, Zurich, and David Zwirner, New York)

Pages 116–117: *Red Sun*, 2000, Videowall, 9 video monitors, 1 DVD player, 1 VVR-1000 video processor, and Lee filters, courtesy of the artist, cat. no. 19

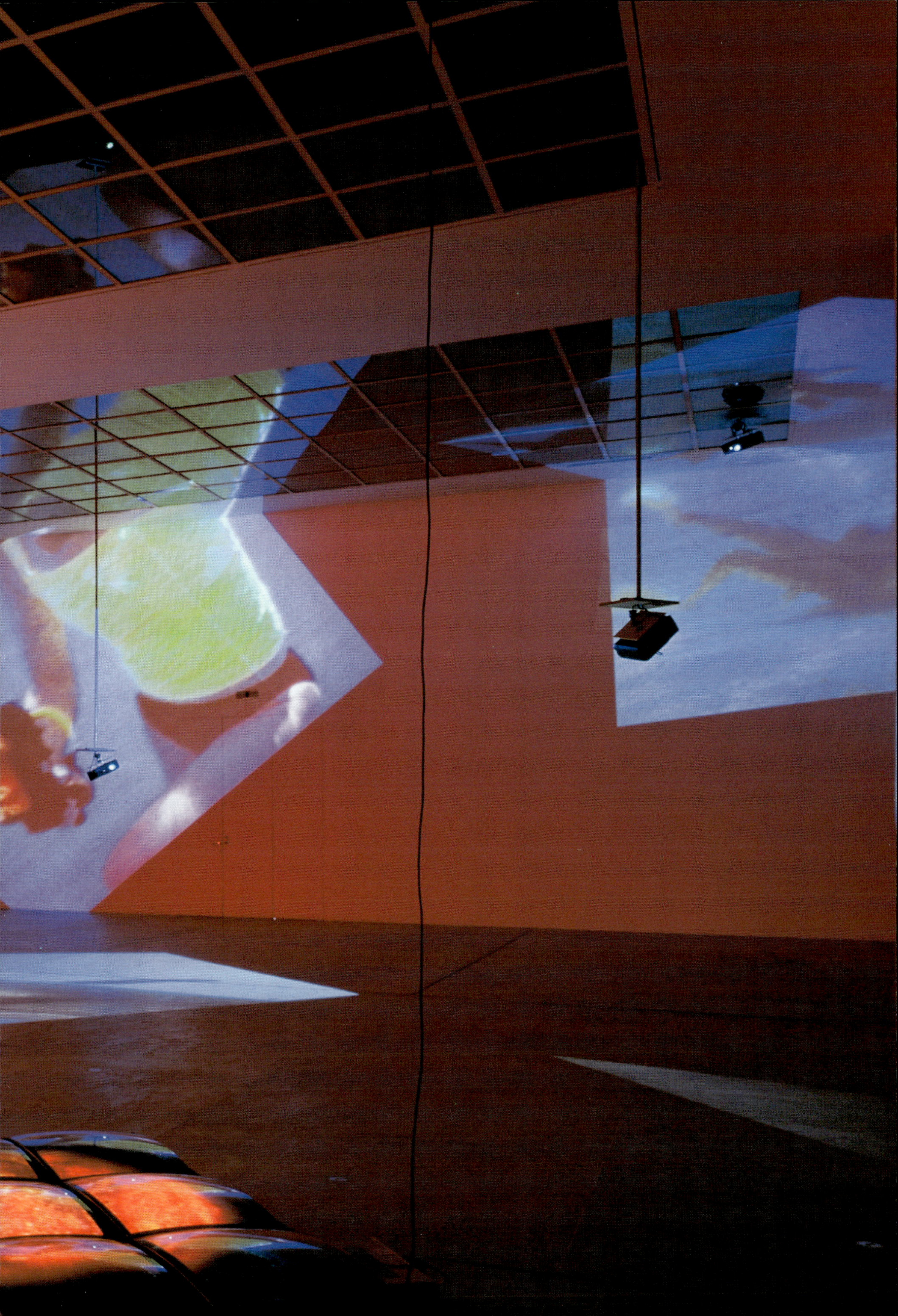

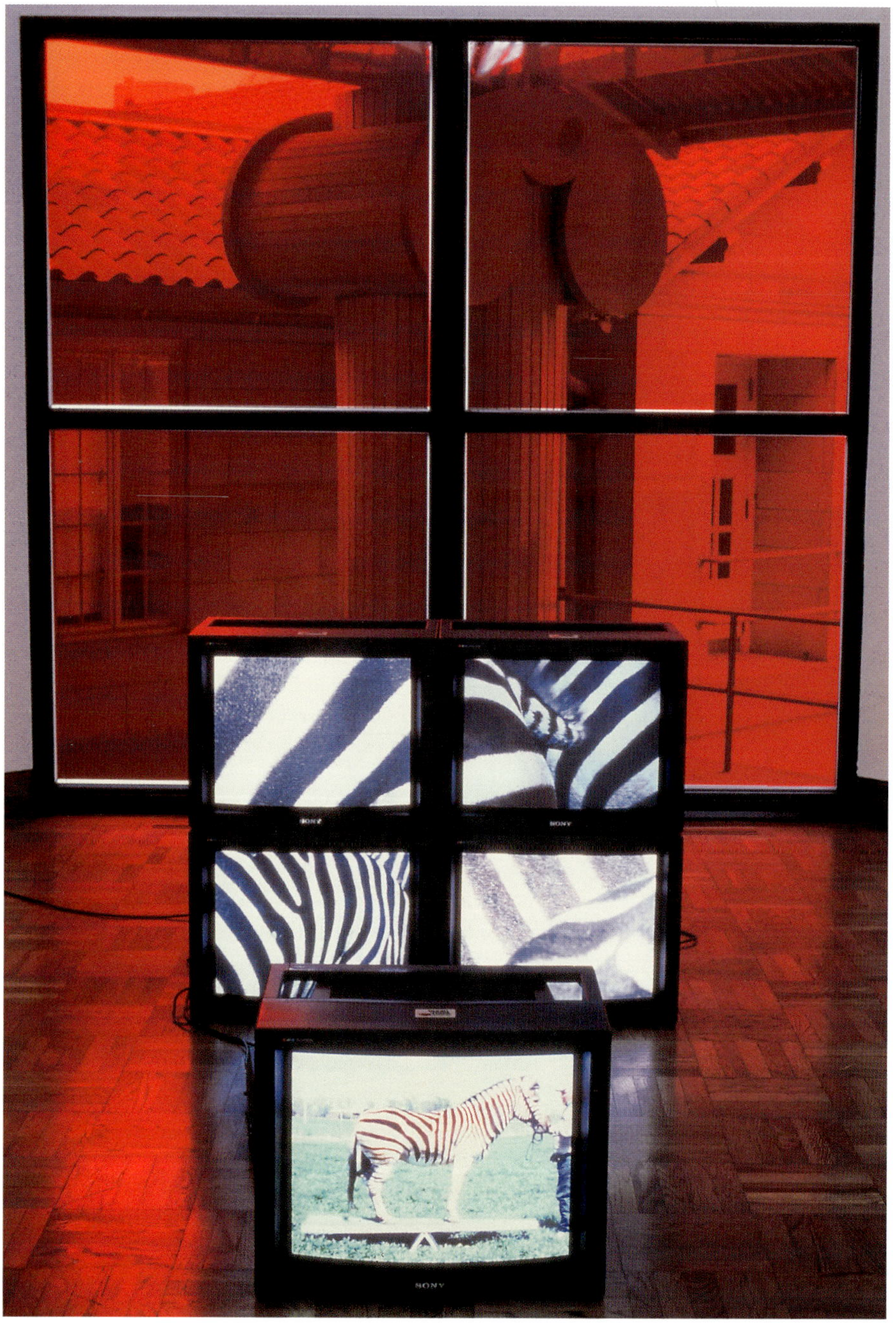

The best animals are the flat animals, 1998, Monitor Stack, 5 video monitors, 5 laserdisc players, 5 laserdiscs, window film, and existing architecture, installation at the Allen Memorial Art Museum, Oberlin, Ohio (photo courtesy David Zwirner, New York)

Yet works of art inevitably contribute to the flattening out and the widening of the world because they are all about the surface; they float on the surface and are only of the surface.[1]

I am looking for something more than the visually arresting. I want to find the spiritually arresting — the ineffable, the sublime moment when the viewer loses herself... and is forced to reconstruct herself, that is, to re-find herself. This is the moment of transformation that is not depicted but is acted. It does not happen in the image — in the pictures — but in the space and in the viewer.[2]

Diana Thater's *Red Sun* came out of her work last year on *Delphine* for the Vienna Secession, a project involving dolphins filmed underwater in their natural environment in the Caribbean. Coronal photographs of the sun, shot with a space telescope for NASA, are broken down into the primary and secondary colours, red, green, and blue, and then into magenta, cyan, and yellow. The images are then further deconstructed by a video processor and distributed onto the screens of a bank of nine television monitors, where they recombine to make a glowing circular image of jewel-like intensity. In the original installation the sun-walls lay on the floor, facing upward, or stood at an angle from the gallery walls, in contrast to the projected images of the swimming dolphins that covered the walls, ceiling, and floor of the space. Coloured gels further transformed the ambient light. Thater's installation offered no fixed point of view and overlapped two distinct kinds of representational space—the dolphins' deep underwater space and the flat outer space of the suns—onto the three-dimensional, rectangular, architectural space of the building. The traditional elements of landscape—land, water, sky—were present in inverted relationship, but one could only take them in by moving into and around the gallery.

Filming the dolphins was the first time Thater had worked underwater, and with free animals. Previously she had filmed wild animals in a nature preserve,

[1] Diana Thater, "Skin Deep," in Peter Noever, ed., *The best animals are the flat animals — the best space is the deep space* (Los Angeles: MAK Center for Art and Architecture, 1998), p. 34. [2] Diana Thater, in "A conversation between Carol Reese and Diana Thater on the occasion of the opening of *Delphine* at the Secession, Vienna, 2000" in *Diana Thater: Delphine* (Vienna: Secession, 2000), p. 28.

or used trained animals such as wolves, horses, and zebras for her shoots, making no attempt to disguise the artifice of the situations. Each of these species occupies a different position with respect to the human iconographical construction of the animal world: wild/romantic, exotic/comic, and domestic/genre. Yet it is not these projections of human consciousness onto the mirror of nature that interests Thater so much as how animals provide instances of other subjectivities and offer other models for negotiating the spatio-temporal world. The structure of her installations exposes the falseness of the usual representations of depth in film and painting, in which the world is shown from the perspective of a single observing consciousness. This is especially clear in the dolphins' fluid underwater environment, where a fixed point of view would be meaningless.

The suns are the other side of this underwater world, and are equally strange. Traditionally in art as well as in everyday experience, the sun is known only indirectly, through its effect on other objects; Claude Monet's series of haystacks painted at different times of day are the great example of this kind of observation of coloured light and atmosphere. The image of the sun, previously unknowable as an object in itself, is tangible evidence of how technology has transformed this earthbound perspective, giving us new points of view as well as new objects. Thater's flat coloured disks, framed and broken up over the surfaces of the television monitors, emphasize this objective presence. Yet while her representations have a strong formal quality, intensified by the non-naturalistic use of colour (although in other contexts the red and magenta of the two sun-walls might suggest the lurid light of the setting sun), the video medium as a source of light-emitting energy mimics and parallels the sun itself, giving the images a conceptual depth that is the result of thinking through technology and making use of its inherent structural and representational qualities.

This way of thinking structurally and conceptually is a distinctive feature of Thater's work. Although its subject is ostensibly the natural world, it does not address nature as a thing in itself, but always as mediated through consciousness and technology. However, the familiar nature/culture opposition is the starting point, not the end of her art. Through it she poses the question of how we construct a point of view, while insisting on the multiplicity of the world and the Other that eludes consciousness.

D.N.

Diana Thater

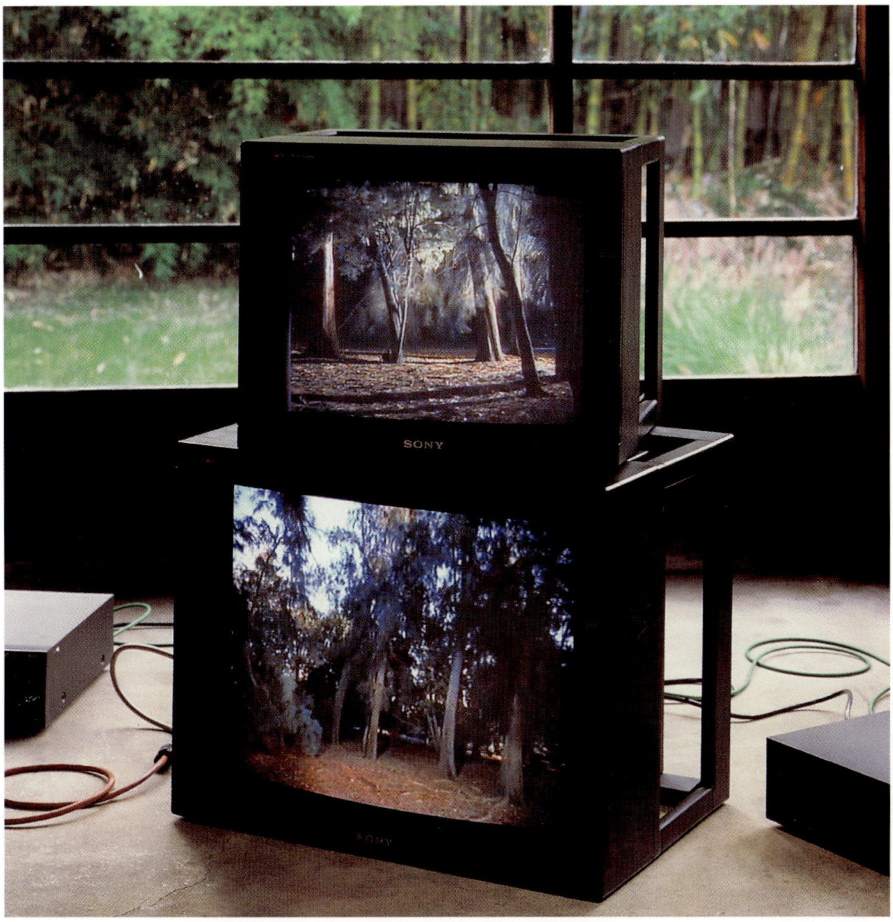

The best outside is the inside, 1998, Monitor Edition, 2 video monitors, 2 laserdisc players, and 2 laserdiscs, installation at the MAK Center for Art and Architecture, Los Angeles (photo Fredrik Nilsen, courtesy David Zwirner, New York)

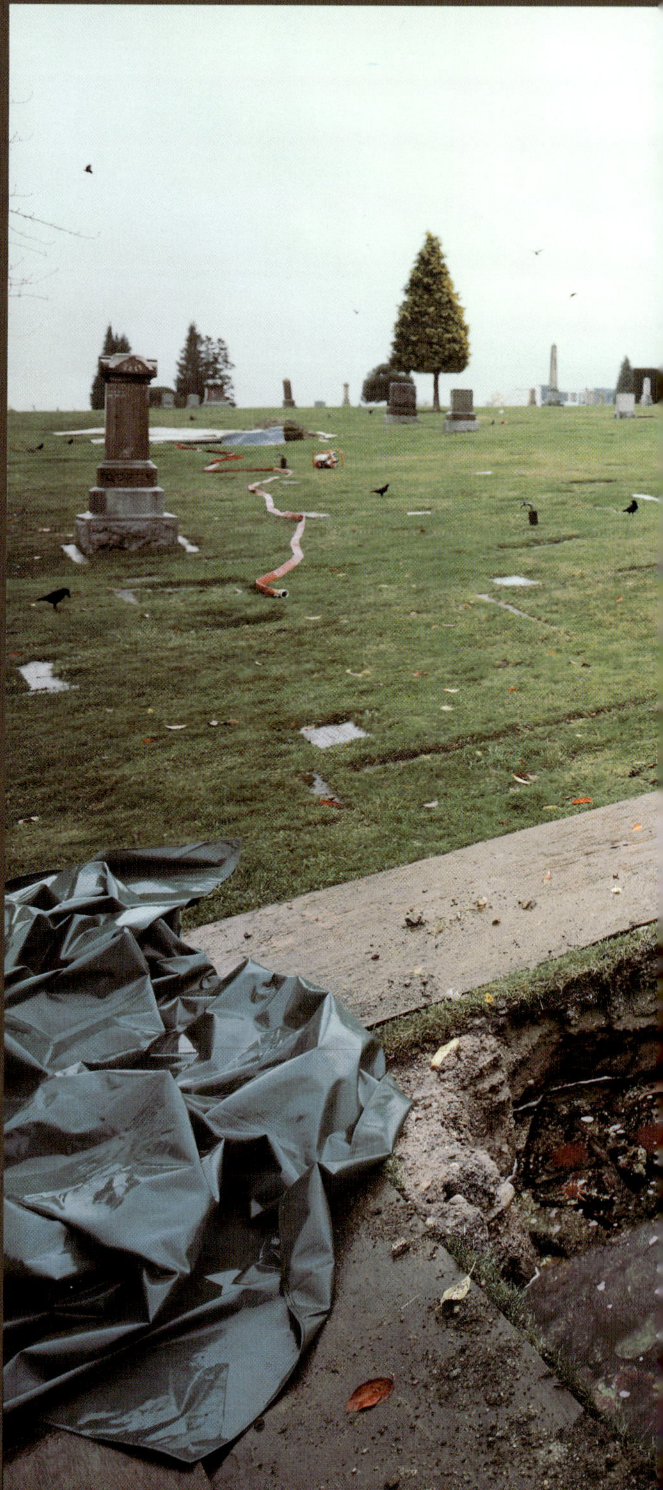

Jeff Wall

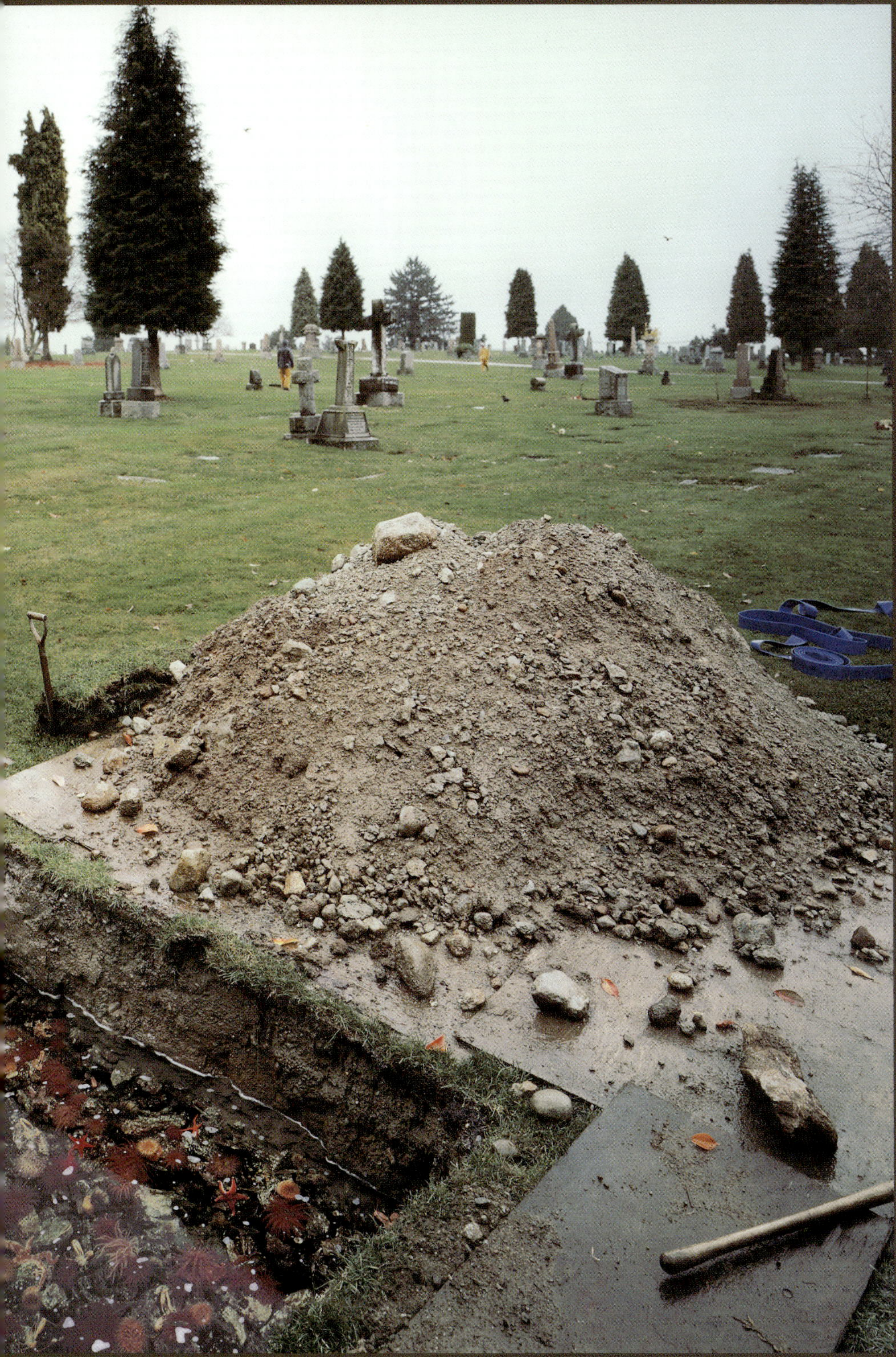

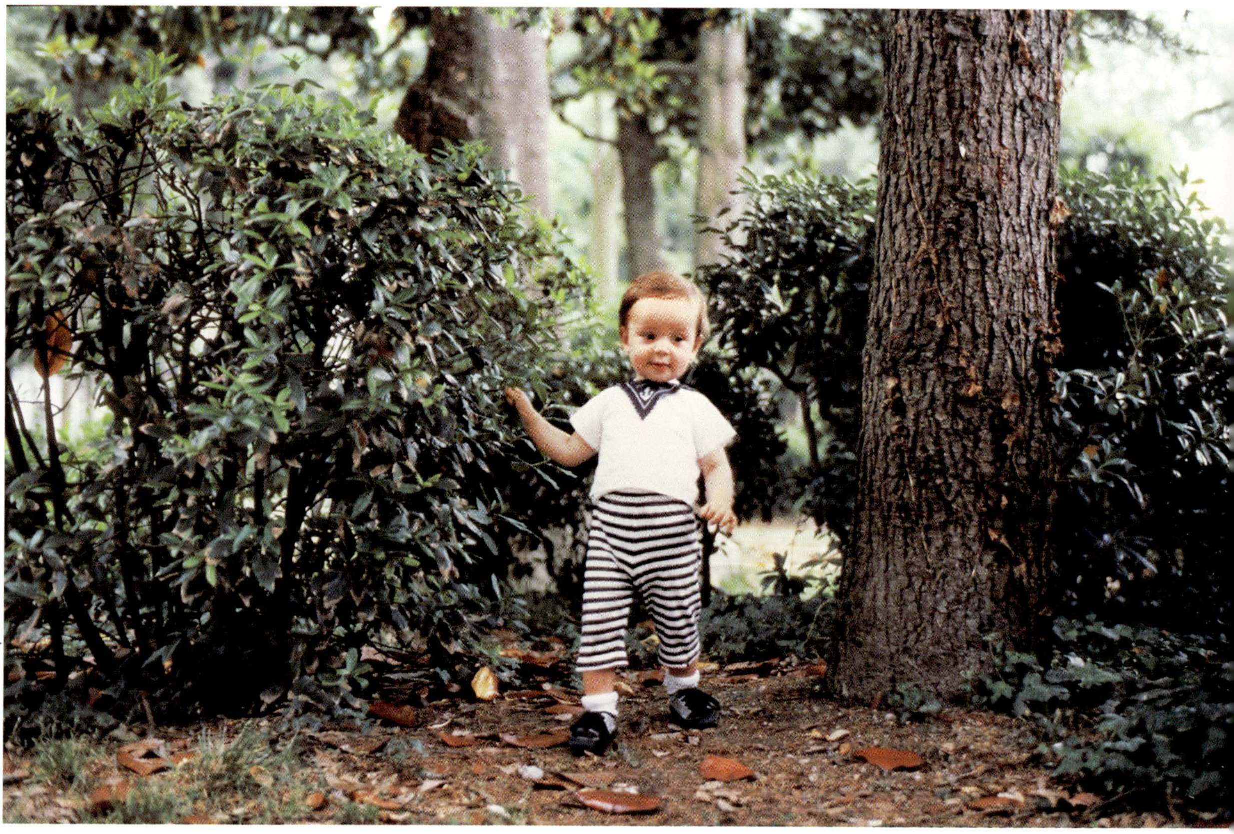

In the Public Garden, 1993, colour transparency in lightbox, 119 x 188 cm, collection of Gary and Tracy Mezzatesta, Los Angeles, cat. no. 23

Pages 124–125: *The Flooded Grave*, 1998–2000, colour transparency in lightbox, 228.6 x 282 cm, courtesy Galerie Jöhnen & Schöttle, Cologne, cat. no. 24

I make landscapes, or cityscapes as the case may be, to study the process of settlement as well as to work out for myself what the kind of picture (or photograph) we call a "landscape" is. This permits me also to recognize the other kinds of picture with which it has necessary connections, or the other genres that a landscape might conceal within itself.[1]

Jeff Wall's interest in landscape can be traced to a very early moment in his career, preceding the large, back-lit transparencies for which he is known, when he published *Landscape Manual* in 1970.[2] The black-and-white photographs illustrating this newsprint pamphlet are formally far removed from his later studied compositions. Taken from the window of a moving car, their central image is the roadway, on either side of which low buildings, trees, and telephone poles fly by, familiar features of the suburban, North American landscape. They provide early, and as yet unfocussed, evidence of the desire to inquire into his immediate social and physical environment and into the act of taking pictures that has characterized his later work. In addition, they point to an incipient concern with the mobility and flux of modern life, so well exemplified by the car, and how this essential feature affects both the subject and the point of view of the picture.

The definition of landscape hinges, as Wall recognizes, on the question of distance in relation to the motif: closer, and you have a history or genre picture, not a landscape; further, and the landscape motif recedes into the background, becoming a view glimpsed from a window or balcony, without independent significance. For him, the specific distance at which the landscape crystallizes as a type of picture "is an example of a threshold-phenomenon or a liminal state. It is a moment of passage, filled with energy, yearning and contradiction."[3] It is also the point at which the communal characteristics of the environment that shapes the individual become recognizable.

Wall's stated wish "to study the process of settlement" draws him to a type of subject that could be called "liminal" not only in terms of distance but also

[1] Jeff Wall, "About Making Landscapes," in Thierry de Duve et al., *Jeff Wall* (London: Phaidon Press, Ltd., 1996), p. 140. [2] Jeff Wall, *Landscape Manual* (Vancouver: Fine Arts Gallery, The University of British Columbia, 1970). [3] Wall, "About Making Landscapes," p. 144.

because of the social and economic tensions it reveals. For example, in spite of the beauty of the luminous panoramic landscape, our eye is inevitably drawn to the signs of logging and other industrial activity which fill the middle ground in *Coastal Motifs*, or to the emblematic orange back-hoe digging up the shoreline almost at the centre of *The Old Prison*. Both are signs of the resource-based economy that is in the process of transforming the landscape even as it fuels development in "beautiful British Columbia" (the motto on the province's licence plates). Often, Wall's landscapes focus on a space which is specifically liminal. In *The Crooked Path* the point of view is that of the edge where one thing ends and another begins, as the straggly openness of the countryside prepares to yield to the random density of the city in the distance. The way through this no-man's land is not direct. Rather, our eye is led along a winding path past a few out-of-place beehives: bucolic remnants that underline the multiple dislocations implicit in the transition to the economic and social space of city life.

While such contrasts of under- and over-development would seem to imply that development eventually sucks up everything in its path, Wall does not limit his landscapes to such dystopic realism. He has often said that he is a maker of tableaux, and frequently works in a more cinematographic mode, not only choosing a viewpoint but constructing an elaborate *mise en scène*. These constructed pictures offer him the freedom to explore landscape's relation to other genres and allow more complex meanings to emerge that engage not only the social but the interior life of the individual. Certain pictures, such as *The Storyteller*, retain elements of pastoral narrative in a lineage that runs from Titian's *Concert champêtre* to Manet's *Déjeuner sur l'herbe*, while *The Vampires' Picnic*, though without direct visual precedent, is a fantastic allegory that may be read as an inverted pastoral. Wall's new work, *The Flooded Grave*, finds a distant iconographic echo in the prominent tombstone and melancholy reference to Arcadia of Poussin's famous painting *The Shepherds of Arcadia*. Though seamless in appearance, it is complex stagecraft and digital technology that allows a story that begins with the ordinary and ends with the fantastic to be told:

The Flooded Grave *depicts a Vancouver cemetery on a wet November day. A newly dug grave has flooded, and the rain has just stopped. Nearby, some workmen are bringing a pump. Under the water surface, you can suddenly see the ocean floor, with all its animals and plants. I thought of the image as a sudden vision, a sort of daydream*

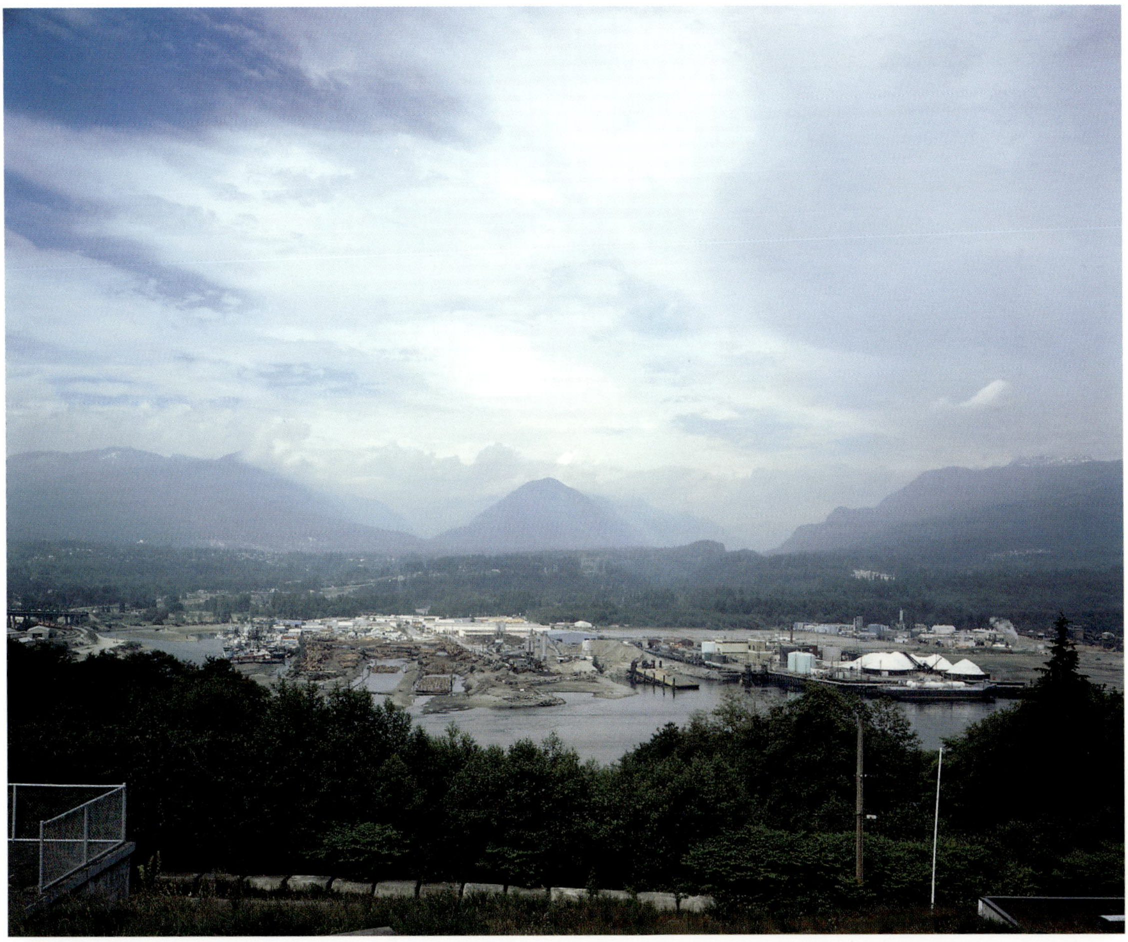

you might have if you were walking through the cemetery, maybe walking your dog, and spent a moment gazing idly into the water.[4]

This moment of reverie is a crucial one. The brief glimpse of the sea floor is an inexplicable, though pleasurable, intrusion into the realism of the depiction which functions—somewhat like the unheard conversations in other pictures but in a manner consistent with the landscape genre—as an assertion of meanings that are necessarily constructed beyond the surface of appearances.

D.N.

[4] Jeff Wall, email to the author, 6 October 2000.

Coastal Motifs, 1989, colour transparency in lightbox, 119 x 147 cm, Mugrabi collection, New York, cat. no. 21

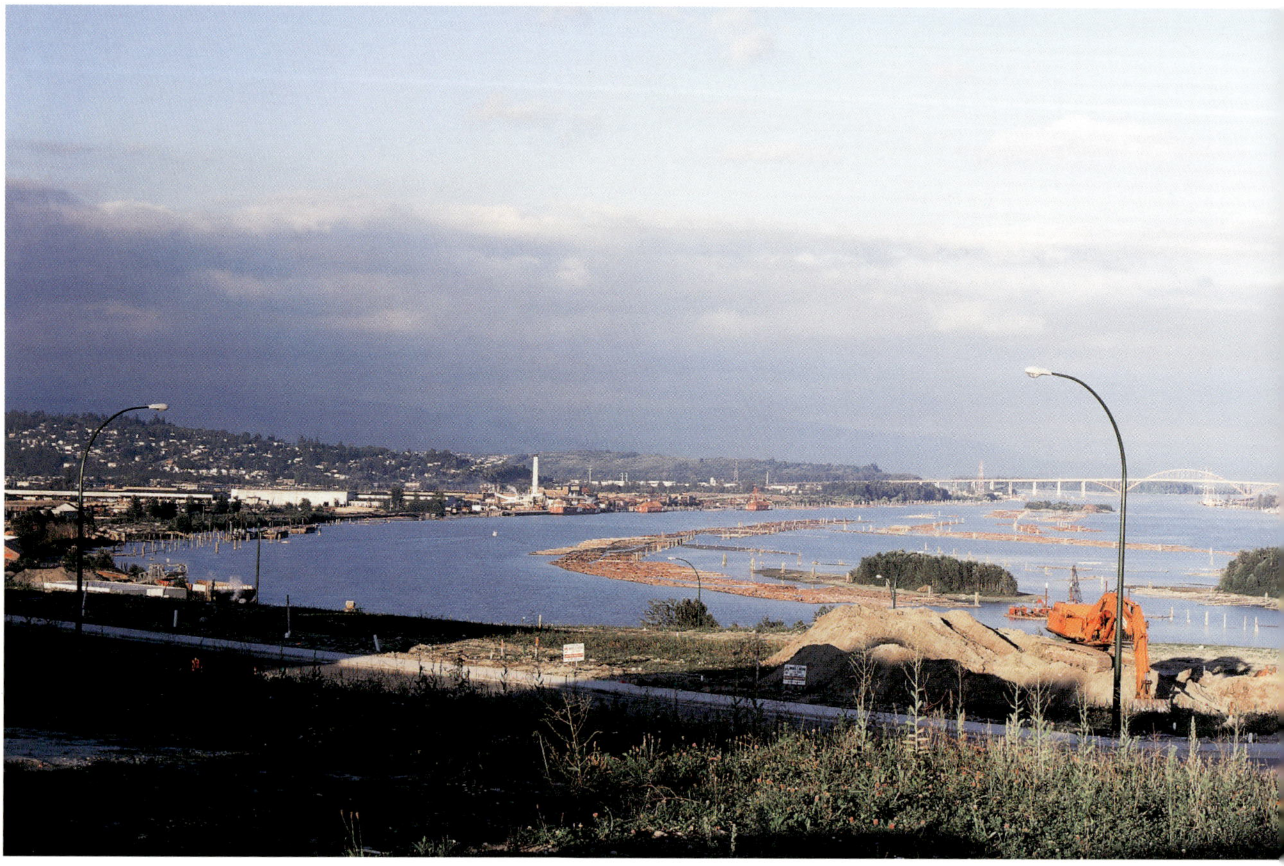

The Old Prison, 1987, colour transparency in lightbox, 70 × 229 cm, collection of Galerie Jöhnen & Schöttle, Cologne, cat. no. 20

Jeff Wall

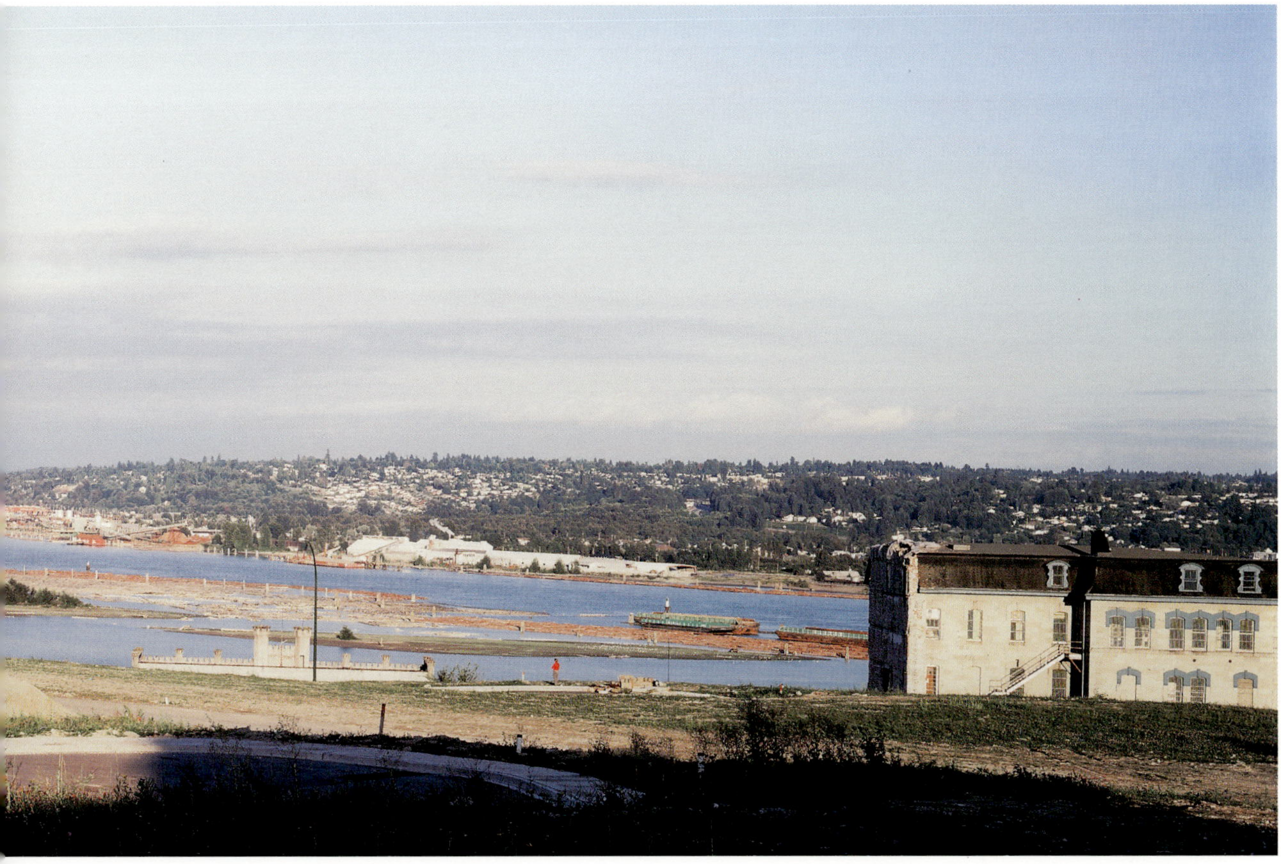

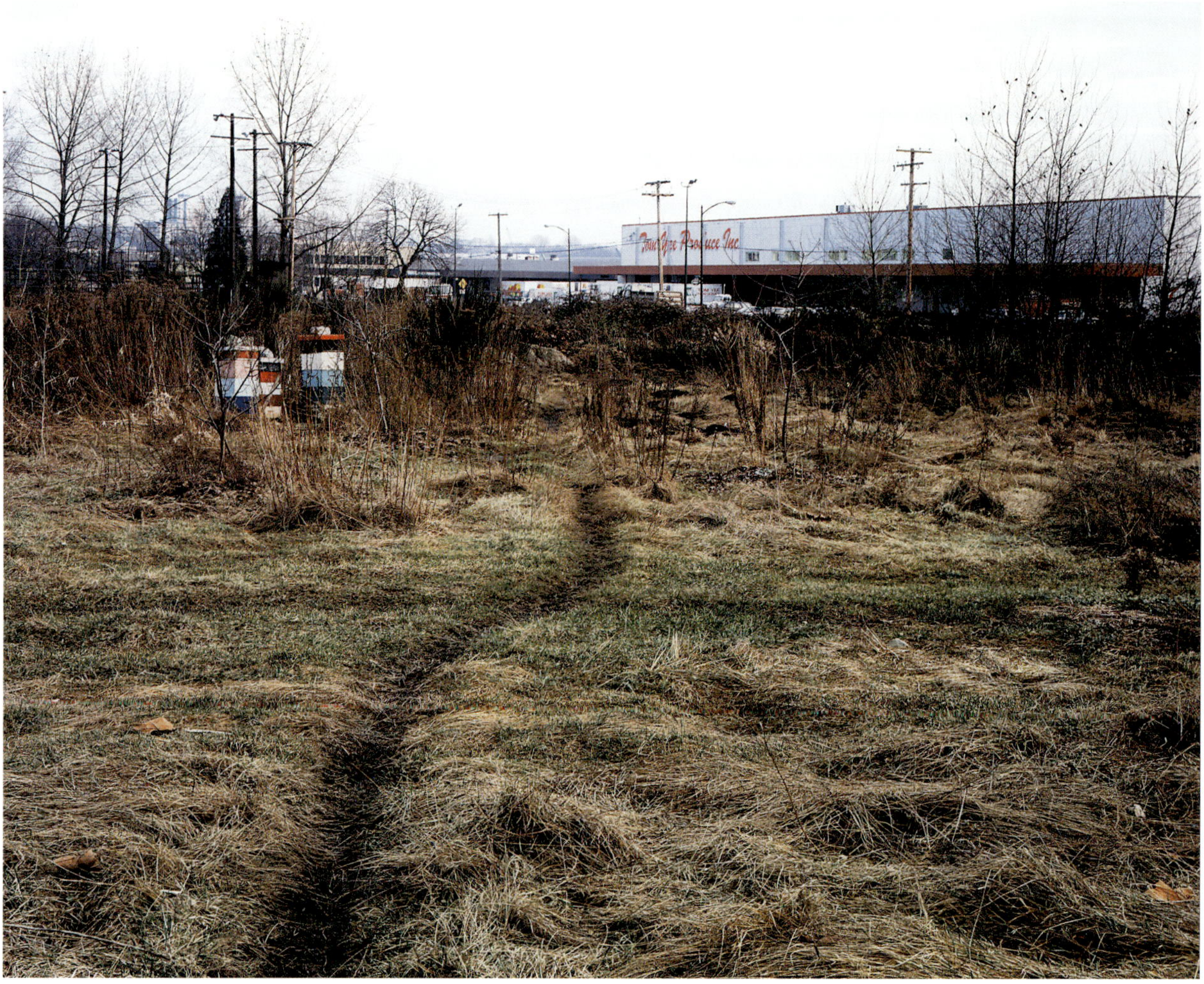

The Crooked Path, 1991, colour transparency in lightbox, 119 × 149 cm, private collection, London, cat. no. 22

Works in the Exhibition

1 **Geneviève Cadieux**
Tears 1995
Edition 2/2
Chromogenic print mounted on plexiglas, with aluminum frame, 182.5 x 277 x 7 cm
Courtesy Galerie René Blouin, Montreal

2 **Geneviève Cadieux**
June 1999
Edition 1/2
Gelatin silver print mounted on panel, with aluminum frame, 216 x 292 x 7 cm
The Bailey Collection, Toronto
Courtesy Jack Shainman, New York

3 **Geneviève Cadieux**
Pour un oui pour un non 2000
Edition 2/2
Gelatin silver print mounted on plexiglas, with aluminum frame, 275 x 366 x 7 cm
Courtesy Galerie René Blouin, Montreal

4 **Janet Cardiff**
Forty-Part Motet 2001
A reworking of "Spem in Alium," 1575, by Thomas Tallis
40-track audio installation
Recorded by SoundMoves. Produced by Field together with the Arts Council of England, the Salisbury Festival and Salisbury Cathedral Choir, Baltic, Now Festival, and The New Art Gallery Walsall. Loudspeakers provided by B&W Loudspeakers (www.bwspeakers.com). Additional production assistance for the North American presentation provided by the National Gallery of Canada.

5 **Tacita Dean**
Banewl 1999
16 mm colour anamorphic film with optical sound, 63 minutes
Courtesy of the artist, Frith Street Gallery, London, and Marian Goodman Gallery, New York and Paris

6 **Liz Magor**
Hollow 1998–1999
Polymerized alpha gypsum, fabric, and foam, 182.8 x 106.7 x 121.9 cm
National Gallery of Canada, Ottawa

7 **Liz Magor**
Burrow 1999
Polymerized alpha gypsum and fabric, 58 x 173 x 137 cm
Vancouver Art Gallery, purchased with the financial support of the Canada Council for the Arts, Acquisition Assistance Program

8 **Liz Magor**
Chee-to 2000
Plaster, resin, and food, 183 x 244 x 61 cm
Art Gallery of Ontario, Toronto, purchased with financial support from the Canada Council for the Arts, Acquisition Assistance Program, and with the assistance of the E. Wallace Fund, 2000

9 **Liz Magor**
Stores 2000
Plaster, resin, and food, 155 x 81 x 36 cm
Courtesy Susan Hobbs Gallery, Toronto

10 **Shahzia Sikander**
Chaman 2000–2001
Acrylic, gouache, and ink on tissue paper
Courtesy of the artist and Deitch Projects, New York

11 **Shahzia Sikander**
Elusive Realities 2000
Vegetable colour, dry pigment, watercolour, and tea on handmade wasli paper, 27.9 x 18.7 cm
The Speyer Family Collection
Courtesy Deitch Projects, New York

12 **Shahzia Sikander**

Riding the Ridden 2000

Vegetable colour, dry pigment, watercolour, and tea on handmade wasli paper, 20.3 × 13.7 cm

Collection of Niva Grill Angel, New York

Courtesy Deitch Projects, New York

13 **Shahzia Sikander**

Riding the Written 2000

Vegetable colour, dry pigment, watercolour, and tea on handmade wasli paper, 20.3 × 14 cm

Private collection, London

14 **Valeska Soares**

Picturing Paradise 2001

Perfume, columns, and engraved copper rings, Installed in the Water Court and in the balcony of the Garden Court

Courtesy Galeria Camargo Vilaça, São Paulo, and LiebmanMagnan, New York

15 **Jana Sterbak**

In collaboration with The Fabric Workshop and Museum, Philadelphia

Oasis 2000

Stainless steel, 297.2 × 396.2 × 304.8 cm

Anonymous loan

With additional production assistance from the National Gallery of Canada and the Canada Council for the Arts

Courtesy of the artist and The Fabric Workshop and Museum, Philadelphia

16 **Yoshihiro Suda**

Tulip 2001

Painted wood

Courtesy Gallery Koyanagi, Tokyo, and Galerie René Blouin, Montreal

17 **Yoshihiro Suda**

Tulip 2001

Painted wood

Courtesy Gallery Koyanagi, Tokyo, and Galerie René Blouin, Montreal

18 **Yoshihiro Suda**

Tulip and Weeds 2001

Painted wood

Courtesy Gallery Koyanagi, Tokyo, and Galerie René Blouin, Montreal

19 **Diana Thater**

Red Sun 2000

Videowall

9 video monitors, 1 DVD player, 1 VVR-1000 video processor, and Lee filters

Courtesy of the artist

20 **Jeff Wall**

The Old Prison 1987

Colour transparency in lightbox, 70 × 229 cm

Collection of Galerie Jöhnen & Schöttle, Cologne

21 **Jeff Wall**

Coastal Motifs 1989

Colour transparency in lightbox, 119 × 147 cm

Mugrabi collection, New York

22 **Jeff Wall**

The Crooked Path 1991

Colour transparency in lightbox, 119 × 149 cm

Private collection, London

23 **Jeff Wall**

In the Public Garden 1993

Colour transparency in lightbox, 119 × 188 cm

Collection of Gary and Tracy Mezzatesta, Los Angeles

24 **Jeff Wall**

The Flooded Grave 1998–2000

Colour transparency in lightbox, 228.6 × 282 cm

Courtesy Galerie Jöhnen & Schöttle, Cologne

Exhibition Histories

Geneviève Cadieux

Born in Montreal, 1955. Lives and works in Montreal. Studied at University of Ottawa, B.F.A., 1977. Represented by Galerie René Blouin, Montreal.

Solo Exhibitions

1977, Saw Gallery, Ottawa; 1981, Galerie France Morin, Montreal; 1982, Agnes Etherington Art Centre, Queen's University, Kingston, Ont., and The Gallery Stratford, Stratford, Ont. (cat.); 1988, Galerie René Blouin, Montreal; 1988, The Power Plant, Toronto (cat.); 1989, Galerie René Blouin, Montreal; 1990, Canadian Pavilion, Venice, XLIV Biennale (cat.); 1990, Galerie René Blouin, Montreal; 1991, Kent Fine Art, New York; 1991, Centre d'art contemporain de Genève, Geneva; 1992, Institute of Contemporary Art, Amsterdam; 1992, Institute of Contemporary Art, London (cat.); 1992, Sagacho Exhibit Space, Tokyo; 1992, Musée départemental d'art contemporain de Rochechouart, Rochechouart, France (cat.); 1993, Musée d'art contemporain de Montréal, Montreal (cat.); 1993, Galerie René Blouin, Montreal; 1994, Nouveau Musée/Institut d'art contemporain, Villeurbanne, France; 1994, Kent Gallery, New York; 1994, Museum van Hedendaagse Kunst Antwerpen, Antwerp; 1994, Bonner Kunstverein, Bonn; 1995, Galerie René Blouin, Montreal; 1995, Tate Gallery (Art Now, 3), London; 1995, Angles Gallery, Santa Monica, Calif.; 1995–1996, Cleveland Center for Contemporary Art, Cleveland, and Pittsburgh Center for the Arts, Pittsburgh, *Body Currents* (cat.); 1997, Galerie René Blouin, Montreal; 1997, Stephen Friedman Gallery, London; 1997, Kunstforeningen, Copenhagen; 1998, Miami Art Museum, Miami; 1998, Galleria S.A.L.E.S., Rome (cat.); 1999, Galerie René Blouin, Montreal; 1999, Morris and Helen Belkin Art Gallery, Vancouver (cat.); 2000, Art Gallery of Hamilton, Hamilton, Ont.; 2000, Montreal Museum of Fine Arts, Montreal; 2000, Americas Society, New York.

Group Exhibitions

1978, Galerie Optica, Montreal, *Cadieux, Duchow, Erskine, Flomen, June*; 1981, Art Gallery of Hamilton, Hamilton, Ont., *Viewpoint: Twenty-Nine by Nine* (cat.); 1984, Montreal Museum of Fine Arts, Montreal, *Theatre of the Imagination* (cat.); 1985, Musée d'art contemporain de Montréal, Montreal, *Les vingt ans du Musée à travers sa collection* (cat.); 1985, Centre international d'art contemporain de Montréal, Montreal, *Aurora Borealis* (cat.); 1985, organized by the Centre international d'art contemporain de Montréal for the Department of External Affairs of Canada, Ottawa, *Traces: Contemporary Canadian Drawings* (cat.), circulated 1987–1989 to Washington, D.C., Alaska, Ohio, and Texas; 1986, Centre international d'art contemporain de Montréal, Montreal, *Lumières: Perception-Projection* (cat.); 1986, Rheinhallen Messegelände (Internationaler Kunstmarkt), Cologne, *Focus: Kanadische Kunst von 1960–1985* (cat.); 1987, Musée d'art contemporain de Montréal, Montreal, *Le geste oublié* (cat.); 1987, Musée d'art contemporain de Montréal, Montreal, *Elementa Naturae* (cat.); 1987, Künstlerhaus Bethanien, Berlin, *Emotope* (cat.); 1987, São Paulo, *19a Bienal Internacional de São Paulo: Ruidos do Norte/Northern Noises* (cat.), organized by the Winnipeg Art Gallery, Winnipeg; 1988, Art Gallery of New South Wales and Pier 2/3, Walsh Bay, Sydney, and National Gallery of Victoria, Melbourne, 7th Biennale, *From the Southern Cross: A View on the World of Art c. 1940–1988* (cat.); 1988, The Power Plant, Toronto, *The Historical Ruse: Art in Montreal* (cat.); 1988, The Power Plant, Toronto, *Enchantment & Disturbance* (cat.); 1989, Nickle Arts Museum, Calgary, *Interior Presence: Projecting Situations* (cat.); 1989, Musée d'art contemporain de Montréal, Montreal, *L'histoire et la mémoire: Acquisitions récentes en art québecois* (cat.); 1989, National Gallery of Canada, Ottawa, Alberta College of Art, Calgary, and Fawbush Gallery, New York, *Canadian Biennial of Contemporary Art* (cat.); 1990, Galerie René Blouin, Montreal,

Oeuvres au noir; 1990, Art Gallery of New South Wales, Sydney, 8th Biennale, *The Readymade Boomerang: Certain Relations in 20th Century Art* (cat.); 1990, National Garden Festival, Gateshead, England, *A New Necessity: First Tyne International 1990* (cat.); 1990, Derry, Glasgow, Newcastle upon Tyne, and Plymouth, U.K., *New Works for Different Places: TSWA Four Cities Project* (cat.); 1990, Montreal Museum of Fine Arts, Montreal, *Acquisitions récentes 1988–1990*; 1990–1992, Centre Georges Pompidou, Musée national d'art moderne, Paris, Fundació Caixa de Pensions, Barcelona, Wexner Center for the Arts, Columbus, Ohio, and San Francisco Museum of Modern Art, San Francisco, *Passage de l'image* (cat.); 1991, Musée du Québec, Quebec City, *Un archipel de désirs: Les artistes du Québec et la scène internationale* (cat.); 1991, New Museum of Contemporary Art, New York, *The Uninterrupted Life* (cat.); 1991, Laing Art Gallery, Newcastle upon Tyne, Ferens Art Gallery, Hull, Camden Arts Centre, London, and Arnolfini Art Gallery, Bristol, England, *Outer Space* (cat.), organized by the South Bank Centre, London; 1991, Art Gallery of York University, Toronto, *Crossroads* (cat.); 1992, Wiener Secession, Vienna, *Skulpturen-Fragmente: Internationale Fotoarbeiten der 90er Jahre* (cat.); 1992, Musée d'art contemporain de Montréal, Montreal, *Pour la suite du monde* (cat.); 1992, Museum of Modern Art, Saitama, Japan, *The Tenth Anniversary Exhibition: Adam and Eve* (cat.); 1993, FRAC Pays-de-la-Loire, Clisson, France, and Musée des beaux-arts, FRAC Franche-Comté, Dole, France, *Canada, une nouvelle génération* (cat.); 1993, Rooseum, Malmö, Sweden, *Passageworks* (cat.); 1993, Frankfurter Kunstverein, Frankfurt, *Das Bild des Körpers* (cat.); 1993, Anderson Gallery, Virginia Commonwealth University, Richmond, Va., and Art Gallery of the University of Maryland, College Park, Md., *Anonymity and Identity* (cat.); 1993, San Sebastian, Spain, *IM=C.299792458'S* (cat.); 1994, Musée des beaux-arts d'Agen, Agen, France, *... Ou les oiseaux selon Schopenhauer*; 1994, Museo Nacional Centro de Arte Reina Sofia, Madrid, *Cocido y crudo*; 1995, Setayaga Art Museum, Tokyo, National Museum of Modern Art, Kyoto, and Hokkaido Museum of Modern Art, Sapporo, *Spirits on the Crossing: Travellers to/from Nowhere — Contemporary Art in Canada 1980–1994* (cat.); 1995, Museum of Contemporary Art, Finnish National Gallery, Helsinki, *ARS 95* (cat.); 1995, New Museum of Contemporary Art, New York, *Human/Nature*; 1995, Musée d'art contemporain de Montréal, Montreal, *Premiers dons 1964–1965 et Dons 1989–1994*; 1995, Pace McGill Gallery, New York, *Large Bodies*; 1995, Angles Gallery, Santa Monica, Calif., *Presences: Recent Portraits*; 1995, Musée d'art contemporain de Montréal, Montreal, *L'effet cinéma*; 1995–1996, Morris and Helen Belkin Art Gallery, Vancouver, and Galerie de l'Université du Québec à Montréal, Montreal, *Seeing in Tongues*; 1996, Musée départemental d'art contemporain de Rochechouart, Rochechouart, France, *Collection/Parcours*; 1996, Museum van Hedendaagse Kunst, Ghent, Belgium, *Fotografische Momenten*; 1996, Kunsthalle Düsseldorf, Düsseldorf, *Happy End*; 1996, Art Gallery of North York, North York, Ont., *Reflections of the Soul*; 1996, National Gallery of Canada, Ottawa, *Odd Bodies*; 1997, Montreal Museum of Fine Arts, Montreal, *Body in the Lens*; 1997, Musée du Québec, Quebec City, *La collection Prêt d'oeuvres d'art: Acquisitions 1997*; 1997, Kelowna Art Gallery, Kelowna, B.C., *Hotel on Fire* (cat.); 1997–1998, Fundaçao Calouste Gulbenkian, Centro de Arte Moderna José de Azeredo Perdigao, Lisbon, and Centro de Fotografia, Porto, Portugal, *From Here to There* (cat.); 1997, Leonard & Bina Ellen Art Gallery, Concordia University, Montreal, *Five Years of Collecting: A Selection of New Acquisitions*; 1998, Palacio de los Condes de Gabia, Granada, *Pasajes de la colección en Santa Fe y Granada* (cat.); 1998, Palazzo Branciforte, Palermo, and Museo di Castelnuovo, Naples, *Disidentico, maschile femminile e altro* (cat.); 1998, Witte de With Center for Contemporary Art, Rotterdam, and Fundació Joan Miró, Barcelona, *Voices* (cat.); 1998, Musée d'art de Joliette, Joliette, Que., *Temps composés, la donation Maurice Forget* (cat.); 1999, Le Fresnoy, Studio national des arts contemporains, Tourcoing, France, *La voix*; 1999, Passage de Retz, Paris, and Centre d'Art Santa Mònica, Barcelona, *Espaces intérieurs: Artistes contemporains du Québec/El cos, la llengua, les paraules, la pell* (cat.); 1999, Massachusetts Museum of Contemporary Art, North Adams, Mass., *Billboard: Art on the Road* (cat.); 1999, New Museum of Contemporary Art, New York, *The Time of Our Lives* (cat.); 1999, Leonard & Bina Ellen Art Gallery, Concordia

University, Montreal, *Redefining the Still Life*; 1999, Leonard & Bina Ellen Art Gallery, Concordia University, Montreal, *Recent Acquisitions: Works from the Permanent Collection*; 2000, Atlanta Contemporary Art Center (The Contemporary), Atlanta, and Leonard & Bina Ellen Art Gallery, Concordia University, Montreal, *Found Wanting*; 2000, Oakville Galleries, Oakville, Ont., and Nickle Arts Museum, Calgary, *Odd Bodies* (cat.), organized by the National Gallery of Canada, Ottawa; 2000, San Diego, *SITE 2000*; 2000, Leonard & Bina Ellen Art Gallery, Concordia University, Montreal, *Concordia Collects: Selected Art Acquisitions 1974–2000*; 2000, Montreal, *La biennale de Montréal*.

Janet Cardiff

Born in Brussels, Ont., 1957. Lives and works in Lethbridge, Alta. Studied at Queen's University, Kingston, Ont., B.F.A., 1980; University of Alberta, Edmonton, M.V.A., 1983. Represented by Luhring Augustine, New York.

Solo Exhibitions

1987, Glendon Gallery, Toronto (cat.); 1988, Macdonald Stewart Art Centre, Guelph, Ont. (cat.); 1989, Latitude 53 Gallery, Edmonton; 1990, Evelyn Aimis Gallery, Toronto; 1991, The New Gallery, Calgary; 1992, YYZ, Toronto; 1992, Eye Level Gallery, Halifax; 1993, Edmonton Art Gallery, Edmonton (cat.); 1993, La Chambre Blanche, Quebec City; 1994, Randolph Street Gallery, Chicago; 1994, Southern Alberta Art Gallery, Lethbridge, Alta. (cat.); 1994, The Power Plant, Toronto; 1995, Walter Phillips Gallery, Banff, Alta. (cat.), collaboration with George Bures Miller; 1995, Eastern Edge Gallery, St. John's, Nfld.; 1995, Front Gallery, Vancouver, collaboration with George Bures Miller; 1996, Galerie Optica, Montreal; 1997, Morris Healy Gallery, New York, collaboration with George Bures Miller; 1997, Raum Aktueller Kunst, Vienna, collaboration with George Bures Miller; 1997, Galerie Barbara Weiss, Berlin; 1999, Side Street Project, Los Angeles, collaboration with George Bures Miller; 1999, Artangel, London, *London Walk*; 2000, Oakville Galleries, Oakville, Ont., *Lakeside Walk*; 2000, Kunstraum Munich, Munich; 2001, P.S.1, Long Island City, N.Y.; 2001, Kunstmuseum des Kantons Thurgau, Warth, Switzerland.

Group Exhibitions

1992, Photographers Gallery, Saskatoon, Sask., *Environment*; 1992, The New Gallery, Calgary, *Intimacies*, performance with Charles Cousins, Nelson Henricks, and John Winet; 1995, Cambridge Library and Art Gallery, Cambridge, Ont., Whitby Arts Inc., Whitby, Ont., and McLaren Art Centre, Barrie, Ont., *A Public Room*; 1995, Erindale College, Toronto, *Think Big*; 1995, Zypressenstrasse 71, Zurich, *A Night at the Show*; 1996, Edmonton Art Gallery, Edmonton, and Glenbow Museum, Calgary, *Alberta Biennial for Contemporary Art*; 1996, Louisiana Museum of Modern Art, Humlebaek, Denmark, "Walking and Thinking and Walking," part of *NowHere* (cat.); 1997, Los Angeles Contemporary Exhibitions, Los Angeles, *Ear as Eye*; 1997, Muttart Art Gallery, Calgary, *Auricle Interchange* (cat.); 1997, A.K.A., Sastkatoon, Sask., *Whisper in My Ear* (cat.); 1997, San Francisco Museum of Modern Art, San Francisco, *Present Tense: Nine Artists in the Nineties* (cat.); 1997, Münster, *Skulpturen Projekte Münster* (cat.); 1998, Edmonton Art Gallery, Edmonton, *Beauty and the Banal*; 1998–2000, Académie de France, Villa Medici, Rome, *La ville, le jardin, la mémoire* (cat.); 1998, Wanås Foundation, Knislinge, Sweden, *Wanås '98* (cat.); 1998, Kulturnämnden, Gothenburg, Sweden, *Places in Gothenburg '98* (cat.); 1998, Witte de With Center for Contemporary Art, Rotterdam, and Fundació Joan Miró, Barcelona, *Voices* (cat.), collaboration with George Bures Miller; 1998, São Paulo, *XXIV Bienal de São Paulo (Roterios, Roterios...)* (cat.); 1999, Trianon Gallery, Lethbridge, Alta., *Stumble*; 1999, Musée régional de Rimouski, Rimouski, Que., *Body and Sound*; 1999, Musée d'art contemporain de Lyon, Lyons, *Musiques en Scène*; 1999, Le Fresnoy, Studio national des arts contemporains, Tourcoing, France, *La voix*; 1999, Fort Asperen, Netherlands, *Divine Comedy* (cat.); 1999, Von der Heydt Museum, Wuppertal, Germany, and Haus der Kunst, Munich, *Talk Show* (cat.); 1999, The Museum of Modern Art, New York, *The Museum as Muse: Artists Reflect* (cat.); 1999, Istanbul, 6th Biennale (cat.); 1999, Carnegie Museum of Art, Pittsburgh, *The Carnegie International*; 2000, Tate Modern, London; 2000, St. Louis Art Museum, St. Louis, Mo., *Wonderland*.

Tacita Dean

Born in Canterbury, England, 1965. Lives and works in London. Studied at Falmouth School of Art, Cornwall; Supreme School of Fine Art, Athens; and Slade School of Fine Art, London. Represented by Frith Street Gallery, London, and Marian Goodman Gallery, New York and Paris.

Solo Exhibitions

1994, Škuc Gallery, Ljubljana, Slovenia, and Umetnostna Gallery, Maribor, Slovenia, *The Martyrdom of St. Agatha and Other Stories*; 1995, Frith Street Gallery, London, *Clear Sky, Upper Air*; 1995, École nationale des beaux-arts, Bourges, France, *Galerie "La Box"* (cat.); 1996, Tate Gallery (Art Now), London, *Foley Artist* (cat.); 1997, Witte de With Center for Contemporary Art, Rotterdam (cat.); 1997, The Drawing Center, New York; 1997, Frith Street Gallery, London (cat.); 1998, Galerie Gebauer, Berlin; 1998, Frith Street Gallery, London; 1998, Basel, *Art Basel 98*; 1998, De Pont Foundation, Tilburg, Netherlands; 1998–1999, Institute of Contemporary Art, University of Pennsylvania, Philadelphia, and Madison Art Center, Madison, Wis. (cat.); 1999, Sadler's Wells, London; 1999, Marian Goodman Gallery, Paris; 1999, Cranbrook Art Museum, Bloomfield Hills, Mich.; 1999, Dundee Contemporary Arts, Dundee, Scotland, *The Sea, with a Ship: Afterwards an Island*; 1999, Newlyn Art Gallery, Penzance, Cornwall, *Banewl*; 1999, Millennium Dome, London, *Millennium Sculpture Project*; 2000, Marian Goodman Gallery, New York; 2000, Museum für Gegenwartskunst, Basel (cat.); 2000, Sala Montcada de la Fundació "la Caixa," Barcelona; 2000, Art Gallery of York University, Toronto; 2001, Tate Britain, London; 2001, Museu d'Art Contemporani de Barcelona, Barcelona.

Group Exhibitions

1992, Newlyn Orion Gallery, Penzance, Cornwall, Cornerhouse, Manchester, Orpheus Gallery, Belfast, Angel Row Gallery, Nottingham, and Bonnington Gallery, Nottingham, U.K., *BT New Contemporaries* (cat.); 1992, Institute of Contemporary Arts, London; 1993, Serpentine Gallery, London, *Barclays Young Artist Award* (cat.); 1993, Benjamin Rhodes Gallery, London, *Peripheral States* (cat.); 1994, Witte de With Center for Contemporary Art, Rotterdam, and Kunsthal, Rotterdam, *Watt* (cat.); 1994, 144 Charing Cross Road and the Agency, London, *Coming Up for Air*; 1994, Institute of Contemporary Arts, London, *Mise en scène* (cat.); 1995, Kampnagel, Hamburg, *Mysterium Alltag, Hammoniale der Frauen* (cat.); 1995, Casino Knokke, Knokke, Belgium, *Kine (kunst) '95*; 1995, Basel, *Video Forum, Art Basel 95*; 1995, London Electronic Arts and London Filmmakers' Co-op, London, *Speaking of Sofas*; 1995, Royal Festival Hall, London, *Whistling Women*; 1995, Ateliers d'artistes de la ville de Marseille, Marseilles, *Videos and Films by Artists*; 1995, Manchester, Edinburgh, and Cardiff, *British Art Show 4* (cat.); 1995, Cubitt Street Gallery, London; 1996, Centre for Contemporary Art, Glasgow, *CCATV*; 1996, Art Node Foundation, Stockholm; 1996, Centrum Beeldende Kunst, Rotterdam, *State of Mind*; 1996, International Festival of the Sea, Bristol, England, *Swinging the Lead* (cat.); 1996, Berwick upon Tweed, England, *Berwick Ramparts Project* (cat.); 1996, Copenhagen, *Container '96* (cat.); 1996, Galerie Paul Andriesse, Amsterdam, *Tacita Dean & Stephen Wilks*; 1996, Klemens Gasser & Tanja Grunert, Cologne, *Found Footage*; 1997, Rotterdam, *International Film Festival* (cat.); 1997, Science Museum, London, *Challenge of Materials*; 1997, Towner Art Gallery, Eastbourne, East Sussex, *A Case for a Collection*; 1997, Sandra Gering Gallery, New York, *Contemporary British Drawings: Marks & Traces*; 1997, Thread Waxing Space, New York, *Celluloid Cave*; 1997, Atheneum, Dijon, *Speaking of Sofas*; 1997, Museum für Gegenwartskunst, Zurich, *Flexible* (cat.); 1997, Museum van Hedendaagse Kunst, Limburg, Netherlands, *The Frame of Time: Openmuseum*; 1997, Sundance Institute, Park City, Utah, *Scriptwriters Lab*; 1997, Henry Moore Institute, Leeds, *At One Remove* (cat.); 1997, Marian Goodman Gallery, New York, *20:20*; 1997, Marian Goodman Gallery, Paris, *Social Space*; 1997, Kerlin Gallery, Dublin, *New Found Landscape*; 1998, Arnolfini Art Gallery, Bristol, Hatton Gallery, Newcastle upon Tyne, and Castle Museum, Nottingham, England, *Voiceover: Sound and Vision in Recent Art* (cat.); 1998, Moderna Museet, Stockholm, *Wounds: Between Democracy and Redemption in Contemporary Art* (cat.); 1998, The Approach

Gallery, London, *A–Z*; 1998, Frith Street Gallery, London, *Video/Projection/Film*; 1998, Musée départemental d'art contemporain de Rochechouart, Rochechouart, France, *La terre est ronde: Nouvelle narration*; 1998, FRAC Bretagne, Châteaugiron, France, *La mer n'est pas la terre*; 1998, Cambridge Darkroom, Cambridge, England, *Disrupting the Scene*; 1998, Marian Goodman Gallery, New York, *Breaking Ground*; 1998, Baden, Austria, *Felsenvilla*; 1998, Tate Gallery, London, *The Turner Prize* (cat.); 1999, Orchard Gallery, Derry, Ireland, *New Media Projects*; 1999, Le Credac, Ivry, France, *1264–1999: Une légende à suivre*; 1999, Frith Street Gallery, London, *Appliance of Science*; 1999, Granship, Shizuoka Convention and Arts Center, Shizuoka, Japan, *Hot Air*; 1999, Marian Goodman Gallery, Paris; 1999, Städtische Galerie im Lenbachhaus, Munich, *Geschichten des Augenblicks* (*Moments in Time*); 1999, Royal College of Art, London, *Go Away* (cat.); 1999, National Maritime Museum, London, *New Visions of the Sea*; 1999, Wexner Center for the Arts, Columbus, Ohio; 1999, Public Art Development Trust at the Royal National Theatre, London, *Fourth Wall*; 1999, Frith Street Gallery, London, *0 TO 60 IN 10 YEARS*; 1999, Antwerpen Open, Antwerp, *Laboratorium*; 1999, Fondation Cartier, Paris, *Un monde réel*; 1999, Dia Center for the Arts, New York, *Tacita Dean, Lee Ranaldo, Robert Smithson*; 2000, ACC Gallery, Weimar, Germany, *Landscape*; 2000, Beaver College Art Gallery, Philadelphia, *The Sea and the Sky*; 2000, Bologna, Italy, *L'ombra della ragione*; 2000, Yerba Buena Center for the Arts, San Francisco, *On the Edge of the Western World*; 2000, Winterthur, Switzerland, *Von Edgar Degas bis Gerhard Richter: Werke auf Papier aus der Sammlung des Kunstmuseums*; 2000, Konstmuseum, Konsthallen, Hasselblad Center, Gothenburg, Sweden, *Amateur/Liebhaber*; 2000, Kunstmuseum Luzern, Lucerne, Switzerland, *Mixing Memory and Desire*; 2000, Deste Foundation, Athens, *Artifice*; 2000, Royal Hibernian Academy, Dublin, *The Sea and the Sky*; 2000, Tate Gallery, London, *New British Art 2000: Intelligence*; 2000, Project Art Centre, Dublin, *Somewhere near Vada*; 2000, Seoul, *Media City*; 2000, Montreal, *La biennale de Montréal*; 2000, Louisiana Museum of Modern Art, Humlebaek, Denmark, *Vision and Reality*.

Liz Magor

Born in Winnipeg, 1948. Lives and works in Vancouver. Studied at University of British Columbia, Vancouver; Parson's School of Design, New York; and Vancouver School of Art, Vancouver. Represented by Equinox Gallery, Vancouver, and Susan Hobbs Gallery, Toronto.

Solo Exhibitions

1977, Art Gallery of Greater Victoria, Victoria, B.C.; 1979, Art Gallery of Greater Victoria, Victoria, B.C.; 1979, Fine Arts Gallery, University of British Columbia, Vancouver; 1979, Southern Alberta Art Gallery, Lethbridge, Alta.; 1980, Vancouver Art Gallery, Vancouver, *Production/Reproduction* (cat.); 1980, Ydessa Gallery, Toronto; 1981, Alberta College of Art, Calgary (cat.); 1981, Ydessa Gallery, Toronto; 1982, Ydessa Gallery, Toronto; 1984, Canada House, London; 1984, Ydessa Gallery, Toronto; 1986, Ydessa Gallery, Toronto; 1986, Art Gallery of Ontario, Toronto (cat.); 1987, Musée d'art contemporain de Montréal, Montreal; 1987, Winnipeg Art Gallery, Winnipeg; 1987, Mendel Art Gallery, Saskatoon, Sask.; 1991, Edmonton Art Gallery, Edmonton, *Constructing Cultural Identity*; 1993, Susan Hobbs Gallery, Toronto; 1993, Oakville Galleries, Oakville, Ont.; 1993, La Chambre Blanche, Quebec City; 1994, Susan Hobbs Gallery, Toronto; 1996, Susan Hobbs Gallery, Toronto; 1996, Toronto Sculpture Garden, Toronto, *Messenger*; 1998, Susan Hobbs Gallery, Toronto; 1999, Equinox Gallery, Vancouver, *Sleeping Rough*; 2000, Contemporary Art Gallery, Vancouver, *Stores*; 2000, Art Gallery of York University, Toronto, *Deep Woods* (cat.); 2000, Susan Hobbs Gallery, Toronto.

Group Exhibitions

1973, Vancouver Art Gallery, Vancouver, *Pacific Vibrations*; 1973, Burnaby Art Gallery, Burnaby, B.C., *Process Editions*; 1973, Burnaby Art Gallery, Burnaby, B.C., *Stand Back You Fools*; 1974, Art Gallery of Greater Victoria, Victoria, B.C., *Librations*; 1975, London Regional Art Gallery, London, Ont., *Young Contemporaries '75*; 1975, Saidye Bronfman Centre, Montreal, *Current Energies*; 1976,

Winnipeg Art Gallery, Winnipeg, *West Coast Waves*; 1977, Fine Arts Gallery, University of British Columbia, Vancouver, *For the Birds*; 1977, Vancouver Art Gallery, Vancouver, *Four Places*; 1978, MacKenzie Art Gallery, Regina, Sask., *Obsessions, Rituals, Controls*; 1978, Saidye Bronfman Centre, Montreal, *Canadian Contemporary Sculpture*; 1981, Winnipeg Art Gallery, Winnipeg, *The Winnipeg Perspective 1981* (cat.); 1982, Vancouver Art Gallery, Vancouver, *Vancouver: Art and Artists 1931–1983*; 1982, Art Gallery of New South Wales, Sydney, 4th Biennale; 1982, Vancouver Art Gallery, Vancouver, *Mise en Scène* (cat.); 1983, Glendon Gallery, Toronto, *Repositioning the Familiar* (cat.); 1983, Glenbow Museum, Calgary, *1×2: Liz Magor and John McEwen* (cat.); 1984, Venice, XLI Biennale, *Ian Carr-Harris/Liz Magor* (cat.); 1985, Winnipeg Art Gallery, Winnipeg, *Recent Canadian Sculpture*; 1985, Centre international d'art contemporain de Montréal, Montreal, *Aurora Borealis* (cat.); 1985, Ydessa Gallery, Toronto; 1986, Rheinhallen Messegelände (Internationaler Kunstmarkt), Cologne, *Focus: Kanadische Kunst von 1960–1985* (cat.); 1986, Contemporary Art Gallery, Vancouver, *Ten Years Later*; 1987, Orangerie, Kassel, Germany, *Documenta 8*; 1987, The Power Plant, Toronto, *Active Surplus: The Economy of the Object* (cat.); 1987, The Power Plant, Toronto, *Toronto: A Play of History*; 1989, Centre international d'art contemporain de Montréal, Montreal, *Les cents jours d'art contemporain*; 1989, Grace Hopper, Toronto, *Inaugural Exhibition*; 1989, Walter Phillips Gallery, Banff, Alta., *Camera Lucida* (cat.); 1989, National Gallery of Canada, Ottawa, *Canadian Biennial of Contemporary Art* (cat.); 1990, Vancouver Art Gallery, Vancouver, Nickle Arts Museum, Calgary, and Art Gallery of York University, Toronto, *Meeting Place: Robert Gober, Liz Magor, Juan Muñoz* (cat.); 1990, YYZ, Toronto, *Salvage Paradigm*; 1991, Spoleto Festival, Charleston, S.C., *Places with a Past: Site Specific Art in Charleston* (cat.); 1991, Walter Phillips Gallery, Banff, Alta., *Between Views and Points of View*; 1992, The Museum of Modern Art, New York, *More than One Photography*; 1992, Musée d'art contemporain de Montréal, Montreal, *Pour la suite du monde* (cat.); 1993, FRAC Pays-de-la-Loire, Clisson, France, and Musée des beaux-arts, FRAC Franche-Comté, Dole, France, *Canada, une nouvelle génération* (cat.); 1994, Southern Alberta Art Gallery, Lethbridge, Alta., *Small Histories*; 1995, Enschede, Netherlands, Foto Biennale, *From Wunderkammer to Cyberspace*; 1995, Fort York, Toronto, *Stone Powder Fort York*; 1995, Stedelijk Museum, Amsterdam, *Notion of Conflict: A Selection of Contemporary Canadian Art*; 1996, Museum of Contemporary Art, Sydney, *Real Fictions: Four Canadian Artists*; 1997, San Diego–Tijuana, *InSITE*; 1997, Museum of Fine Arts, Florida State University, Tallahassee, *The Gun as Image*; 1998, McMaster Museum of Art, Hamilton, Ont., *Points of View*; 1999, Edmonton Art Gallery, Edmonton, *Model Homes: Explorations on Alternate Living*; 2000, Oakville Galleries, Oakville, Ont., *Beaver Tales*; 2000, Diefenbunker, Carp, Ont., *Singular FISSION*.

Shahzia Sikander

Born in Lahore, Pakistan, 1969. Lives and works in New York. Studied at National College of Arts, Lahore, Pakistan, B.F.A., 1992; Rhode Island School of Design, Providence, R.I., M.F.A., 1995. Represented by Deitch Projects, New York.

Solo Exhibitions

1993, Embassy of Pakistan, Washington, D.C.; 1994, Sol Koffler Gallery, RISD, Providence, R.I., *Veil: In Their Minds and on Our Heads*; 1996, Project Row Houses, Houston, *Knock Knock, Who's There? Mithilia, Mithilia Who?*; 1997, Hosfelt Gallery, San Francisco, *A Kind of Slight and Pleasing Dislocation*; 1997, Deitch Projects, New York, *Miniatures and Murals*; 1998, The Renaissance Society, University of Chicago (cat.); 1998–1999, Kemper Museum of Contemporary Art and Design, Kansas City, Mo. (cat.); 2000, Hirshhorn Museum and Sculpture Garden, Washington, D.C. (cat.); 2000, Whitney Museum of American Art, Philip Morris Branch, New York, *Acts of Balance* (cat.).

Group Exhibitions

1992, Rhotas Gallery, Islamabad, Pakistan, *New Artists, Recent Works*; 1994, Pacific Asia Museum, Pasadena, Calif., *A Selection of Contemporary Paintings from Pakistan* (cat.); 1994–1995, Bradford City Museum, Bradford, England, *An Intelligent Rebel-*

lion: Women Artists of Pakistan (cat.); 1996, Sarah Campbell Blaffer Gallery, University of Houston, Houston, *1996 Houston Area Exhibition*; 1996, Glassell School of Art, Museum of Fine Arts, Houston, *Core 1996 Exhibition* (cat.); 1997, Laing Art Gallery, Newcastle upon Tyne, England, *Eastern Edge*; 1997, Glassell School of Art, Museum of Fine Arts, Houston, *Core 1997 Exhibition* (cat.); 1997, The Drawing Center, New York, *Selections Spring '97*; 1997, Whitney Museum of American Art, New York, *Biennial Exhibition* (cat.); 1997, Caldas da Rainha, Portugal, Biennale; 1997, Lehman Maupin Gallery, New York, *Project Painting* (cat.); 1997, Johannesburg, Biennale, *Transversions*; 1997, Yerba Buena Center for the Arts, San Francisco, *Three Great Walls*; 1997, Queens Museum of Art, Flushing Meadows, N.Y., *Out of India* (cat.); 1998, Forum for Contemporary Art, St. Louis, Mo., *On the Wall* (cat.); 1998, Center for Curatorial Studies, Bard College, Annandale-on-Hudson, N.Y., *Liberating Tradition*; 1998, Ludwig Museum, Cologne, *I Love New York*; 1998, Deste Foundation, Athens, *Global Vision: New Art from the 90's—Part 2* (cat.); 1998, Aldrich Museum of Contemporary Art, Ridgefield, Conn., *Pop Surrealism*; 1998–1999, Thomas Healy Gallery, New York, *Hedge: Between Time and Intent*; 1998–1999, Museo de la Ciudad de México, Mexico City, *Cinco Continentes y una ciudad* (cat.); 1999, Blanton Museum of Art, Austin, Tex., *Negotiating Small Truths* (cat.); 1999, Ludwig Museum, Cologne, *Art-Worlds in Dialogue* (cat.); 1999, Queensland Art Gallery, Brisbane, Australia, *Third Asia-Pacific Triennial of Contemporary Art* (cat.); 1999, Whitney Museum of American Art, New York, *The American Century* (cat.); 2000, P.S.1, Long Island City, N.Y. *Greater New York*; 2000, Barbara Gladstone Gallery, New York, *00* (cat.).

Valeska Soares

Born in Belo Horizonte, Minas Gerais, Brazil. Lives and works in Brooklyn, New York. Studied architecture at Universidade Santa Ursula, Brazil, B.A.; Pontifícia Universidade Católica, Rio de Janeiro, post-graduate studies in art and architecture history; Pratt University, New York, M.F.A.; School of Education, New York University, New York, candidate for Doctor of Arts. Represented by Galeria Camargo Vilaça, São Paulo, and LiebmanMagnan, New York.

Solo Exhibitions

1991, Centro Cultural Sérgio Porto, Rioarte, Rio de Janeiro (cat.); 1992, Centro Cultural São Paulo, São Paulo; 1994, Information Gallery, New York (cat.); 1994, Galeria Camargo Vilaça, São Paulo (cat.); 1995, New Museum of Contemporary Art, New York, *Discontinuous Teasers*; 1996, Christopher Grimes Gallery, Santa Monica, Calif.; 1996, Laumeiar Sculpture Park, Saint Louis, Mo., Galeria Camargo Vilaça, São Paulo, *Strangelove* (cat.); 1997, Galeria Luis Adelantado, Valencia, Spain, *Personagens*; 1998, Public Art Fund, New York, *Histórias*; 1998, Portland Institute of Contemporary Art, Portland, Oreg., *Vanity*; 1998, Christopher Grimes Gallery, Santa Monica, Calif.; 1998, Galeria Camargo Vilaça, São Paulo, *Vanishing Point* (cat.); 1999, Galerie Papillon-Fiat, Paris; 1999, Paço Imperial, Rio de Janeiro, *Projeto Finep*; 1999, Museum of Contemporary Art, San Diego.

Group Exhibitions

1988, Museu de Arte Moderna, Belo Horizonte, XX Salão Nacional de Artes Plásticas; 1989, Funarte, Rio de Janeiro, XI Salão Nacional (cat.); 1990, Fundição Progresso, Rio de Janeiro, *Arqueos*; 1990, Solar Grandjean de Montigny, Rio de Janeiro, *Possível Imagem*; 1990, São Paulo, VII Salão Paulista de Arte Contemporânea; 1991, Parque Lage, Rio de Janeiro, Salão Carioca de Artes Plásticas; 1991, Pavilhão da Fundação Bienal, São Paulo, *Programa de Exposições 91: Centro Cultural São Paulo*; 1991, Museu Municipal de Arte, Curitiba, Brazil, *80/90 Formas Tridimensionais: A Questão Orgânica*; 1991, Funarte, Rio de Janeiro, *EAV Processo no. 738.765-2*; 1991, Museu de Arte Moderna, Rio de Janeiro, *7XAR* (cat.); 1991, Museu de Arte Moderna, São Paulo, *Panorama*; 1991, Galeria Casa Triângulo, São Paulo; 1991, Havana, IV Bienal de la Habana (cat.); 1991, Espaço Cultural Sérgio Porto, Rio de Janeiro, *Imagem sobre Imagem* (cat.); 1992, Paço das Artes, São Paulo, *Polaridades e Perspectivas* (cat.); 1992, Galeria Camargo Vilaça, São Paulo; 1993, MAC-USP, São Paulo, *A Presença do Ready-Made 80 Anos*; 1993, Stux Gallery, New York, *Lingua Latina Regina Est*;

1993, Valenzuela Klenner Galeria, Bogotá, *Brasil Hoy* (cat.); 1993–1994, Mitchell Museum, Mount Vernon, Ill., Table Arts Center, Eastern Illinois University, Charleston, Ill., and University Museum, Southern Illinois University, Carbondale, Ill., *International Critic's Choice* (cat.); 1993, Bronx Museum, New York, *Artists in the Marketplace* (cat.); 1993, Sidney Mishkin Gallery, New York, *ABC: Contemporary Art from Argentina, Brazil and Colombia* (cat.); 1994, Paço Imperial, Rio de Janeiro, *Escultura Carioca* (cat.); 1994, Museu de Arte Moderna, São Paulo, *Espelhos e Sombras* (cat.); 1994, Centro Cultural São Paulo, São Paulo, *Fotografia Contaminada* (cat.); 1994, Information Gallery, New York, *Perceptions* (cat.); 1994, São Paulo, XXII Bienal Internacional (cat.); 1995, Palazzo Pamphili, Roma, *L'Educazione dei Cinque Sensi*; 1995, Galeria da Universidade Federal Fluminense, Niterói, Brazil, *Brasil na Bienal*; 1995, Centro Cultural Banco do Brasil, Rio de Janeiro, *Espelhos e Sombras* (cat.); 1995, Site Santa Fe, Santa Fe, N. Mex., *Longing and Belonging* (cat.); 1995, White Columns, New York, *The Education of the Five Senses*; 1995, Haus der Kulturen der Welt, Berlin, *Havana–São Paulo: Junge Kunst aus Lateinamerika* (cat.); 1995, Stark Gallery, New York, *Dark Room*; 1996, Paço Imperial, Rio de Janeiro; 1996, Museu de Arte Moderna, Rio de Janeiro, *Transparencias* (cat.); 1996, Paço Imperial, Rio de Janeiro, and Centro Cultural Alumni, São Paulo, *Pequenas Mãos*; 1996, Galeria Camargo Vilaça, São Paulo, *Camargo Vilaça Bis*; 1996, Rhona Hoffman Gallery, Chicago, *Visions*; 1996, Christopher Grimes Gallery, Santa Monica, Calif., *The Tailor's Dummy*; 1996, Hospício de Las Cabanas, Guadalajara, Mexico, *To Live Is to Leave Traces* (cat.); 1996, Galleria Marabini, Bologna, Italy, *Collective Soul* (cat.); 1996, Galeria Luis Serpa, Lisbon, *6 Women in Red* (cat.); 1997, Knoedler & Company, New York, *Art Foundry Editions Santa Fe at Knoedler New York*; 1997, Johannesburg, Biennale, *Life's Little Necessities* (cat.); 1997, Centro Cultural de Arte Contemporaneo, Mexico City, *Esto Es: Arte Objeto e Instalación de Iberoamérica* (cat.); 1997, Royal College of Art, London, *You Are Here* (cat.); 1998, Museu de Arte Moderna, Rio de Janeiro, and Haus der Kulturen der Welt, Berlin, *Anos 90: Coleção Gilberto Chateaubriand* (cat.); 1998, São Paulo, XXIV Bienal Internacional (cat.); 1998, Centro Cultural Itau, São Paulo, *Fronteiras*; 1998–2000, Track 16 Gallery, Santa Monica, Calif., Christopher Grimes Gallery, Santa Monica, Calif., Contemporary Arts Center, Cincinnati, Biblioteca Luis Arango, Bogotá, and Contemporary Art Museum, University of South Florida, Tampa, *Amnesia* (cat.); 1998, Museo de Bellas Artes, Caracas, *Desde el Cuerpo: Alegorias de lo Feminino*; 1999, Rena Bransten Gallery, San Francisco, *Not There*; 1999, Centro Cultural Mar del Plata, Mar del Plata, Argentina, *La Metamorfose de Las Manos*; 1999, Centro Cultural Banco do Brasil, Rio de Janeiro and Gota, Brazil, *Ums e Outros*; 1999, Casa de America, Madrid, *A Vuelta com los Sentidos* (cat.); 1999, Bronx Museum, New York (cat.); 1999, Institut de Cultura, Barcelona, *Double Vidas* (cat.); 2000, P.S.1, Long Island City, N.Y., *Greater New York*; 2000, Bronx Museum, New York, *Good Business Is the Best Art*; 2000–2001, Museum of Contemporary Art, San Diego, and Modern Art Museum of Fort Worth, Fort Worth, Tex., *Ultrabaroque: Aspects of Post-Latin American Art* (cat.); 2000, San Diego–Tijuana, *InSITE 2000*; 2001, Museo Nacional Centro de Arte Reina Sofia, Madrid, *Ficcoenes*.

Jana Sterbak

Born in Prague, 1955. Lives and works in Montreal and Barcelona. Studied at Concordia University, Montreal, B.F.A., 1975. Represented by Galeria Toni Tàpies, Barcelona.

Solo Exhibitions

1978, Pumps Art, Vancouver; 1980, YYZ, Toronto; 1980, Galerie Optica, Montreal, *Travaux récents*; 1981, Main Exit, Vancouver, *How Things Stand Up*; 1982, Mercer Union, Toronto, *Golem: Objects as Sensations*; 1985, Ydessa Gallery, Toronto; 1987, Ydessa Gallery, Toronto; 1987, Galerie René Blouin, Montreal; 1988, The Power Plant, Toronto (cat.); 1989, The Western Front, Vancouver; 1989, MacKenzie Art Gallery, Regina, Sask. (cat.); 1989, Galerie René Blouin, Montreal; 1990, Donald Young Gallery, Chicago; 1990, New Museum of Contemporary Art, New York (cat.); 1991, Galerie René Blouin, Montreal, *Sisyphe II*; 1991–1992, National Gallery of Canada, Ottawa, List Visual

Arts Centre, Cambridge, Ont., Contemporary Arts Center, Cincinnati, Nickle Arts Museum, Calgary, and San Diego Museum of Contemporary Art, San Diego, *States of Being* (cat.); 1992, The Museum of Modern Art, New York, *Project Room* (cat.); 1992, Galerie Croussel-Robelin/BAMA, Paris; 1993, Louisiana Museum of Modern Art, Humlebaek, Denmark (cat.); 1993, Fundació "la Caixa," Barcelona, *I Want You to Feel the Way I Do* (cat.); 1993, Galerie René Blouin, Montreal, *Lénine rétréci*; 1994, Musée des beaux-arts de Nantes, Nantes, France, *Déclaration* (cat.); 1994, Musée d'art contemporain de Montréal, Montreal, *Déclaration* (cat.); 1995, Donald Young Gallery, Seattle; 1995–1996, Musée d'art moderne de Saint-Étienne, Saint-Étienne, France, Fundació Antoni Tàpies, Barcelona, and Serpentine Gallery, London, *VELLEITAS* (cat.); 1996, Donald Young Gallery, Seattle, *New Photoworks*; 1996, Galerie René Blouin, Montreal, *Trichotilomania III*; 1997, David Winton Bell Gallery, Brown University, Providence, R.I., *Metamorphosis* (cat.); 1998, Museum of Contemporary Art, Chicago; 1998, Galerie René Blouin, Montreal; 1998, Galeria Toni Tàpies, Edicions T, Barcelona; 1999, Fabric Workshop and Museum, Philadelphia; 2000, Centro Cultural de la Fundació "la Caixa" de Lleida, Lleida, Spain, *Direccions*; 2000, Galerie Erna Hécey, Luxembourg; 2000, Galerie Barbara Gross, Munich; 2000, Canadian Embassy and the LOFT, Beijing, *Drawings*; 2001, Konsthall, Malmö, Sweden.

Group Exhibitions

1978, Galerie Optica, Montreal, *5 Artists*; 1979, Powerhouse, Montreal, *Bookworks*; 1981, The New YYZ, Toronto; 1982, Simpson Gallery, Toronto, *Four Artists*; 1982, Musée d'art contemporain de Montréal, Montreal, *Menues manoeuvres* (cat.); 1982, YYZ, Toronto, *Monumenta*; 1982, Galerie France Morin, Montreal, *Photos by Artists*; 1983, San Diego University Gallery, San Diego, *Small Works*; 1983, Pomona University Gallery, Pomona, Calif., *Small Works*; 1983, International Exposure, Toronto, *Unaffiliated Artists*; 1984, 49th Parallel, New York, *Canada/New York* (cat.); 1984, YYZ, Toronto, *Influencing Machines* (cat.); 1984, 49th Parallel, New York, *Canadian Paintings and Sculptures: Works Selected by David Rabinowich*; 1985, Glendon Gallery, Toronto, *Ida Applebroog and Jana Sterbak* (cat.); 1985, Michael Katz Gallery, New York, *Anadromous*; 1986, Southern Alberta Art Gallery, Lethbridge, Alta., *Postmarked New York* (cat.); 1986, Musée d'art contemporain de Montréal, Montreal, *Sept sculpteurs canadiens*; 1986, The 49th Parallel, New York, and Nexus Gallery of Contemporary Art, Atlanta, *Jana Sterbak/Krzysztof Wodiczko* (cat.); 1986, National Gallery of Canada, Ottawa, *Songs of Experience* (cat.); 1986, Galerie René Blouin, Montreal, *Oeuvres ex-centrées*; 1987, 56 Bleeker Gallery, New York, *Subject/Object*; 1988, The Power Plant, Toronto, *Enchantment & Disturbance* (cat.); 1988, Dia Art Foundation, New York, *Group Material*; 1988, Winnipeg Art Gallery, Winnipeg, *Identity, Identities* (cat.); 1988, Winnipeg Art Gallery, Winnipeg, and Vancouver Art Gallery, Vancouver, *Impossible Self* (cat.); 1989, Artists Space, New York, *Dark Rooms* (cat.); 1989, National Gallery of Canada, Ottawa, *Canadian Biennial of Contemporary Art* (cat.); 1990, Art Gallery of York University, Toronto, *Diagnosis* (cat.); 1990, Venice, Biennale, *Aperto '90* (cat.); 1990, Museum of Fine Arts, Boston, *Figuring the Body*; 1990, Galerie René Blouin, Montreal; 1990, Derry, Glasgow, Newcastle upon Tyne, and Plymouth, U.K., *New Works for Different Places: TSWA Four Cities Project* (cat.); 1990, Donald Young Gallery, Chicago; 1990, Centre international d'art contemporain de Montréal, Montreal, and Vancouver Art Gallery, Vancouver, *Goya to Beijing*; 1991, Galerie Crousel-Robelin/BAMA, Paris, *Vanitas*; 1991, Glenbow Museum, Calgary, *The Embodied Viewer* (cat.); 1991, Axe Néo-7, Hull, Que., *En hommage à un cadeau d'Eva Hesse à Sol Lewitt*; 1991, Donald Young Gallery, Chicago; 1991, Ikon Gallery, Birmingham, *With this ring...* (cat.); 1991, Musée du Québec, Quebec City, *Un archipel de désirs: Les artistes du Québec et la scène internationale* (cat.); 1991, Galerie Crousel-Robelin/BAMA, Paris, *Interiors*; 1991, Barbican Art Gallery, London, *Un-Natural Traces: Contemporary Art from Canada* (cat.); 1991, Centre for Contemporary Art, Ujazdowski Castle, Warsaw, *The Wealth of Nations* (cat.); 1992, Betty Rymer Gallery, Chicago, and Donald Young Gallery, Seattle, *Power Play* (cat.); 1992, Saarbrucken, Germany, *Internationale Künstlerplakate* (cat.); 1992, P.P.O.W., New York, *Between the Sheets*; 1992, Marian Goodman Gallery, New York; 1992, Istanbul, 3rd Biennale; 1992, Galerie nationale du

Jeu de Paume, Paris, *GÉNÉRIQUE I: DÉSORDRES* (cat.); 1993, Louisiana/Museum of Modern Art, Humlebaek, Denmark, *At the Edge of Chaos: New Images of the World*; 1993, Galerie Barbara Weiss, Berlin,... *Just to Name a Few*; 1993, FRAC Pays-de-la-Loire, Clisson, France, and Musée des beaux-arts, FRAC Franche-Comté, Dole, France, *Canada, une nouvelle génération* (cat.); 1993, Munich, *Ordnung und Zerstörung* (cat.); 1993, Tate Gallery Liverpool, Liverpool, *Elective Affinities* (cat.); 1993, Centre d'art contemporain du domaine de Kerguéhennec, Locminé, France, *De la main à la tête, l'objet théorique*; 1993, Americas Society, New York, and Center for the Fine Arts, Miami, *Space of Time: Contemporary Art from the Americas* (cat.); 1993, Bonner Kunstverein, Bonn, *Über Leben* (cat.); 1994, Galerie René Blouin, Montreal, *Séduction*; 1994, O'Vertigo, Montreal, *Scénographie-danse*, with Javier Pérez; 1994, Walker Art Center, Minneapolis; 1994, Musée des beaux-arts d'Agen, Agen, France,... *Ou les oiseaux selon Schopenhauer*; 1994, Donald Young Gallery, Seattle; 1994, Centre Georges Pompidou, Musée national d'art moderne, Paris, *Hors limite* (cat.); 1994, Galerie Chantal Crousel, Paris, *Trans*; 1994, Montclair Art Museum, Montclair, N.J.; 1994, Kröller-Müller Museum, Otterlo, Netherlands, *Heart of Darkness*; 1994, Beaver College Art Gallery, Glenside, Pa., *Social Fabric*; 1995, Setagaya Art Museum, Tokyo, National Museum of Modern Art, Kyoto, and Hokkaido Museum of Modern Art, Sapporo, *Spirits on the Crossing: Travellers to/from Nowhere — Contemporary Art in Canada 1980–94* (cat.); 1995, Theater Am Turm, Frankfurt, *Bildende Künstler im TAT, Phase 1*; 1995, Swiss Institute, New York, *Chocolate!*; 1995, Zerynthia, Serre di Rapolano, Tuscany, *Images in Perspectives*; 1995, Musée d'art contemporain de Montréal, Montreal, *Premiers dons 1964–1965 et Dons 1989–1994*; 1995, Kanaal Art Foundation, Kortrijk, Belgium, *Inside the Visible*; 1995, Tate Gallery, London, *Rites of Passage* (cat.); 1995, Knokke Video Festival, Knokke, Belgium; 1995, Musée d'art de Joliette, Joliette, Que., *Traces de la danse*; 1995, Thaddaeus Ropac Gallery, Salzburg, Austria, *Die Muse?*; 1995, Angles Gallery, Santa Monica, Calif.; 1995, Institute of Contemporary Art, Philadelphia, *PerForms: Janine Antoni, Charles Ray, Jana Sterbak* (cat.); 1995, Kwangju, Korea, Biennale, *Beyond the Borders* (cat.); 1995, Galerie Thaddaeus Ropac, Paris, *Muse?*; 1995, Centre Georges Pompidou, Musée national d'art moderne, Paris, *Féminin-Masculin, le sexe de l'art* (cat.); 1995, Padua, Italy, Biennale, *Picola Scultura*; 1995, Arteleku, San Sebastian, Spain, *Colisiones-Collisions*; 1996, Institute of Contemporary Art, Boston, and Whitechapel Art Gallery, London, *Inside the Visible* (cat.); 1996, Österreichisches Museum für angewandte Kunst, Vienna, *Mässig und Gefrässig* (cat.); 1996, Musée départemental d'art contemporain de Rochechouart, Rochechouart, France, *Collection/Parcours*; 1996, MAC, Galeries contemporaines des musées de Marseille, Marseilles, *L'Art au corps* (cat.); 1996, Louisiana Museum of Modern Art, Humlebaek, Denmark, *NowHere*; 1996, Independant Curators Incorporated, New York, *Embedded Metaphor*; 1996, Florence, Biennale, *Il tempo e la moda* (cat.); 1996, Musée d'art contemporain de Montréal, Montreal, *L'oeil du collectionneur* (cat.); 1996, National Gallery of Canada, Ottawa, *Odd Bodies*; 1997–1998, Arizona State University Art Museum, Tempe, Ariz., and Cranbrook Art Museum, Bloomfield Hills, Mich., *Art on the Edge for Fashion*; 1997, Art Gallery of Western Australia, Perth, *Inside the Visible*; 1997, Museu d'Art Contemporani de Barcelona, Barcelona, *Introvertions*; 1997, Montreal Museum of Fine Arts, Montreal, *Body in the Lens*; 1997, Guggenheim Museum SoHo, New York, *Art/Fashion* (cat.); 1997, Villa de Noailles, Hyères, France, *Le songe de Constantin*; 1997, Tochigi Prefectural Museum of Fine Arts, Tochigi, Japan, *Floating Images of Women in Art History* (cat.); 1997, Institute of Contemporary Art, Portland, Maine, *The Quiet in the Land*; 1997–1998, Plimsoll Gallery, University of Tasmania, Hobart, Australia, Australian Centre for Contemporary Art, Melbourne, Brisbane City Gallery, Brisbane, Auckland Art Gallery, Auckland, New Zealand, and John Curtin Gallery, Curtin University of Technology, Perth, Australia, *Love Hotel* (cat.), organized by the National Gallery of Australia; 1997, Palazzo delle Albere, Trento, Italy, *Trash: Quando i rifiuti diventano arte*; 1997, Istanbul, 5th Biennale (cat.); 1997, Leonard & Bina Ellen Art Gallery, Concordia University, Montreal, *Five Years of Collecting*; 1998, Museo de Bellas Artes, Caracas, Venezuela, *Desde el Cuerpo: Alegorias de lo Femenino*; 1998, Mitsubishi-jisho Atrium/Nishinippon,

Fukuoka, Japan, *The Secret Life of Clothes* (cat.); 1998, Palazzo Branciforte, Palermo, Italy, *Disidentico: Maschile femminile e altro* (cat.); 1998, Thread Waxing Space, New York, and Museum of Contemporary Art, North Miami, *Spectacular Optical* (cat.); 1998, Institute of Contemporary Art, Boston, *The Quiet in the Land*; 1998, Galerie Chantal Crousel, Paris, *Oeuvres récentes*; 1998, National Gallery of Canada, Ottawa, *Crossings* (cat.); 1998–1999, Hayward Gallery, London, and Kunstmuseum Wolfsburg, Wolfsburg, Germany, *Addressing the Century*; 1999, PAC, Milan, *Rosso Vivo* (cat.); 1999, Fabric Workshop and Museum, Philadelphia, *As Above, So Below: The Body at Work*; 1999, Galeria Palma Dotze, Vilafranca del Penedès, Barcelona, *Denuncias*; 1999, Passage de Retz, Paris, and Centre d'Art Santa Mònica, Barcelona, *Espaces intérieurs: Artistes contemporains du Québec/El cos, la llengua, les paraules, la pell* (cat.); 1999, Israel Museum, Jerusalem, *Skin-deep* (cat.); 1999, ATA Center for Contemporary Art, Sofia, Bulgaria, *Un certain art de vivre*; 1999, National Museum of Modern Art, Kyoto, and Museum of Contemporary Art, Tokyo, *Visions of the Body: Fashion or Invisible Corset* (cat.); 1999, Institut de Cultura de Barcelona, Barcelona, *Dobles Vides*; 1999, Leonard & Bina Ellen Art Gallery, Concordia University, Montreal, *Redefining the Still Life*; 2000, Food Pavilion, Universal Exhibition, Hannover, Germany, *Egg DreemMuseum*; 2000, Diefenbunker, Carp, Ont., *Singular FISSION*; 2000, Museo Pablo Serrano, Zaragoza, Spain, *Luis Bunuel: Los enigmas de un sueno*; 2000, Galerie Erna Hécey, Luxembourg; 2000, Galerie du TNB, Rennes, France, *Ici on peut toucher*, in collaboration with FRAC Bretagne; 2000, Oakville Galleries, Oakville, Ont., and Nickle Arts Museum, Calgary, *Odd Bodies* (cat.), organized by the National Gallery of Canada, Ottawa; 2000, Manès Gallery, Prague, *TRANSGLOBE*; 2000, Kunstverein, Munich, *Die verletzte Diva*; 2000, Walker Art Center, Minneapolis, and Harward Film Archive, Boston, *Magnetic North*; 2000, ARKEN Museum for Moderne Kunst, Copenhagen, *MAN—Body in Art from 1950 to 2000*; 2001, National Gallery of Canada, Ottawa, *Condition* (video installation); 2001, Galerie de l'Université du Québec à Montréal, Montreal, *Nancy Spero, Jana Sterbak*; 2001, Museum of American Folk Art, New York, *The Quiet in the Land*.

Yoshihiro Suda

Born in Yamanashi, Japan, 1969. Lives and works in Tokyo. Studied at Tama Art University, Hachioji, Tokyo, B.F.A., 1992. Represented by Galerie René Blouin, Montreal, and Gallery Koyanagi, Tokyo.

Solo Exhibitions

1993, 1st to 4th blocks, Ginza District, Tokyo, *Ginza Weed Theory*; 1994, Daiwa Parking Area, Tokyo, *Tokyo Installation*; 1995, Gallery K, Tokyo, *Tokyo Installation 2*; 1996, Gallery 360, Tokyo, *Tokyo Installation 2 2/3*, 1996, Gallery K, Tokyo, *Tokyo Installation 3*; 1997, Gallery Koyanagi, Tokyo; 1997, Galerie Wohnmaschine, Berlin; 1998, Caisse des Dépôts et Consignations, Paris; 1999, Hara Museum of Contemporary Art, Tokyo, *Hara Document 6: Tree of Calm Mountain*; 1999, Galerie Wohnmaschine, Berlin; 1999, Gallery Koyanagi, Tokyo, *Ma*; 2000, CN Gallery, Osaka; 2000, D'Amelio Terras Gallery, New York; 2000, Galerie René Blouin, Montreal; 2000, Gallery Koyanagi, Tokyo (cat.); 2001, Entwistle Gallery, London.

Group Exhibitions

1996, Galeria Rasen, Tokyo, *Flowers for Mururoa Project*; 1996, Sakura City Art Museum, Chiba, Japan, *Art Now 96: Artificial Paradise* (cat.); 1997, Tama Art University Gallery, Hachioji, Tokyo, *Tama Vivant 97*; 1997, Mitaka City Arts Foundation, Tokyo, *The Secret Garden*; 1997, Gallery 360, Tokyo, *Geijutsu to Keizai* (*Art and Economy*); 1997, D'Amelio Terras Gallery, New York, *Spaces Between*; 1997, D'Amelio Terras Gallery, New York, *Two Men Show with Luca Pancrazzi*; 1998, Taipei Fine Arts Museum, Taipei, Biennale, *Site of Desire* (cat.); 1998, Sydney, 11th Biennale, *Everyday* (cat.); 1998, Galerie Michael Zink, Regensburg, Germany, *Little Creatures*; 1998, Art Gallery of New South Wales, Sydney, and Museum of Contemporary Art, Sydney; 1998, École nationale supérieure des beaux-arts, Paris, *Donai-Yanen! Et maintenant!* (cat.); 1998–1999, Meguro Museum of Art, Tokyo, National Museum of Art, Osaka, and Korean Culture and Art Foundation, Seoul, *Between the Unknown Straits: Art Now in Japan and Korea* (cat.); 1999, Mattress Factory, Pittsburgh, *Installations by*

Asian Artists; 1999, Gallery TAF, Kyoto; 2000, Toyota City Museum, Nagoya, *Vacant Space* (cat.); 2000, Serpentine Gallery, London, *Greenhouse Effect* (cat.); 2000, Kunsthalle, Baden-Baden, and Haus am Waldsee, Berlin, *Yome no Alto* (cat.); 2000, Basel, *Art 31 Basel* (cat.); 2000, Montreal, *La biennale de Montréal*; 2000, Centre for Contemporary Art, Ujazdowski Castle, Warsaw, *Japanese Contemporary Art: Between Body and Space* (cat.); 2001, Museum of Contemporary Art, Miami; 2001, Hayward Gallery, London.

Diana Thater

Born in San Francisco, 1962. Lives and works in Los Angeles. Studied at New York University, New York, B.A., Art History, 1984; Art Center College of Design, Pasadena, Calif., M.F.A., 1990. Represented by David Zwirner, New York.

Solo Exhibitions

1991, Dorothy Goldeen Gallery, Santa Monica, Calif., *Dogs and Other Philosophers*; 1992, Bliss House, Pasadena, Calif., and Shoshana Wayne Gallery, Santa Monica, Calif., *Up the Lintel*; 1993, 1301, Santa Monica, Calif., *Abyss of Light*; 1993–1994, David Zwirner, New York, *Late and Soon: Occident Trotting*; 1994, Friesenwall 116a, Cologne, *Ginger Kittens*; 1994, Witte de With Center for Contemporary Art, Rotterdam; 1995, Schipper & Krome, Cologne, *Crayons & Molly Numbers 1 through 10*; 1995, The Renaissance Society, University of Chicago, Chicago, and Le Creux de l'Enfer, Centre d'art contemporain de Thiers, Thiers, France, *China*; 1996, David Zwirner, New York, *China, Crayons & Molly Numbers 1 through 10*; 1996, Salzburger Kunstverein, Salzburg, Austria, *Electric Mind*; 1996, Kunsthalle Basel, Basel, *The individual as a species, the object as a medium: Selected Works 1992–1996*; 1996, Temporary Contemporary Series for the Baltic Flour Mills, Gateshead, England, *The Wicked Witch of the West*; 1996–1997, Portland Art Museum, Portland, Oreg., SITE, Sante Fe, N. Mex., McKinney Avenue Contemporary, Dallas, Tex., and University Gallery, University of Massachusetts, Amherst, Mass., *Electric Mind and Recent Works* (cat.); 1997, Kunstverein in Hamburg, Hamburg, *The individual as a species, the object as a medium: Selected Works 1992–1996*; 1997, Walker Art Center, Minneapolis, *Orchids in the Land of Technology*; 1998, School of the Museum of Fine Arts, Boston; 1998, Patrick Painter, Inc., Santa Monica, Calif.; 1998, ArtPace, San Antonio, Tex.; 1998, MAK Center for Art and Architecture, Los Angeles, *The best animals are the flat animals—the best space is the deep space*; 1998, Allen Memorial Art Museum, Oberlin College, Oberlin, Ohio, *The best space is the deep space*; 1998, The Museum of Modern Art, New York, *Projects 64: The best animals are the flat animals*; 1999, Galerie Ghislaine Hussenot, Paris; 1999, Carnegie Museum of Art, Pittsburgh, *The best space is the deep space*; 1999, Saint Louis Art Museum, Saint Louis, Mo., *The best outside is the inside*; 1999, Art Gallery of York University, Toronto, *The best sense is the non sense*; 2000–2001, Tensta Konsthall, Stockholm; 2000, 1301PE Gallery, Los Angeles; 2000, Galerie Hauser & Wirth, Zurich, *Delphine*; 2000, Galleria Emi Fontana, Milan, *The Caucus Race*; 2000, Wiener Secession, Vienna, *Delphine*; 2001–2002, Dia Center for the Arts, New York, *Knots and Surfaces*.

Group Exhibitions

1990, Fahey/Klein Gallery, Los Angeles, *Heart in Mouth*; 1991, Los Angeles Airport International Terminal, Los Angeles, *Rhythms of Earth and Water*; 1992, 1301, Santa Monica, Calif., *Into the Lapse*; 1992, Shoshana Wayne Gallery, Santa Monica, Calif., *Very, Very, Very*; 1993, Anderson O'Day Gallery, London, *The Time*; 1993, Long Beach Museum of Art, Long Beach, Calif., *Sugar n' Spice*; 1993, California State University, Los Angeles, *Emblazoned Ciphers of the Visible*; 1994, David Zwirner, New York, *Stan Douglas, Jason Rhoades, Diana Thater, Franz West*; 1994, American Center, Paris, and Museum of Contemporary Art, Los Angeles, *Pure Beauty*; 1994, Deichtorhallen, Hamburg, *Temporary Translation(s): Sammlung Schürmann* (cat.); 1995, Lyons, Biennale (cat.); 1995, Museum Fridericianum, Kassel, Germany, *Surroundings* (cat.); 1995, Kwangju, Korea, Biennale (cat.); 1995, Fundação de Serralves, Porto, Portugal, *Threshold / Recent American Sculpture* (cat.); 1995, Whitney Museum of American Art, New York, *Biennial Exhibition* (cat.); 1996, Kunstverein in Hamburg, Hamburg, *Wunderbar*; 1996, National Gallery and Alexandros Soutzos Museum, Athens, *Art at the*

End of the 20th Century: Selections from the Whitney Museum of American Art (cat.); 1996, Albright-Knox Art Gallery, Buffalo, N.Y., *Being and Time: The Emergence of Video Projection* (cat.); 1996, Sydney, 10th Biennale, *Jurassic Technologies Revenant* (cat.); 1996, Magasin 3, Rooseum, Stockholm and Malmö, Sweden, *Painting: The Extended Field* (cat.); 1997, Castello di Rivoli, Museo d'Arte Contemporanea, Turin, Museo d'Arte Contemporanea, Milan, and Kunstmuseum Bonn, Bonn, *American Art from the Whitney Museum: 1975–1995: Multiple Identity* (cat.); 1997, Cranbrook Art Museum, Bloomfield Hills, Mich., and Contemporary Arts Museum, Houston, *Being and Time: The Emergence of Video Projection* (cat.); 1997, Münster, *Skulpturen Projekte Münster* (cat.); 1997, Whitney Museum of American Art, New York, *Biennial Exhibition* (cat.); 1997, Louisiana Museum of Modern Art, Humlebaek, Denmark, and Kunstmuseum Wolfsburg, Wolfsburg, Germany, *Sunshine & Noir: Art in L.A. 1960–1997* (cat.); 1997, Henry Art Gallery, University of Washington, Seattle, *Between Lantern and Laser*; 1997, Johannesburg, Biennale, *Trade Routes: History and Geography*; 1998, Jewish Museum, New York, *Light x Eight: The Hanukkah Project*; 1998, Kunsthalle Zürich, Zurich, *Auf der Spur*; 1998, Castello di Rivoli, Museo d'Arte Contemporanea, Turin, and UCLA at the Armand Hammer Museum of Art, Los Angeles, *Sunshine & Noir: Art in L.A. 1960–1997* (cat.); 1998, Artspace, Auckland, Govett-Brewster Art Gallery, New Plymouth, New Zealand, and Centre for Contemporary Photography, Melbourne, *Span*; 1998, Mary Boone Gallery, New York, *View One*; 1998, David Zwirner, New York, *Five Years 1993–1998*; 1999, California College of Arts and Crafts, Oakland, Calif., *Consciousness at the Millennium*; 1999, Arizona State University Art Museum, Tempe, Ariz., *Sites around the City: Art and Environment*; 1999, Museum van Hedendaagse Kunst Antwerpen, Antwerp, *Trouble Spot Painting*; 1999, Städtische Galerie, Karlsruhe, Germany, *Herausforderung Tier*; 1999, David Zwirner, New York, *Gallery Artists Summer Show*; 1999, Rosamund Felsen Gallery, Los Angeles, *Art/Journalism*; 1999, California College of Arts and Crafts, San Francisco, *Searchlight*; 1999, Whitney Museum of American Art, New York, *The American Century*; 1999, Institut d'art contemporain, Villeurbanne, France, *Collection FRAC Rhônes-Alpes*; 1999, Carnegie Museum of Art, Pittsburgh, *Carnegie International 1999/2000*; 2000, Städtische Galerie, Karlsruhe, Germany, *The Animal Horror*; 2000, Museum Villa Stuck, Munich, *L.A.—Indoor Street*; 2000, Art Gallery of Hamilton, Hamilton, Ont., *Thinking Space: Selections from the Ann and Marshall Webb Collection*; 2000, Palm Beach Institute of Contemporary Art, Lake Worth, Fla., *Making Time: Considering Time as a Material in Contemporary Video and Film*; 2000, Orange County Museum of Art, Newport Beach, Calif., *Lasting Legacy: Recent Additions to the Collection*; 2000, Museum of Modern Art Oxford, Oxford, England, *Enclosed and Enchanted*; 2000, Villa Merkel, Esslingen, Germany, *Electronic Images: Videokunst 1965–2000*; 2001, Museum of Contemporary Art, Los Angeles, *Public Offerings* (cat.).

Jeff Wall

Born in Vancouver, 1946, where he lives and works. Studied at University of British Columbia, Vancouver, B.A., M.A., 1970; Courtauld Institute, London, 1970–1973. Represented by Marian Goodman Gallery, New York, and Galerie Jöhnen & Schöttle, Cologne.

Solo Exhibitions

1978, Nova Gallery, Vancouver; 1979, Art Gallery of Greater Victoria, Victoria, B.C. (cat.); 1982, David Bellman Gallery, Toronto; 1983, The Renaissance Society, University of Chicago, Chicago (cat.); 1984, Institute of Contemporary Arts, London, and Kunsthalle Basel, Basel, *Transparencies* (cat.); 1986, Ydessa Gallery, Toronto; 1986, Galerie Jöhnen & Schöttle, Cologne; 1987, Galerie Ghislaine Hussenot, Paris; 1987, Galerie Jöhnen & Schöttle, Cologne; 1987, Museum für Gegenwartskunst, Basel, *Young Workers* (cat.); 1988, Westfalischer Kunstverein, Münster (cat.); 1988, Nouveau Musée, Villeurbanne, France (cat.); 1989, Galerie Jöhnen & Schöttle, Cologne; 1989, Marian Goodman Gallery, New York (cat.); 1989–1990, Marian Goodman Gallery, New York, Galerie Roger Pailhas, Marseilles, FRAC Rhônes-Alpes, Lyons, Galerie Chantal

Boulanger, Montreal, and Santa Barbara Contemporary Arts Forum, Santa Barbara, Calif., *The Children's Pavilion*, collaborative project with Dan Graham (cat.); 1990, Carnegie Museum of Art, Pittsburgh (cat.); 1990, Ydessa Hendeles Art Foundation, Toronto; 1990, and *Jeff Wall–Dan Graham: Pavillon des Enfants*; 1990, Vancouver Art Gallery, Vancouver, Art Gallery of Ontario, Toronto (cat.); 1991, Galleria Christian Stein, Milan; 1991, Galerie Meert Rihoux, Brussels; 1991, Galerie Jöhnen & Schöttle, Cologne; 1991, San Diego Museum of Contemporary Art, San Diego (cat.); 1992, Palais des beaux-arts, Brussels; 1992, Marian Goodman Gallery, New York; 1992, Louisiana Museum of Modern Art, Humlebaek, Denmark (cat.); 1993, Galerie Roger Pailhas, Marseilles; 1993, Fondation Cartier pour l'art contemporain, Jouy-en-Josas, France; 1993, Museum Boijmans Van Beuningen, Rotterdam, and Le Magasin, Centre National d'Art Contemporain, Grenoble, *The Children's Pavilion*; 1993–1994, Kunstmuseum Luzern, Lucerne, Switzerland, Irish Museum of Modern Art, Dublin, and Deichtorhallen, Hamburg (cat.); 1994, Galerie Jöhnen & Schöttle, Cologne; 1994, Städtische Kunsthalle, Düsseldorf (cat.); 1994, The White Cube, London; 1994, De Pont Foundation, Tilburg, Netherlands (cat.); 1994, Galerie Rüdiger Schöttle, Munich; 1994, NGBK, Berlin (cat.); 1994, Museo Nacional Centro de Arte Reina Sofia, Madrid (cat.); 1995, Marian Goodman Gallery, New York; 1995–1996, Museum of Contemporary Art, Chicago, Galerie nationale du Jeu de Paume, Paris, Museum of Contemporary Art, Helsinki, and Whitechapel Art Gallery, London (cat.); 1996, Städtische Galerie im Lenbachhaus, Munich (cat.); 1996, Kunstmuseum Wolfsburg, Wolfsburg, Germany (cat.); 1997, Hirshhorn Museum and Sculpture Garden, Smithsonian Institution, Washington, D.C., Museum of Contemporary Art, Los Angeles, and Art Tower Mito, Mito, Japan (cat.); 1998, Galerie Rüdiger Schöttle, Munich, *Transparencies*; 1998, Galerie Jöhnen & Schöttle, Cologne, *Photographs*; 1998, Museum für Gegenwartskunst, Basel, *Fotografien des modernen Lebens/Photographs of Modern Life* (cat.); 1998, Henry Moore Institute, Leeds, *Here and Now* (cat.); 1998, Marian Goodman Gallery, New York; 1999, Musée d'art contemporain de Montréal, Montreal (cat.); 2000, Galeria Helga de Alvear, Madrid; 2001, Marian Goodman Gallery, New York.

Group Exhibitions

1969, Bau-Xi Gallery, Vancouver, *Focus '69*; 1969, S.U.B. Art Gallery, University of British Columbia, Vancouver, *Photo Show*; 1969–1970, Seattle Art Museum, Seattle, *557,087*, and Vancouver Art Gallery, Vancouver, *955,000* (cat.); 1970, Fine Arts Gallery, University of British Columbia, Vancouver, *Four Artists: Tom Burrows, Duane Lunden, Jeff Wall, Ian Wallace*; 1970, Allen Memorial Art Museum, Oberlin College, Oberlin, Ohio, *Art in the Mind* (cat.); 1970, The Museum of Modern Art, New York, *Information* (cat.); 1970, Whitechapel Art Gallery, London, *3 to Infinity: New Multiple Art*; 1971, Fine Arts Gallery, University of British Columbia, Vancouver, *Collage Show* (cat.); 1971, Prague, *New Art*; 1971, Bad Salzdetfurth, Germany, *Ecological Art*; 1971, Sir George Williams University, Montreal, and Saidye Bronfman Centre, Montreal, *45° 30' N – 73° 36' W* (cat.); 1973, Vancouver Art Gallery, Vancouver, *Pacific Vibrations* (cat.); 1980, Hal Bromm Gallery, New York, *New Work: Mac Adams, Roger Cutforth, Dan Graham, John Hillard, Jeff Wall*; 1980, Photo Gallery, National Film Board of Canada, Ottawa, *Cibachrome*; 1980, National Gallery of Canada, Ottawa, *Pluralities 1980* (cat.); 1981, Hirshhorn Museum and Sculpture Garden, Washington, D.C., and Sarah Campbell Blaffer Gallery, University of Houston, Houston, *Directions 1981* (cat); 1981, Rheinhallen Messegelände, Cologne, *Westkunst: Zeitgenössische Kunst seit 1939* (cat.); 1982, Museum Fridericianum, Kassel, Germany, *Documenta 7* (cat.); 1983, Simon Fraser Gallery, Burnaby, B.C., *David MacWilliam, Greg Snider, Jeff Wall*; 1984, Coquitlam Centre Mall, Coquitlam, B.C., *Poco Rococo*; 1984, Städtische Kunsthalle, Düsseldorf, *A Different Climate: Aspects of Beauty in Contemporary Art* (cat.); 1984–1985, New Museum of Contemporary Art, New York, The Renaissance Society, University of Chicago, Chicago, Institute of Contemporary Art, London, and List Visual Arts Center, Massachusetts Institute of Technology, Cambridge, Mass., *Difference: On Representation and Sexuality* (cat.); 1985, Aorta, Amsterdam, *Cover/Doppelgänger* (cat.); 1985, Stedelijk Museum, Amsterdam, *Günther Förg & Jeff Wall: Photoworks*; 1985, Centre international d'art contemporain de Montréal, Montreal, *Aurora Borealis* (cat.); 1985, London Regional Art Gallery,

London, Ont., Art Gallery at Harbourfront, Toronto, Laurentian University Museum and Arts Centre, Sudbury, Ont., and Mendel Art Gallery, Saskatoon, Sask., *Subjects and Subject Matter* (cat.); 1985, Grande Halle du Parc de la Villette, Paris, *La nouvelle biennale de Paris* (cat.); 1985, Third Eye Centre, Glasgow, Graves Art Gallery, Sheffield, N.B., and Canada House Cultural Centre Gallery, London, *Visual Facts: Photography and Video by Eight Artists in Canada* (cat.); 1985, 49th Parallel, Center for Contemporary Canadian Art, New York, *Rodney Graham, Ken Lum, Jeff Wall, Ian Wallace* (cat.); 1985–1987, Galerie der Künstler, Munich, Vereinkunsthalle, Zurich, and FRAC Rhône-Alpes, Saint-Étienne, France, *Louis XIV Tanzt/Louis XIV Dances*; 1986, Galerie Rüdiger Schöttle, Munich, *Zwei Landschaften: Glenn Branca, Jeff Wall*; 1986, Or Gallery, Vancouver, *Camera Works*; 1986, Rheinhallen Messegelände (Internationaler Kunstmarkt), Cologne, *Focus: Kanadische Kunst von 1960–1985* (cat.); 1986, Frankfurter Kunstverein and Schirn Kunsthalle, Frankfurt, *Prospect 86* (cat.); 1986, Vancouver Art Gallery, Vancouver, *Making History: Recent Art of the Pacific West* (cat.); 1987, De Appel, Amsterdam, *Nightfire* (cat.); 1987, Künstlerwerkstatt, Munich, *Theatergarten/Bestiarium* (cat.); 1987, Christine Burgin Gallery, New York, *Dan Graham, Rodney Graham, Robert Smithson, Jeff Wall*; 1987, Galerie Ralph Wernicke, Stuttgart, *Kunst mit Photographie*; 1987, Museum Fridericianum, Kassel, Germany, *Documenta 8* (cat.); 1987, Centre Georges Pompidou, Musée national d'art moderne, Paris, *L'époque, la mode, la morale, la passion: Aspects de l'art d'aujourd'hui, 1977–1987* (cat.); 1987–1988, Württembergischer Kunstverein, Stuttgart, Haus am Waldsee, Berlin, Kunstverein in Hamburg, Hamburg, Kunstverein Hannover, Hannover, and Frankfurter Kunstverein, Frankfurt, *Zeitgeschichten/Blow-up* (cat.); 1988, Studio Casoli, Milan, *Rodney Graham, Robert Kleyn, Jeff Wall, Ian Wallace* (cat.); 1988, Galleri Contur, Stockholm, *John Hilliard, Barbara Kruger, Ken Lum, Richard Prince, Jeff Wall*; 1988, Galerie Rüdiger Schöttle, Munich, *Landschafts-Ansichten: Stephan Balkenhol, Michael van Ofen, Jeff Wall, Giovanni Battista Piranesi*; 1988, Carnegie Museum of Art, Pittsburgh, *Carnegie International* (cat.); 1988, FRAC Champagne-Ardenne, Reims, France, *À l'hotel de la région*; 1988, Tomoko Liguori Gallery, New York, *Dennis Adams, Alfredo Jaar, Jeff Wall*; 1988, Monika Spruth Gallery, Cologne, *Das Licht von der anderen Seite, II: Fotografie* (cat.); 1988, Padiglione d'Arte Contemporanea, Milan, *Presi per Incantamento: L'Immagine Fotografica nelle Nuove Tendenze Internazionali* (cat.); 1988, Guiness Hop Store, Dublin, Royal Hospital Kilmainham, Dublin, *Rosc '88*; 1988, Galerie Roger Pailhas, Marseilles, *Éléments manifestes*; 1988, Barbara Gladstone Gallery, New York, *Robert Mapplethorpe, Richard Prince, Thomas Ruff, Jeff Wall*; 1988, Art Gallery of New South Wales and Pier 2/3, Walsh Bay, Sydney, and National Gallery of Victoria, Melbourne, 7th Biennale (cat.); 1988, Galerie Jöhnen & Schöttle, Cologne, *Krieg, Liebe, Geld: Katharina Fritsch, Michel van Ofen, Jeff Wall*; 1988, Kaiser Wilhelm Museum, Krefeld, Germany, and CAPC Musée d'art contemporain, Bordeaux, *Bilanz/Balance* (cat.); 1988, Institute of Contemporary Art, Boston, *Utopia Post Utopia* (cat.); 1989, P.S.1, Long Island City, N.Y., Teatro Lope de Vega, Casino de la Exposicion, Seville, and Galerie du Confort Moderne, Poitiers, France *Theatergarten/Bestiarium: The Garden as Theater as Museum* (cat.); 1989, Mai 36 Galerie, Lucerne, Switzerland, *Arrangements I*; 1989, Musée d'Art Moderne de la Ville de Paris, Paris, *Images Critiques: J. Wall, D. Adams, A. Jaar, L. Jammes* (cat.); 1989, Galerie Rüdiger Schöttle, Munich, *Ken Lum, Jeff Wall*; 1989, Centre National des Arts Plastiques, Paris, and Centro per l'Arte Contemporanea Luigi Pecci, Prato, Italy, *Une autre objectivité/Another Objectivity* (cat.); 1989, Marian Goodman Gallery, New York; 1989, Centre Georges Pompidou, Musée national d'art moderne, Paris, and Grand Halle du Parc de la Villette, Paris, *Les magiciens de la terre* (cat.); 1989, Rooseum, Malmö, Sweden, *What Is Contemporary Art?* (cat.); 1989, Musée d'art contemporain de Montréal, Montreal, *Tenir l'image à distance* (cat.); 1989, Galerie Grita Insam, Vienna, and Museum of Contemporary Art, 's Hertogenbosch, Netherlands, *Vis à Vis der Kamera: Aspekte der Aktuellen Porträt-Fotografie*; 1989, Barbara Gladstone Gallery, New York, *Selected Photographs from the Donnelley Collection*; 1989, Staatsgalerie, Stuttgart, *Foto-Kunst* (cat.); 1990, National Garden Festival, Gateshead, England, *A New Necessity: First Tyne International 1990* (cat.);

1990, Hirshhorn Museum and Sculpture Garden, Washington, D.C., *Culture and Commentary: An Eighties Perspective* (cat.); 1990, Centre Georges Pompidou, Musée national d'art moderne, Paris, Fundació Caixa de Pensions, Barcelona, and San Francisco Museum of Modern Art, San Francisco, *Passages de l'image* (cat.); 1990, Israel Museum, Jerusalem, *Life Size: A Sense of the Real in Recent Art* (cat.); 1990, Museum Haus Lange and Museum Haus Esters, Krefeld, Germany, *Weitersehen 1980–1990* (cat.); 1990, Musée des beaux-arts/FRAC Nord–Pas de Calais, Tourcoing, France, *La diaphane*; 1991, Centre international d'art contemporain de Montréal, Montreal; 1991, Marian Goodman Gallery, New York, *This Land…*; 1991, Ginny Williams Gallery, Denver, *Photography*; 1991, Martin-Gropius-Bau, Berlin, *Metropolis* (cat.); 1991, Castello di Rivoli, Museo d'Arte Contemporanea, Turin, *Sguardo di Medusa* (cat.); 1991, Vancouver Art Gallery, Vancouver, *Lost Illusions: Recent Landscape Art* (cat.); 1992, Museum Haus Lange and Museum Haus Esters, Krefeld, *In anderen Räumen*; 1992, Circulo de Bellas Artes, Madrid, and Centre d'Art Santa Mònica, Barcelona, *Cameras indiscretes* (cat.); 1992, Salas del Arenal, Seville, *The Last Days* (cat.); 1992, Borås Konstmuseum, Borås, Sweden, *What Is Contemporary Art?*; 1992, Kunst- und Austellungshalle der Bundesrepublik Deutschland, Bonn (cat.); 1992, Institut du Monde Arabe, Paris, *Images Métisses*; 1992, Städtische Kunsthalle, Düsseldorf, *Avantgarde & Kampagne*; 1992, Walter Phillips Gallery, Banff, Alta., *Queues, Rendezvous and Riots: Questioning the Public*; 1992, Musée d'art contemporain de Montréal, Montreal, *Pour la suite du monde* (cat.); 1992, Stux Gallery, New York; 1992, Musée Communal d'Ixelles, Brussels, *The Binary Era: New Interactions* (cat.); 1993, Kunsthalle, Vienna, *Binera: 14 Interaktionen — Kunst und Technologie* (cat.); 1993, FRAC Pays-de-la-Loire, Clisson, France, and Musée des beaux-arts, FRAC Franche-Comté, Dole, France, *Canada, une nouvelle génération* (cat.); 1993, Norwich Gallery, Norfolk Institute of Art and Design, Norfolk, England *Renegotiations: Class, Modernity, Photography* (cat.); 1993, FAE Musée d'art contemporain, Pully, Switzerland, Castello di Rivoli, Museo d'Arte Contemporanea, Turin, Deste Foundation, Athens, and Deichtorhallen, Hamburg, *Post-Human*; 1993, Center for the Fine Arts, Miami; 1993, Århus Kunstmuseum, Århus, Denmark; 1993, Parachute Magazine, Montreal, *Bestiarium/Endangered Species*; 1993, Bayerische Staatsgemäldesammlungen, Munich; 1993, Foundation Still/Archipel Apeldoorn, Rotterdam; 1993, Charles H. Scott Gallery, Emily Carr College of Art and Design, Vancouver, *Beneath the Paving Stones: Art, Architecture, City* (cat.); 1993, Marian Goodman Gallery, New York, *A Group Show*; 1994, Paula Cooper Gallery, New York, *Pictures of the Real World (In Real Time)*; 1994, Public Art Fund, New York, and Payne Webber Art Gallery, New York, *Urban Paradise: Gardens in the City*; 1994, Marian Goodman Gallery, New York, *A Painting Show*; 1994, Artimo Foundation, Amsterdam, and Netherlands Red Cross, Amsterdam, *Ik + de Ander: Dignity for All — Reflections on Humanity*; 1994, Hayward Gallery, London, *The Epic and the Everyday: Contemporary Photographic Art* (cat.); 1994, Gimpel Fils, London; 1994, Deichtorhallen, Hamburg, *The Century of the Multiple: From Duchamp to the Present*; 1994, Institut Français de Madrid, Madrid, *Le corps en scène*; 1994, Institute of Contemporary Arts, London, *The Institute of Cultural Anxiety: Works from the Collection*; 1994, Angles Gallery, Los Angeles, *Rodney Graham, Stephen Prina, Jeff Wall*; 1994, MIT List Visual Arts Center, Cambridge, Mass., *The Ghost in the Machine* (cat.); 1994, Nicole Klagsburn, New York, *Ashley Bickerton, Jimmie Durham, Walton Ford, Jeff Wall*; 1994, Kunstmuseum Luzern, Lucerne, Switzerland, *Prospect/Retrospect: Contemporary Art from the Collection*; 1994–1995, National Museum of Contemporary Art, Seoul, and Fine Art Museum of Taipei, *Fondation Cartier: A Collection*; 1995, Centro per l'Arte Contemporanea Luigi Pecci, Prato, Italy, *L'immagine riflessa: A Selection of Contemporary Photography from the LAC Collection, Switzerland* (cat.); 1995, American Center, Paris, and Israel Museum, Jerusalem, *Micromegas*; 1995, Setayaga Art Museum, Tokyo, Museum of Modern Art, Kyoto, and Hokkaido Museum of Art, Sapporo, *Spirits on the Crossing — Travellers to/from Nowhere: Contemporary Art in Canada 1980–1994* (cat.); 1995, Ydessa Hendeles Art Foundation, Toronto, *Projections*; 1995, Art Institute of Chicago, Chicago *About Place: Recent Art of the Americas* (cat.); 1995, San Francisco Museum of Modern Art, San Francisco, *Public Information: Desire, Disaster, Docu-*

ment (cat.); 1995, Whitney Museum of American Art, New York, *Biennial Exhibition* (cat.); 1995, Centre Georges Pompidou, Musée national d'art moderne, Paris, *Féminin-Masculin, le sexe de l'art* (cat.); Centre Georges Pompidou, Musée national d'art moderne, Paris, *Face à l'histoire 1933–1996: L'artiste moderne face à l'événement historique* (cat.); 1996, Museum of Contemporary Art, Los Angeles, Wexner Center for the Arts, Columbus, Ohio, Palazzo delle Esposizioni, Rome, and Museum of Contemporary Art, Chicago (cat.); 1997, Yokohama Museum of Art, Yokohama, Japan, *Absolute Landscape: Between Illusion and Reality*; 1997, Centre d'art contemporain, Geneva, *Veronica's Revenge* (cat.); 1997, Museum Fridericianum, Kassel, Germany, *Documenta X* (cat.); 1998, XXIV Bienal de São Paolo, São Paolo, Brazil (cat.); 1998, Kunsthalle Zürich, Zurich, *Auf der Spur*; 1998, Marian Goodman Gallery, New York, *Breaking Ground*; 1999, Kaiser Wilhelm Museum, Krefeld, Germany, *Am Horizont*; 1999, Kunst-Werke Berlin, Berlin, *Warten*; 1999, Thread Waxing Space, New York, *Foul Play*; 1999, Castellón Contemporary Arts Center (EACC), Castellón, Spain, *Jeff Wall, Pepe Espaliú: Suspended Time*; 1999, The Museum of Modern Art, New York, *The Museum as Muse: Artists Reflect* (cat.); 1999, Carnegie Museum of Art, Pittsburgh, *1999/2000 Carnegie International*; 1999, San Francisco Museum of Modern Art, San Francisco, *Seeing Time: Selections from the Pamela and Richard Kramlich Collection of Media Art*; 2000, Palais des beaux-arts, Brussels, *Voici, 100 ans d'art contemporain* (cat.); 2000, Kunsthaus, Zurich, *Hypermental: Rampant Reality 1950–2000: From Salvador Dali to Jeff Koons* (cat.); 2000, Padiglione d'Arte Contemporanea di Milano, Milan, *La Forma del Mondo/La Fine del Mondo* (cat.); 2000, Neues Kunstmuseum Luzern, Lucerne, Switzerland, *Mixing Memory and Desire/Wunsch und Erinnerung* (cat.); 2000, National Gallery, London, *Encounters: New Art from Old* (cat.); 2000, Sydney, Biennale (cat.); 2000, Palais des Papes, Avignon, France, *La beauté in fabula* (cat.); 2000, Americas Society, New York, *Icon + Grid + Void: Art of the Americas from the Chase Manhattan Collection*; 2000, P.S.1, Long Island City, N.Y., *Around 1984: A Look at Art in the Eighties* (cat.); 2000, Queens Museum of Art, New York, *Art at Work: Forty Years of the Chase Manhattan Collection*; 2000, Bonakdar Jancou Gallery, New York, *Staged*; 2000, Art Gallery of Western Australia, Perth, *Home* (cat.); 2000, Centro Andaluz de Arte Contemporaneo, Seville, and Centre de Cultura Contemporània de Barcelona, Barcelona, *Architecture without Shadow* (cat.); 2000, Neuberger Museum of Art, New York, *Inner Eye: Contemporary Art from the Marc and Livia Straus Collection*.

Published in conjunction with the exhibition *Elusive Paradise: The Millennium Prize*, organized by the National Gallery of Canada and presented in Ottawa from 9 February to 13 May 2001.

Catalogue produced by the Publications Division of National Gallery of Canada, Ottawa.

Chief: Serge Thériault
Editors: Usher Caplan, Claire Rochon
Production: John Barton

Designed and typeset in Granjon by Emmeline Debay of Timmings & Debay, Aylmer. Printed by St. Joseph/MOM Printing, Ottawa, on Mohawk Superfine and Sappi Opus paper.

National Library of Canada Cataloguing in Publication Data

Nemiroff, Diana.
Elusive paradise : the Millenium prize.
Exhibition catalogue.
Issued also in French under title: Paradis insaisissables.

ISBN 0-88884-720-3

1. Art, Modern–20th century–Exhibitions.
2. Art–Awards–Canada–Exhibitions. 3. Arcadia in art–Exhibitions.
I. Sloan, Johanne. II. National Gallery of Canada. III. Title.

N395 C3 N45 2001 709'.05'007471384 C2001-986000-5

All photographs courtesy of the owners of the works, except where otherwise indicated.

Available through your local bookseller or from:

The Bookstore
National Gallery of Canada
380 Sussex Drive, Box 427, Station A, Ottawa K1N 9N4
ngcbook@gallery.ca

Cover: **Janet Cardiff**, *Forty-Part Motet* (cat. no. 4)